JESUS AND THE
SERVANT

JESUS AND THE SERVANT

THE INFLUENCE OF THE
SERVANT CONCEPT OF DEUTERO-ISAIAH
IN THE NEW TESTAMENT

BY

MORNA D. HOOKER, M.A.

WIPF & STOCK · Eugene, Oregon

Wipf and Stock Publishers
199 W 8th Ave, Suite 3
Eugene, OR 97401

Jesus and the Servant
The Influence of the Servant Concept of Deutero-Isaiah in the New Testament
By Hooker, Morna D.
Copyright©1959 SPCK
ISBN 13: 978-1-60899-410-6
Publication date 2/15/2010
Previously published by SPCK, 1959

This Edition reprinted by Wipf and Stock Publishers
by arrangement with SPCK, London.

TO THE MEMORY
OF MY GRANDFATHER
H. J. HOOKER
1872–1957

Ἀνὴρ ἀγαθος
καὶ πλήρης Πνεύματος Ἁγίου
καὶ πίστεως

NOTE

Except where otherwise stated, the English translations of Biblical passages are taken from The Revised Standard Version of the Bible, copyrighted in 1946 and 1952, by permission of The National Council of Churches, New York, and Thomas Nelson and Son, Ltd., Edinburgh.

CONTENTS

Foreword by Professor C. K. Barrett, D.D.   *page* ix

Introduction   xi

Abbreviations   xiii

1   GENERAL SURVEY OF RECENT WORK ON THE PROBLEM   1
    1 Introduction   1
    2 Opponents of the traditional view   2
    3 Exponents of the traditional view   6
    4 Petrine influence   16
    5 The need for further investigation   18
    6 Method of investigation   21
    7 The significance of the problem   23

2   THE SERVANT PASSAGES: THEIR MEANING AND BACKGROUND   25
    1 Introduction   25
    2 The Songs in relation to their context   25
    3 Deutero-Isaiah in relation to Hebrew prophecy   30
    4 The Servant   41
    5 The problem of Isa. 53   45
    6 Objections to the collective theory   48

3   JEWISH INTERPRETATION OF THE SERVANT   53
    1 The Servant in Jewish literature   53
    2 The neglect of the Servant concept   58

4   THE SERVANT IN THE SYNOPTIC GOSPELS   62
    1 Basis of study   62
    2 Passages for consideration   64
    3 Group 1 (*a*): Words or phrases used of the person or work of Jesus   65
    4 Group 1 (*b*): Details in the Passion narrative   86
    5 Group 2: References by Jesus to his suffering   92
    6 Conclusion   101

CONTENTS

5 THE SERVANT IN THE EARLY CHURCH   *page* 103

   1 Introduction   103
   2 The Fourth Gospel   103
   3 The Acts of the Apostles   107
   4 The Epistles of St Paul   116
   5 The Epistle to the Hebrews   123
   6 1 Peter   124
   7 Revelation   126
   8 Conclusion   126
   Appendix   128

6 THE CONCEPT OF SUFFERING   134

   1 Introduction   134
   2 Suffering in the New Testament: The Synoptic Gospels   134
   3 Suffering in the New Testament: Books other than the Synoptic Gospels   137
   4 The concept of suffering in Jewish thought   140
   5 The Son of Man   142

7 THE SERVANT CONCEPT IN THE THOUGHT OF JESUS AND THE EARLY CHURCH   147

   1 The results of our investigation   147
   2 The absence of the 'Servant' in early Christian thought   154
   3 The pattern of suffering and exaltation   159

Notes   164

Bibliography   201

Indexes

   1 Biblical, Apocryphal, and other ancient writings   211
   2 Hebrew and Aramaic words   224
   3 Greek words   225
   4 Modern authors   226
   5 Subjects   228

FOREWORD

I first made the acquaintance of Miss Hooker's study of *Jesus and the Servant* when I helped to examine it as a dissertation submitted for a degree in the University of Bristol. I was immediately impressed by the unusual maturity of Miss Hooker's scholarship, and I am glad to have played a small part in securing the publication of her first book. I am honoured by her request to introduce it in a Foreword.

It has become almost an axiom of recent New Testament study that most of the New Testament writers, and probably our Lord himself, were controlled in their Christological thinking by the figure of the Suffering Servant of the Lord, depicted in Isa. 52. 13–53. 12. In this figure (so it is widely held) is to be found the clue to both the Person and the work of Jesus: so he conceived of himself, and so he was proclaimed by the early Church. It is to be feared that there are some (though not of course among the best scholars) with whom this axiom has become an unexamined assumption, taken for granted as an 'assured result' of New Testament theology. Miss Hooker has ventured to examine this assumption, and to judge it in accordance with the evidence. Her competence to do this needs no commendation from me, for her scholarship speaks for itself in the following pages, in which the Biblical material is accurately set out and acutely discussed. They must be taken seriously by all students of the New Testament. I do not commit myself to every opinion she expresses, but I believe that she has made out her main point. It may be too much to hope that her arguments will meet with universal agreement; but if any dissent they encounter is to be effective, it will have to be based upon evidence and reason, and not upon prejudice.

C. K. BARRETT

Durham, 1958

Jesus and the Servant

Errata

p. v	ἀγαθος should read ἀγαθὸς
p. xi, line 14	add ; after 'theory'
p. 104	טָלֵח should be טָלַח (bis)
p. 125, fifth line of Greek	δικαιοσύνη should read δικαιοσύνη
p. 170, line 8	a is reversed
last line	׳ is reversed
p. 175, half way down	נֶעֱרָה should be נֶעֱרָה (after 'Niph'al')
p. 185, three lines up	'laügnen' should be leugnen'
pp. 80, 186, 202 and 226	A. E. Abbott should be E. A. Abbott

INTRODUCTION

A great deal has been written about the Servant Songs. Most writers, however, have concentrated on the original meaning of the passages and have devoted little attention to a problem which has much more vital consequences, namely the question whether or not the relevance of the Servant Songs to his Passion was accepted by Jesus himself. It is with this question that the present study is concerned.

In view of the wide influence which the Servant Songs have had upon Christian thought over many centuries, it is surprising that an aspect of the subject which has far-reaching implications has never been really thoroughly investigated. This is not to say that the problem has been by any means neglected, for almost every writer on the New Testament has some comment to make upon it. Some scholars, taking it for granted that Jesus saw in himself the fulfilment of the Servant Songs, quote evidence which they regard as supporting this theory others, who take the opposite view, deny the validity of the evidence. Neither side, however, appears to have examined critically all the available material.

I have, therefore, ventured in the following pages to undertake a detailed examination of all the passages in the New Testament which are relevant to this question. As might be expected from the contrary nature of the theories about these passages, they are not in themselves sufficient basis for the resolution of the problem, and I have therefore attempted to consider it also against the background of both New Testament and Jewish thought about suffering. An interpretation of the Servant Songs has also been included, in order to trace the concept from the beginning.

Two things, I believe, emerge from these studies. One is that Jesus' understanding of his own sufferings can be comprehended only when they are seen against a pattern of suffering which, while it includes the Servant Songs, is much wider in its scope. The other is that there is a consistent interpretation of the 'Servant' which stretches from Deutero-Isaiah, through Judaism, to Jesus himself: an interpretation which arises, not from the concept of the 'Servant', but from the thought of the mission of the people of God to the world.

I am glad to acknowledge the help and encouragement which have been given to me by the Reverend Professor S. B. Frost, M.Th., Ph.D., and the Reverend Kenneth Grayston, M.A., who have devoted considerable time and trouble to discussing the problem with me, and who have offered helpful criticism of my work. I should also like to thank my father and the Reverend E. J. Sharpe, B.A., for their help in compiling the indexes and correcting proofs.

M. D. HOOKER

ABBREVIATIONS

B.A.S.O.R.   *Bulletin of the American Schools of Oriental Research.*

B.D.B.   F. Brown, S. R. Driver and C. A. Briggs, *Hebrew Lexicon of the Old Testament*, Oxford, 1906.

B.J.R.L.   *Bulletin of the John Rylands Library*, Manchester.

E.R.E.   *Encyclopaedia of Religion and Ethics*, ed. by J. Hastings, 12 vols. and index, 1908–21.

E.T.   *The Expository Times*, Edinburgh.

G.T.   C. L. W. Grimm, *Greek-English Lexicon*, trans. and revised by J. H. Thayer, 4th ed., Edinburgh, 1901.

H.D.B.   *Hastings' Dictionary of the Bible*, 4 vols. and extra vol., 1909.

J.B.L.   *Journal of Biblical Literature*, Philadelphia, U.S.A.

J.T.S.   *Journal of Theological Studies*, Oxford and London.

L.S.   H. G. Liddell and R. Scott, *Greek-English Lexicon*, new ed. by H. Stuart Jones, Oxford, 1925.

N.T.S.   *New Testament Studies*, London and New York.

T.W.B.   *A Theological Word-book of the Bible*, ed. by A. Richardson, London, 1950.

T.W.N.T.   *Theologisches Wörterbuch zum Neuen Testament*, ed. G. Kittel and G. Friedrich, Stuttgart, 1933– .

V.T.   *Vetus Testamentum*, Leiden.

Beginnings   *The Beginnings of Christianity*, part 1, 5 vols., ed. F. Jackson and K. Lake, London, 1920–33.

G. F. Moore, *Judaism*   *Judaism in the First Centuries of the Christian Era*, 3 vols., Cambridge, 1927–30.

C. R. North, *The Suffering Servant*   *The Suffering Servant of Deutero-Isaiah*, Oxford, 1948.

S.-B. *Kommentar*   H. L. Strack and P. Billerbeck, *Kommentar zum Neuen Testament aus Talmud und Midrasch*, 4 vols., Munich, 1922–8.

CHAPTER 1

GENERAL SURVEY OF RECENT WORK ON THE PROBLEM

I. INTRODUCTION

It is universally recognized that the concept of the Servant found in Deutero-Isaiah plays some part in New Testament theology, although there is considerable difference of opinion as to the extent and importance of its influence. The real problem is to discover at what point the identification of Jesus with the Servant came into Christian thought: whether it was inherent in the teaching of Jesus, or whether it was introduced by the Church to explain his death; and if the latter, at what stage this was done.

This problem has been recognized by many writers. The use of the idea of the Suffering Servant in 1 Peter is taken by Hoskyns and Davey[1] as an illustration of the problem of discovering whether the particular significance which is attached to the history of Jesus by the New Testament writers is due to some extraneous influence, or 'whether there is evidence that the significance was embedded in the concrete, historical living of the life and in the concrete, historical dying of the death, and, moreover, actually conditioned the course of the one and the fact of the other': this is, in fact, 'the real problem with which all New Testament exegesis is ultimately faced'.

F. C. Burkitt sets out the same problem in a different way when he says: 'From what did Jesus derive the conviction that He was destined to suffer, to be rejected, to be killed? The popular answer is that He identified Himself with the Suffering Servant of the Lord depicted by the Prophets, in other words that He derived it from a study of Isa. 53.'[2]

This 'popular' view had normally been held without question by the older commentators: for example, an article entitled 'Our Lord's use of the Old Testament'[3] described the attitude of Jesus in these words: 'He regards it as rich in prophecies of Himself, of His Passion and Resurrection, and of the preaching of His Gospel to the world.' The writers who held this view realized that it was subject to the difficulty that Jesus interpreted the Scriptures in a way foreign to the original meaning of the authors; they did not, however, normally question the correctness of the assumption that Jesus quoted the Old Testament passages. Even those who did not take this assumption for granted accepted the traditional answer as the most probable, without serious consideration of any alternative; thus J. E. Carpenter, writing of the suffering aspect of the Messianic character, said: 'When we try to trace it back to its source, shall we be wrong if we ascribe it, at least provisionally, to Jesus Himself?'[1]

2. OPPONENTS OF THE TRADITIONAL VIEW

The first serious challenge to this view was made by F. Jackson and K. Lake in their book *The Beginnings of Christianity*.[2] They recognized two distinct difficulties in connection with the New Testament words about the sufferings of Jesus. The first was the problem whether those sayings which connected the figure of the Son of Man with suffering were originally spoken by Jesus, or whether they represented the interpretation given to his words by the Church. They point out that the explicit predictions of his death by Jesus are not consistent with the behaviour of his disciples when those predictions were fulfilled; and further, that their context suggests that the disciples did not understand their meaning at the time. This evidence implies that the sayings were originally far more vague and obscure than they are in their present form, and Jackson and Lake therefore reach the conclusion that, while Jesus did speak of his rejection, it was not with the detail which is ascribed to him.

The other problem, which they take as being quite independent of the first, is whether this 'amplification of the connotation of Son of Man' to include the idea of suffering is due to literary influence or to the facts of the Passion. Literary influence, they say, must mean the figure of the Suffering Servant. They hold that references to the Servant are scanty in the New Testament, being confined to the more Hellenistic writings, and that therefore 'it was the knowledge of the Passion, whether prophetic or historic, not the interpretation of Isa. 53, which produced the gospel narrative'.[3] In an examination of the use of the concept in the various New Testament sources they maintain that the only possible references to the Servant in Mark are the use of παραδίδωμι —a word which they regard as the most natural one in the context— in 14. 18, 21, etc., and a possible allusion in 10. 45, where, however, the words used are quite different from the Greek version of Isa. 53. 12. In Q there is a possible allusion to Isaiah in the message of Jesus to John the Baptist (Matt. 11. 5 = Luke 7. 22), but if so it is to Isa. 61, and not to the concept of suffering. There are two definite quotations in Matthew (8. 17 and 12. 17 ff.), but both refer to healing miracles, not to vicarious suffering. It is not until Luke–Acts that the connection with the Suffering Servant is made. In Luke 4. 18 and Acts 10. 36 Jesus is clearly identified with the figure of Isa. 61, with again no thought of suffering, but in Luke 22. 37[1] and Acts 8. 32 quotations from Isa. 53 are applied to the Passion. They conclude: 'It is tempting to suggest that the interpretation of Isa. 53 as a prophecy of Jesus was first introduced by Hellenistic Christians, for there is no positive evidence of its existence in sources which certainly represent the thought of the first disciples in Jerusalem, but it was clearly part of the teaching of Philip.'[2]

This view was supported by F. C. Burkitt, who pointed out in *Christian Beginnings* that, while Paul, John, the Apocalypse, Mark, and Q show no influence of the Servant concept, nevertheless that influence was very soon felt in the New Testament, namely in Matthew, 1 Peter, Hebrews, and above all in Luke–Acts. 'That is to say, the writers who use the Greek Bible exclusively are on one side, while those who, like Saint Paul, have access to Semitic forms and interpretations of the Old Testament are on the other.' From this evidence Burkitt feels that there is 'a strong presumption that the application of Isa. 53 as a prediction of the Passion of Jesus was the work of Gentile Christians, familiar only with the Bible in Greek'.[3] In support of this he maintains that no one could have thought of Jesus as God's slave, which is the meaning of the Hebrew עֶבֶד translated by the Greek παῖς, whereas he might quite well have been regarded as παῖς by non-Jews, since in Greek the word carries no offensive meaning. Burkitt concludes, therefore, that the application of the Isaian concept of the Servant to Jesus was due to Greek-speaking Christians who did not realize that the original word meant 'slave'. This is 'a very early stage of Greek-speaking Christianity, but it is not quite primitive or apostolic'.[4]

H. J. Cadbury[1] also followed Jackson and Lake in their belief that Jesus was not influenced by the figure of the Suffering Servant, and he too supported this view by studying the use of the word παῖς in the New Testament. This word, when applied to Jesus, is generally taken as being a reference to his role as the Servant of Deutero-Isaiah, but Cadbury endeavoured to show that it has no such specialized meaning, but is an Old Testament form of expression with no implication of any one particular figure. Cadbury supports Jackson and Lake in maintaining that references to Isa. 53 are very few in the New Testament: 'Paul and Luke refer frequently in a general way to the Scriptural expectation of Christ's passion, but Paul never uses Isaiah's words and Luke but once (Acts 8. 32 f.).' Further, Cadbury maintains that Luke 'not only omits any vicarious phrases found in Mark, but the one time he does quote Isa. 53 almost unbelievably escapes all the vicarious phrases with which that passage abounds'.[2]

The position of these writers is similar to that maintained by certain continental scholars. Thus W. Bousset[3] considers it noteworthy that Isa. 53 exerted so little influence at first upon the Christian imagination, especially as the rest of the book was clearly influential. He notes that Paul shows no essential trace of the chapter, and that the early Christian title 'Lamb of God' need not be derived from this source; Matthew quotes from Isa. 53, but relates it to the healing miracles, not to the death of Jesus, and Bousset holds it to be very doubtful whether it would have been possible, in view of Jewish Messianic belief, to interpret this chapter in terms of a suffering Messiah. Like the scholars whose work has been discussed above, he draws attention to the fact that only 1 Peter and Acts (8. 32) quote the chapter in detail, and he concludes that the Old Testament has not played a very great part in shaping the gospel narrative apart from the passion story. Here, however, Old Testament prophecies and detailed predictions of his suffering have, so Bousset claims, been put into Jesus' mouth by the early Church, so that much of the story is reduplicated; moreover the history, as well as the predictions, has been elaborated by the primitive community, for 'man hat nicht nur Weissagung im Leben Jesu erfüllt gefunden sondern der Weissagungsbeweis hat selbst Geschichte gemacht'.[4] In particular, Pss. 22 and 69 have been influential here, though there are possible details also from Isa. 53. 12 and 50. 6.

A more radical position than that of Jackson and Lake is maintained by R. Bultmann,[1] who writes: 'The predictions of the passion, which represent his suffering and death as willed by God and necessary to salvation, were put in his mouth subsequently by the church.' He holds that the Church has rightly understood forgiveness as an event, but is wrong in seeing this event, 'the decisive act of deliverance, in the death of Jesus, or in his death and resurrection'. Like Jackson and Lake, Bultmann attributes these predictions of suffering, put into the mouth of Jesus, to Hellenistic Christianity: 'Moreover, Jesus did not speak of his death and resurrection and their redemptive significance. Some sayings of such a character are indeed attributed to him in the gospels, but they originated in the faith of the church—and none of them even in the primitive church, but in Hellenistic Christianity.' After examining what he considers to be the two most important of these sayings (Mark 10. 45 and 14. 24), and dismissing them as Hellenistic variations, he concludes: 'It is then certain that Jesus did not speak of his death and resurrection as redemptive acts.' Inevitably, Bultmann must reject also the idea that Jesus fused the two concepts of Son of Man and Servant of God; thus he writes elsewhere: 'The tradition of Jesus' sayings reveals no trace of a consciousness on his part of being the Servant of God of Isa. 53.'[2]

Bultmann thus denies the authenticity, not only of the details contained in the predictions of suffering, but of those predictions themselves. With regard to the question of their dependency on the Servant passages, however, he adopts a position similar to that of Jackson and Lake and of Bousset. For while he recognizes that the Passion narrative itself is full of details which have been deduced from the Old Testament,[3] he finds no reference to Isa. 53 in the earliest strata. Regarding the predictions of suffering attributed to Jesus, he claims that they 'obviously do not have Isa. 53 in mind; otherwise why is it nowhere referred to?'[4] On this question, therefore, these scholars are all agreed in maintaining that it was the Hellenistic Church which was responsible for the identification of Jesus with the Suffering Servant of Isa. 53.[5]

3. EXPONENTS OF THE TRADITIONAL VIEW

In spite of this serious attack made upon the traditional interpretation, the evidence brought against it seems to have been largely ignored by many scholars who still accept the use of Isa. 53 by Jesus without question. Thus Engnell[1] speaks of the 'indisputable role that the 'Ebed Yahweh figure and its ideological world played for Jesus and his messianic interpretation of himself', and writes: 'It should not be doubted that our Lord saw himself as the Messiah victorious and exalted by way of suffering, and interpreted his own situation and task in the light of this belief.' Similarly, E. O. James declares: 'While it has yet to be proved that the Isaianic Servant was originally identified with the Messiah, that Christ Himself so applied the prophecies is beyond reasonable doubt.'[2] Bultmann's categorical statements that Jesus did not speak of his death or regard himself in terms of the Servant are thus balanced by equally emphatic statements of the opposite view.

Among those who have recognized the seriousness of the problem, however, there are some who have attempted to find reasonable proof in support of the traditional view, although they have not answered all the evidence brought forward in opposition. Thus E. Hoskyns and N. Davey, as has been noted above, see in this question an example of the supreme problem of New Testament exegesis. Nevertheless they do not examine the evidence concerning the use of the Servant passages in particular, or answer the details of Jackson and Lake's attack. From an examination of the gospel narrative they argue that Jesus is throughout set against an Old Testament background, and that the authors of the gospels always had this background in mind. Assuming that the Evangelists had a definite purpose in writing—that of proclaiming the gospel of Jesus Christ, in whom the promises of the Old Testament were fulfilled—Hoskyns and Davey ask why this particular form was chosen.[3]

> Did the needs of the primitive church, its preaching, its manner of apologetic, its spiritual experience, the innate conception of its non-Jewish converts or the peculiar theologizing of St Paul, cause [Mark] to complicate the simple story of the vigorous life and tragic death of a Jewish reformer, and to invest them with this heavy significance? Or was there a complication

in the material itself which drove him so to order it that clearer expression might be given to the interpretation which it inevitably and unmistakably demanded? Why, for instance, did he again and again, in portraying his subject, use the medium of Old Testament aspiration? Was it because the apostolic age had been driven to do so in the hope of compelling the attention of the Jewish world? Or was it that Old Testament aspiration did in fact condition the teaching and action of Jesus, so that he went to his death consciously in order that the scripture might be fulfilled, and ordered his ministry to that end? In other words, is the particular Marcan ordering an imposition upon the original history, or the very essence of it?

In order to answer this question Hoskyns and Davey undertake an investigation of the Synoptic Problem, because they feel that if

analysis should reveal a steady unity of direction: if the four great blocks of material show a general agreement, and the editors are found to be mainly engaged in exposing a significance already contained in the material that they are handling, then, however awkward the result may be, it is difficult to avoid the conclusion that this unity of direction was set in motion, not by the creative faith of the primitive church, but by the teaching and actions of Jesus of Nazareth.[1]

After a comparison of the three authors of the Synoptics and then of the various sources used by them, they find that the same basic Christology and Old Testament background are common to them all. The references to the Old Testament in Matthew and Luke do not represent a radical change from the Marcan gospel, but are an attempt to clarify Mark's somewhat obscure allusions to the biblical background.[2] Hoskyns and Davey therefore conclude that

The interpretation put upon the actions and life and death of Jesus did not originate in the minds of the men who compiled the gospels in their present form. Their records have a clear and conscious purpose. That is obvious. But they extracted their purpose from the traditions they received: they did not impose it roughly upon a material unable to bear it. Their editing did not complicate the material, but simplified it.[3]

They continue:

Jesus acted as he did act and said what he did say because he was consciously fulfilling a necessity imposed upon him by God through the demands of the Old Testament. He died in Jerusalem, not because the Jews hounded him thither and did him to death, but because he was persuaded that, as messiah, he must journey to Jerusalem in order to be rejected and to die.

This conclusion is based upon the acceptance of the Four-document hypothesis, and not upon Form Criticism, the results of which have seriously modified the value of comparing sources. But an examination of the miracles, parables and aphorisms of Jesus leads them to the conclusion that these too have the same Christological significance— a significance in all cases rooted in the Old Testament.

V. Taylor was concerned with the problem of the influence of the Servant concept in the careful examination of the Passion-sayings which he made in his book *Jesus and His Sacrifice*. He regards it as 'hyper-criticism' to doubt that Isa. 53 is in mind in Mark 9. 12b, and holds that the reference here confirms those in Mark 8. 31, 9. 31 and 10. 33–4;[1] similarly, this chapter underlies the concepts expressed in Mark 10. 45 and 14. 24.[2] Taylor believes that Jesus had so far identified the Son of Man with the Servant 'that He can say of the Son of Man what, as far as the text of Scripture is concerned, is true only of the Servant'.[3] The presence of a quotation from Isa. 53. 12 in Luke 22. 37 'confirms the view that Jesus had deeply pondered the description of the Suffering Servant and saw it as a foreshadowing of His own experience of suffering and death'.[4] Such an interpretation of his vocation makes it incredible, Taylor maintains, that Jesus could have ignored the vicarious and representative aspects of the Servant's sufferings.[5]

In a recent article Taylor has examined the Servant problem more closely, again in relation to the Marcan Passion-sayings, which he regards as reflecting the influence of Isa. 53.[6] He argues that the Suffering Servant idea, as applied to Jesus, is almost wholly lacking in the later epistles, and appears in Paul only in passages taken over from a previous tradition; in Acts it is found in what appear to be early Aramaic sources, in the title 'Servant', and in the story of the Ethiopian eunuch. It is on the basis of this evidence that Taylor deems it probable that the Servant Christology was at its height 'in the period A.D. 30–50, and in the earlier of the two decades more than in the later'.[7] Moreover, the further conclusion that this doctrine comes from Jesus himself rather than from the early community is supported by the originality of the concept, and the reasonableness of the view that Jesus must have thought and taught about his probable rejection. It is on the belief that the Servant theme goes back to Jesus himself, therefore, that Taylor here establishes his case for the authenticity of the sayings.

It should be noted that Taylor—like many other scholars—does not seriously doubt the influence of Isa. 53 on the Passion-sayings; his concern is rather with the genuineness of the sayings themselves. His method is thus the reverse of that adopted by Jackson and Lake, since he uses an affirmative answer to the question of influence by Isa. 53 to prove that the predictions of suffering were spoken by Christ: they, on the other hand, treat the problem of Isa. 53 as quite independent of the question of the authenticity of the Passion-sayings.

Rudolf Otto, in *The Kingdom of God and the Son of Man*,[1] argued that the words of Mark 9. 12 are proof of Jesus' awareness that he was the Suffering Servant of Isa. 53, and that they become intelligible only when regarded as a quotation from that chapter. Similarly, he saw in Mark 10. 45 'a clear synthesis of the Son of Man and Isaiah's Servant of God', and it was in the light of this identification that Otto understood the meaning of Christ's death.

C. J. Cadoux set forth his conviction that Jesus applied the Servant passages to himself in *The Historic Mission of Jesus*.[2] He holds the evidence to be adequate, although not abundant; it is to be found in the echo of Isa. 42. 1 at the Baptism and Transfiguration, in the reading of Isa. 61. 1–2 by Jesus at Nazareth (Luke 4. 17–21), in Jesus' application of Isa. 53. 12 to himself at the Last Supper (Luke 22. 37), and in the echo of Isa. 53. 11–12 in the word 'many' in Mark 10. 45 and 14. 24 (cf. Matt. 20. 28, 26. 28). In view of the fact that the method of quotation at that time paid little attention to context, however, and his belief that Messianic interpretation of the Servant passages by the Jews was post-Christian, Cadoux disagrees with those many commentators who regard evidence that Jesus identified himself with some characteristics of the Servant as sufficient to prove also his acceptance of Isa. 53 as his destiny. He holds it improbable that Jesus had the later songs in mind at the very beginning of his ministry, and maintains rather that his use of these passages was a developing one, which embraced the picture given in Isa. 53 only as his hopes of success changed to the expectation of suffering.[3]

H. W. Wolff[4] has made a detailed study of the fourth Servant Song and its influence in the early Church. Supporting the traditional view, Wolff maintains that both the frequency with which Jesus refers to Deutero-Isaiah, and his constant occupation with the fate of John the

Baptist and the prophets, make it very unlikely that he could have ignored Isa. 53. He examines those sayings in which he finds the influence of this chapter (Luke 22. 37, Mark 10. 45, 14. 24, 9. 12b), and puts forward important arguments for their authenticity. Further, although in Luke 22. 37 only a few words from Isa. 53 are quoted, and these do not speak of the significance of Jesus' death, Wolff finds this significance expressed in Mark 10. 45 and 14. 24, where words are echoed from Isa. 53, although he admits that there is no actual quotation. In the light of these two passages he feels justified in referring Mark 9. 12b primarily to the same background. From this evidence Wolff concludes that Isa. 53 played an important role in Jesus' thought about his death: the fact that there is nevertheless so little direct evidence of its importance he attributes to the fact that Jesus—in contrast to his contemporaries—used the Scriptures in a 'synthetic' rather than 'atomistic' manner; his quotation of Isa. 53 in Luke 22. 37 is therefore not the use of words torn from their context, but implies the concepts of the whole prophecy.

W. Manson, in his book *Jesus the Messiah*,[1] admits that Jesus never actually designated himself as 'Servant', but maintains nevertheless that he regarded his vocation in the light of Isaiah's prophecies, and that in the sayings of Jesus himself 'it is made clear that the spirit, the example, the obedience, and the self-renunciation of the Isaianic Servant possessed a high significance for him, and exercised a profoundly formative influence on his interpretation of his work and destiny'. For although the Servant is nowhere 'the subject of any pronouncement of Jesus about his personal vocation or fortunes', yet this figure does supply 'the predicate', and Jesus 'sees the way marked out for him by the practice of the Servant'. Manson suggests two possible explanations for this avoidance of the direct application of the term 'Servant' to himself: either that the name 'Servant' was too general to convey a sense of the authority of Jesus; or, more likely, that the 'Son of Man' symbol had come for Jesus to absorb all other aspects of the Messianic idea. But though the name of 'Servant' is not adopted by Jesus, the concept finds expression in his teaching: the Servant can be seen, both in Jesus' teaching about his sacrifice, since the glory of the Son of Man was to come about only through the sufferings of the Servant; and in his teaching on righteousness, where the Servant affords the supreme example, so that Manson writes that it 'was dyed in the grain with reminiscence of the Servant. The evangelist has perhaps touched up the colouring of the original saying of Jesus, but that is all.'

J. W. Bowman sums up the importance of the Servant problem when he says: '*The Church cannot indefinitely continue to believe about Jesus what he did not know to be true about himself!* The question, accordingly, of his Messianic consciousness is the most vital one the Christian faith has to face.'[1] Bowman holds that when the Church confesses Jesus as 'the crucified Saviour' and as 'Lord of the Church', these expressions are the Greek equivalent of the Hebrew 'Suffering Servant' and 'Messiah of the Remnant', so that the idea implied by the combination of the two terms, although they themselves are found together only in the words of the *Bath Qôl* at Jesus' Baptism, nevertheless 'forms the very foundation of the New Testament theology'. These two phrases, in isolation,

became the stock-in-trade of the prophetic strand of Hebrew culture centuries before the Christian Era. But *who first brought these terms together into a fertilizing union?* This question is of cosmic significance. The answer to it is the name of the originator of Christianity as we know it. He is the creator of the New Testament faith and of the Christian Church.

Essentially it is the answer to this question that students of the New Testament have been earnestly seeking for the past hundred years and more.[2]

This combination, Bowman maintains, appears at the very beginning of Jesus' ministry, and as the reference to Ps. 2 at his Baptism confirmed his consciousness of Messiahship, so the reference to Isa. 42 defined its nature as one of suffering and death; this is further seen in the fact that Jesus—like the Servant—is anointed with the Spirit. This experience was continued in the Temptation, which could come only to one who knew himself to be Messiah and yet realized that he was destined to suffer; for there could be no temptations facing a Messiah of the traditional pattern.

The problem of Jesus' Messianic consciousness has been answered at one extreme by those who say he held himself to be the Messiah of traditional Jewish expectation, and at the other by those who maintain that he did not believe himself to be the Messiah at all. Bowman rejects both these solutions and suggests that Jesus did know himself to be the Messiah, but that his conception of Messiahship was not the popular one, but was based upon the prophetic ideas of the Messiah of the Remnant and the Suffering Servant. He argues that the originality shown in the combination of these two ideas must be due to an individual—that is to Jesus—and not to a community, which could not be so brilliantly creative. But at the same time this uniqueness was not something without foundation, but shows a 'deep-seated continuity with the best and highest in the Hebraic culture, namely, with the prophetic strand of that culture'.[1] Jesus' background is that of the prophetic literature, not of any of the Jewish sects, and his teaching and work show how he was at once unique and the continuation of the prophetic promises.

Bowman then examines the teaching of Jesus and notes his winsomeness, authority and wisdom, contrasting his words with those of the Rabbis. Speaking of his works, Bowman stresses their importance as an expression of Jesus' person; he refused to perform signs as proof of his Messiahship when asked to do so by the Pharisees, because such signs would have proved him to be the popular Messiah. Nevertheless his works were signs of his Messiahship, though they were not recognized as such, since his conception of his vocation was not the accepted one; '*both word and work were intended in Jesus' view to serve precisely the same function in his ministry*'. When John the Baptist doubts whether Jesus is the true Messiah, the latter's answer to him (in the form of a quotation from Isa. 35 and 61) is that he is to 'think of his activity as a *saving* one in terms of the description of the Suffering Servant'.[2]

From this evidence Bowman concludes:

it may be said now, without any reservation, that either: (*a*) Jesus did not conceive himself to be the Messiah at all, or (*b*) if he did, then his conception of the Messiahship was radically different from every other held in his time! It went back, that is to say, to the old prophetic conceptions of the Messiah of the Remnant and the Suffering Servant of the Lord.[3]

Bowman next examines the title 'Son of Man', which he accepts as having a Messianic meaning in pre-Christian times, and finds that it is used both of exaltation and of humiliation. Of these 'the exaltation motif attaching to the term was by no means original with Jesus. *What was new with him was that to the Son of Man, Messiah concept he brought the motif of humiliation, of suffering and death!*'[4] Bowman presumes that this idea of humiliation was introduced by the Suffering Servant concept, since Jesus must have recognized the power of love within himself to be the character of the Suffering Servant. So Jesus was responsible for the fusion of the three figures of Messiah, Son of Man and Suffering Servant. As proof that Jesus knew himself to be the Suffering Servant, Bowman refers[1] to the scene in the synagogue at Nazareth where 'it was the role of the Suffering Servant which our Lord said he was about to assume', and to the answer to John the Baptist, when 'our Lord once more represented the nature of his mission in terms of the labours of the Suffering Servant'. Bowman regards these two events, taken with the Baptism, as 'irresistible testimony to Jesus' understanding of the Father's will for him in line with the portrait of the Suffering Servant'. He then notes that the humiliation motif at times became detached from the Suffering Servant concept and could stand alone, so that Jesus could speak of his suffering without actually referring to the Servant, and the idea of humiliation became part of the title by which he chose to designate himself—that of 'Son of Man'.

C. R. North summarizes the argument of Jackson and Lake and seeks to answer it in his study *The Suffering Servant in Deutero-Isaiah*.[2] Supporting the traditional view that Jesus regarded himself as the Servant, North argues that even allowing for the expansions of the Evangelists, there are still indications that Jesus clearly foresaw his destiny, in the sayings of the cup and baptism.[3] Further, the words heard by Jesus at his baptism, and his application of Isa. 61 to himself in Luke 4. 21, show that he thought of himself in terms of the Old Testament Messiah—a concept which for him included both Son of Man and Servant—from the very beginning of his ministry. North claims that even if there are no indisputable references to Isa. 53 by Jesus, this passage is the only basis which can account for the Church's belief that 'Christ died for our sins according to the scriptures', and he quotes with approval the words of Wheeler Robinson: 'That which explains the faith of the disciples might with equal justice be used to explain the shaping of the conviction in the mind of their Master.'[4] Outside the gospels there are few references, and these, North admits, are not clear, although Acts 8 and 1 Peter 2 show that 'the early Church did interpret the cross in the light of Isa. 53', and he therefore concurs with the judgement of V. Taylor: 'In the records of primitive Christian belief we can trace a diminishing emphasis upon an idea which for Jesus Himself was central and determinative.'[1] North therefore arrives at a conclusion which is the direct opposite of that reached by the opponents of the traditional view.

The problem is discussed by Joachim Jeremias in the article 'παῖς Θεοῦ' in *Theologisches Wörterbuch zum Neuen Testament*.[2] While he agrees with the judgement that many of the gospel passages which show Jesus as applying the 'Servant of Yahweh' sayings to himself bear the marks of influence by the early Church, he maintains that this does not justify the dismissal of them *en bloc*. The Evangelists' assertion that Jesus reckoned with the likelihood of violent death possesses great historical probability. It is confirmed by the situation of danger in which Jesus continually found himself; by the fact that he saw himself as standing in the succession of the prophets, and that martyrdom was at that time held to be part of the prophetic office; and by the fact that Jesus' predictions of suffering for himself contain many details which were not fulfilled, and so cannot have been composed by the Church.

Jeremias argues that if Jesus did realize the probability of his death, then he must also have given thought to its meaning: it is highly probable that he found the key to this in Isa. 53, as the sources maintain, and such an interpretation would be in keeping with his frequent use of Isa. 40 ff. Proof of this supposition is seen by Jeremias in the following observations. First, the tradition is a pre-Hellenistic one, showing no certain influence of the LXX except in Luke 22. 37, and in many cases definitely depending on a Hebrew or Aramaic background.[3] Secondly, the sayings are often of so general a nature that they cannot have been composed *ex eventu*; moreover, these passages omit any mention of the Resurrection.[4] Thirdly, many of the passages are rooted firmly in their context and are found on investigation to be an essential part of the pericope.[5] Fourthly, the Marcan version of the Last Supper contains an old tradition of Isa. 53: this account is held by Jeremias to be older than the Hellenistic form of Paul's which is found in 1 Corinthians.

Finally, Jeremias suggests that a possible explanation of the paucity of passages which contain references by Jesus to the Servant may be that it was only to his own disciples, and not openly, that he entrusted the secret that he believed himself to have been sent by God to fulfil this prophecy.

T. W. Manson sets out the problem of the use of the Old Testament in the New in these words:

> The claims of the kerygma were supported by appeals to Old Testament texts, the so-called Testimonia, and by detailed accounts of the Ministry and Passion. It is here that we are brought face to face with the main question concerning the gospels as historical documents. It is this. Were the stories told in the gospels created in order to provide fulfilment for the Messianic prophecies or were the prophecies sought out of the Old Testament in order to provide a *raison d'être* in the purposes of God for the particular incidents that went to make up the Ministry of Jesus? Has the evidence been faked to support the theory or has the theory been devised to suit the evidence?[1]

Manson does not, however, offer any evidence to support his contention that 'the figure of the Son of Man...in the teaching of Jesus combines the characteristics of the servant of Jehovah in Deutero-Isaiah and the Son of Man in Daniel',[2] or that Jesus defines 'Son of Man in terms of the Servant of the Lord portrayed in Isa. 40-55'.[3] He points out the tension which existed between the popular Messianic hope of the time —a longing for a Messiah who should be Son of David—and the Messianic purposes of Jesus, who saw his vocation in terms of Son of Man and Servant of the Lord.

H. E. W. Turner has discussed the problem in his book *Jesus, Master and Lord*.[4] In support of the view that the identification with the Suffering Servant goes back to Jesus himself, Turner writes:

> the Primitive Church was, Paul apart, not so fruitful in profound and original ideas as to invent one of great and rich significance and then to allow it so quickly to recede into the background. And it is more likely that the marginalia of the Evangelists are drawing out the significance of what was for Jesus already there rather than importing into the facts a significance which they did not possess.[5]

Turner agrees with F. C. Burkitt that the references to the Suffering Servant in the gospels seem to take the form of marginal references, but he refuses to admit that this means that they are glosses; rather he sees in them 'footnotes drawing out and making explicit what was already involved in the actions and sufferings of our Lord'. He finds further evidence in Mark 10. 45, the words of the voice at the Baptism and the Transfiguration, and in 'the silences and indirectness of claim which Jesus imposed upon Himself'.[1]

One of the most recent defences of the belief that the Servant concept can be traced back to Jesus is made by R. H. Fuller in *The Mission and Achievement of Jesus*.[2] Fuller says that since—as he endeavours to show—Jesus related his healing miracles to his proclamation of the Kingdom, it would be incredible if he did not relate his death also to that proclamation. While some details in the five Marcan Passion sayings— 8. 31, 9. 12, 9. 31, 10. 33, 10. 45—may be the result of subsequent reflection on past events, many of them do not refer to details recounted in the Passion narrative, and can therefore be taken as genuine words of Jesus. These sections, Fuller maintains, when placed together form a clear description of the Suffering Servant of Isa. 53, and some of the phrases are direct reproductions of the Hebrew text. He thus distinguishes between 'a pre-Hellenistic stratum in which Jesus is represented as foretelling his sufferings partly in general terms and partly in language derived from the Hebrew text of Isa. 53, and a later stratum (whether editorial or pre-Markan, we cannot say for certain) in which the prophecies have been expanded in the light of subsequent events'.[3]

While Fuller admits that it is impossible to answer with absolute certainty the question whether this older stratum goes back to Jesus himself, he finds confirmation for an affirmative answer in Mark 1. 11, Luke 12. 49–50, 13. 32–3, and the sayings at the Last Supper. He believes that Jesus' consciousness was primarily one of Sonship—the fulfilment of 'the mission and destiny of Israel'—and that this Sonship was defined for him at the Baptism in terms of the Servant.[4] The concepts of Servant and Son of Man are not conflated, since the period of obedience, as Servant, belongs to Jesus' earthly life, and he will become Son of Man only after his death: for the Cross is the decisive event which inaugurates the Kingdom, and Jesus the Servant stands in the same relationship to the glorified Son of Man as his earthly ministry does to the Coming Kingdom.[5]

4. PETRINE INFLUENCE

Several scholars have made a suggestion which deserves separate consideration: they maintain that the application of the Servant theme to Jesus by the early Church was due primarily to Petrine influence. This theory is based upon their claim that the doctrine is found only in the very primitive tradition, and mainly in those sources which are connected with the name of Peter. This is the position which is adopted by O. Cullmann in *Peter: Disciple, Apostle, Martyr*;[1] he notes that the four occasions in Acts when the title παῖς Θεοῦ is applied to Jesus all occur in one section, in chapters 3 and 4.[2] Of these, '*two stand in speeches which are ascribed to the Apostle Peter* and two in a prayer spoken in unison by the Jerusalem group of disciples when Peter is present'. Confirmation that the belief is associated with Peter is to be seen in the extensive quotation of the fourth Servant Song in 1 Pet. 2. 21 ff., quite independently of whether this epistle is genuine. Cullman holds that Peter, who at Caesarea Philippi had denied the necessity for Christ's suffering, was later, with typical impetuosity, the first to preach it, and could find no better way of expressing this conviction than by adopting the very concept of the Servant which had been used by his master.

A similar interpretation is made by L. L. Carpenter, who, in his book *Primitive Christian Application of the Doctrine of the Servant*, makes a careful examination of 'all references to, or even hints in regard to, the Servant passages or the Servant idea' over a period of six centuries.[3] His work covers both Jewish and Christian application of the Servant passages in biblical and extra-canonical writings. He accepts most of the passages examined as being genuinely influenced by the Servant concept, which he finds underlying even those books which do not make an open use of the idea. His examination, however, is an attempt to discover the origin and use of the concept by the Church, rather than to solve the problem of whether Jesus himself was conscious of the idea, although he constantly reiterates his belief that the application must go back to Jesus. He finds confirmation for this in the association of the concept with Peter, and holds that it became prominent for him through his experience of forgiveness after the Resurrection.[4] Furthermore, Peter is expressly mentioned in 1 Cor. 15. 3 ff., the one occasion when Paul used this concept, where he listed it as something which he had received from his predecessors in the faith.[5]

Even if we accept Carpenter's conclusion that the idea of the Servant is present throughout so much of the New Testament, the fact that his followers may have seen the relevance of Isa. 53 cannot, of course, be taken as proof that Jesus himself did. The suggestion that Peter is primarily responsible may, however, be important in discussing this problem, since it is reasonable to suppose that Peter, the leader of the disciples, was a reliable witness to the words of Jesus. Even the supporters of the Petrine view are divided on this question, however, and B. W. Bacon,[1] while he also holds that the doctrine can be traced to Peter, nevertheless finds evidence for attacking the traditional view upheld by Cullman and Carpenter.

5. THE NEED FOR FURTHER INVESTIGATION

It has been possible in this short discussion to summarize only a few representative views on a subject concerning which a great deal has been written. The fact that the vast majority of scholars have declared themselves supporters of the traditional view might suggest that the problem has been resolved: and, indeed, if their arguments can be substantiated it is clear that there will be no cause for further investigation. It will therefore be desirable at this point to examine the arguments of a typical exponent of the traditional view in more detail. For this purpose it is convenient to select J. W. Bowman, since he sets out clearly the fundamental importance of the problem and makes one of the most noteworthy and detailed attempts to show the significance which he believes the Suffering Servant concept to have had for the mind of Jesus.

The starting-point of Bowman's claim is the uniting of the concepts of 'Messiah of the Remnant' and 'Suffering Servant', which he finds combined by the voice at the Baptism, in quotations from Ps. 2 and Isa. 42. But do the words which he believes come from Ps. 2—a psalm typical of Israel's political hopes—really convey the prophetic concept of the 'Messiah of the Remnant'? For Bowman himself says: 'The "Messiah of the Remnant" concept was an ethico-spiritual one, as far as possible removed from the nationalistic Messiah of the popular thought.'[2] Is it then clear that the words 'Thou art my Son' are meant to apply specifically to the prophetic rather than to the popular idea? Furthermore, are we justified in assuming with Bowman that a reference which he finds here to the Servant of Isa. 42 implies the mission of the Suffering Servant of Isa. 53? If not, we cannot accept the thesis that a fusion is made here between these two prophetic concepts. We may note also that it is doubtful whether these two figures were ever quite as important in prophetic thought as Bowman maintains. But if Jesus did indeed combine them in his understanding of his own mission, then he chose a very roundabout manner of expression in handing on to his disciples what was to become 'the very foundation of New Testament theology': for Bowman admits that this is the only occasion when these two terms, in their Hebrew form, are in fact combined.

The fact that Bowman shows Jesus to be a unique teacher can tell us nothing about whether he is the Suffering Servant. Although Jesus does indeed define his work by quoting from the book of Isaiah, in neither case where he does so—in the synagogue at Nazareth and in his reply to John—is it a passage about the Suffering Servant, or even a passage from Deutero-Isaiah, which he quotes. There may be 'an awareness on Jesus' part of continuity with the prophetic heritage of Israel',[1] but this does not prove that he necessarily thought of himself as the Suffering Servant. Bowman's assertion that on these two occasions Jesus represented his mission in terms of that figure is scarcely justified when we consider, not only that Jesus does not refer to a Servant passage, but that nowhere in these descriptions is there the slightest hint about suffering: the close association of Isa. 35 and 61 with the element of vicarious suffering in Isa. 53 is an entirely modern development.[2] Similarly, when speaking about the gift of the Spirit at Jesus' Baptism, Bowman assumes without justification that a possible reference to the Servant concept confirms Jesus as the *Suffering* Servant; but the one figure does not necessarily imply the other. Further, even if we agree that the alternatives are either that Jesus did not conceive himself to be the Messiah at all, or that his idea of Messiahship was radically different from all others, this does not inevitably mean, as Bowman maintains, that in the second case the concept must have been derived from the Suffering Servant and the Messiah of the Remnant.

Bowman argues that the idea of humiliation was introduced into the 'Son of Man' concept by Jesus, and then assumes that this must have been by the fusion of this figure with those of the Messiah and the Suffering Servant. We are not, however, obliged to assume that the figure of the Servant was the link between the concepts of Son of Man and Messiah, or that it was the only possible source for the idea of suffering and humiliation: Isa. 53 is not the only passage in the Old

Testament which speaks of suffering. Bowman is thus assuming the answer to his question before he has proved his case. He goes on to show how the idea of suffering became detached and could stand alone apart from the concept of the Suffering Servant: this, however, supports the exact opposite of Bowman's thesis—it suggests that the humiliation motif never depended on the Servant concept but was independent from the beginning, and that it was only later that the aptness of the Isaian figure was noticed and the parallel drawn.

The approach of Bowman is typical of the exponents of the traditional view in general: far too often they tend to beg the question rather than to make a fair critical analysis of the evidence, and the arguments of Jackson and Lake remain unanswered. Indeed, it may be seriously questioned whether the material has been examined sufficiently thoroughly to warrant on either side such categorical conclusions as those which have frequently been advanced. For, on the one hand, those who attack the tradition examine only those few passages where they admit the possible influence of the Servant idea, and completely ignore as unworthy of attention the numerous other references which their opponents claim; bringing forward good arguments against the few texts which they examine, they then point out the dangers of building a whole Christology on references which are so few and of so precarious a nature. The defenders of the traditional view, on the other hand, have been equally unwilling to examine the evidence, but whereas their opponents have examined a few passages in detail and ignored the rest, these scholars quote numerous references, and rely on the number as sufficient support to their claim. They begin with a tacit assumption of the influence of the Servant on the thought of Jesus, and then show how well this fits in with their interpretation of his life and death; once the influence has been assumed, it is easy to find numerous passages which appear to support it.[1] The difference in the approach of the two schools is illustrated by the fact that whereas in Mark the authors of *The Beginnings of Christianity* consider only 14. 18, 21 and 10. 45, C. H. Dodd claims at least nine references.[2]

6. METHOD OF INVESTIGATION

To answer the question raised by Jackson and Lake it is not enough to rely solely upon general arguments concerning Old Testament influence or the character of Jesus: before any judgement can be made, it is essential to examine in detail each of the New Testament passages concerning which claims for the influence of the Servant concept have been advanced.[1] The diversity of opinion on the problem suggests beforehand that such an examination may, of itself, provide insufficient evidence upon which to base any conclusions. Nevertheless, while verbal similarity or dissimilarity alone cannot solve the problem of the significance of the Servant figure in New Testament thought, we have already seen that similarity of thought, without any linguistic evidence, is equally inconclusive. Our study must therefore include this detailed investigation of individual passages, as well as an examination of the Old Testament background of the Servant concept and its use in first-century Judaism, before we can consider the place of the Servant in the wider context of Jesus' own conception of his mission.

The suggestion of a linguistic examination, however, immediately raises the question of the manner in which the early Christians used passages of scripture. C. H. Dodd[2] has made a brief examination of the particular New Testament passages which concern our study, in support of his contention that certain passages in the Old Testament were regarded by the early Church as setting forth the determinate counsel of God which had now been fulfilled in the gospel facts, and that these passages are, moreover, common to all the main portions of the New Testament. Furthermore, Dodd claims that these sections are regarded as wholes by the New Testament writers, so that the quotation of one verse does not stand alone, but is a pointer to the whole context of the Old Testament passage. In this he is defending a view of scripture which has been attacked by H. J. Cadbury as a modern approach quite alien to the attitude of the New Testament authors. Thus with regard to the Servant concept Cadbury writes:

Even where parts of Isa. 53 are plainly quoted by early Christians it is important not to assume that the whole chapter is in the quoter's mind. The Christian use of Old Testament passages usually called attention to the actual part quoted, or even less than the whole quotation, in a quite verbal and literal sense. Thus Matt. 8. 17 quotes Isa. 53. 4a, b, of Jesus' cures, Matt. 12. 17f. quotes Isa. 42. 1f. of his avoidance of publicity, Luke at 22. 37 quotes Isa. 53. 12d, the phrase καὶ μετὰ ἀνόμων ἐλογίσθη, and Acts 8. 32f. applies Isa. 53. 7f. to Jesus in some sense not clear to us. Only in 1 Pet. 2. 22–4 do we have a continuous application to Jesus of several successive items from Isa. 53.

In their atomistic use of Scripture the early Christians were very different from the modern theologian who, gathering together the four 'servant passages' of Isaiah, derives from them a complete concept, treating them as a whole, and then assumes that this Christological concept underlies the passages mentioned, and even such passages as have no more echo of Isaiah than the simple παῖς.[1]

Dodd lists a large number of places in the New Testament where he finds references to the Servant passages, including those which are discussed by Jackson and Lake. He admits that some of these are doubtful and have no clear reference, but argues that taken together they have considerable weight. But this is surely a circular argument, for the strength of Dodd's evidence depends on the very point he is trying to prove. If we accept his theory that each reminiscence, however small, is meant to conjure up the whole corpus of the Messianic picture, then the number of references supports the theory we have already accepted; but if we adopt Cadbury's position, then the scattered and scanty nature of the evidence does not seem to carry much weight; for Dodd quotes no passage—apart from that in 1 Pet. 2—where there is any sustained interpretation of Jesus as Servant. The references are admittedly widely diffused among the New Testament writers—but they are indeed so widely diffused that there are no two in such proximity as to justify, with regard to Deutero-Isaiah, Dodd's claim that words from different verses of an Old Testament passage occurring throughout a section in the New show that the whole passage is in mind, and not just those verses which are actually quoted.

Clearly the value which we attach to possible references to the Servant passages depends largely on our answer to this problem of the New Testament use of Scripture. If we adopt Dodd's viewpoint, then we must attach far more importance to the Servant references than if we hold that the writers used the Old Testament in a purely atomistic way.[2] This question must be borne in mind, therefore, during our examination of the linguistic evidence. Unless we find any evidence to support Dodd's claim, however, either in a unified interpretation by the Jews of the whole Isaianic Servant concept, or in the New Testament passages themselves, we must assume that he has failed to prove his case, and that the 'atomistic' interpretation is therefore the correct one. Dodd's conclusions would not, of course, even if they were substantiated, solve the basic problem with which we are concerned, since his analysis deals only with the extent to which the Servant passages are used in the New Testament, and is not meant to decide with whom this use originated.

7. THE SIGNIFICANCE OF THE PROBLEM

The problem of the influence of Isa. 53 on the thought of Jesus is not a purely academic one. The supreme importance of the question is witnessed to by the vast amount of labour which has been expended on attempts to come to a solution: for the whole Christian doctrine of Atonement is involved in this problem. This was clearly put forward by Hastings Rashdall in his 1915 Bampton Lectures.[1] Rashdall there sought to show that in the words of Jesus there is no trace of any teaching that his death is in any way uniquely efficacious or necessary for the forgiveness of sins;[2] the repentance of the sinner is the only requirement a loving God needs. While he admitted that it is just possible that the words of Mark 10. 45 and 14. 21–4 are genuine utterances of Jesus, Rashdall maintained that even they do not speak of any vicarious punishment or sacrifice, although he believed that they echo words about vicarious suffering from Isa. 53. The belief that forgiveness of sins depended on faith in the saving power of Christ's death developed, therefore, some time between the Resurrection and the conversion of St Paul, and in Hellenistic, as opposed to Judaistic, Christianity.[3] Rashdall maintained that this was derived primarily from a study of the Scriptures by those who sought to solve the enigma of the scandal of the Cross; nothing was more natural than that they should find in Isa. 53 the answer to this very real problem, even if that chapter had not before been applied to the Messiah, or if Jesus himself had not used the Servant language: and this doctrine was confirmed by the experience of the early Christians, who associated their faith in Jesus as the Messiah with their release from the burden of sin.

It may, however, be argued that it was Jesus himself who offered this solution to the enigma of the Cross, but that he came to this recognition of himself as a suffering, redeeming Messiah, not by a close study of Isa. 53, but by the realization that God's salvation is always accomplished through suffering, and that his own life must of necessity fulfil this same pattern. Thus a decision that the Suffering Servant concept was not influential in the thought of Jesus will not necessarily lead to the conclusion that he attached no atoning significance to his death, unless it can also be shown that there is no other evidence in the Gospels that he did so. Nor, on the other hand, will a decision that Jesus did use the Servant passages lead us to believe that he interpreted the meaning of his death in their light, if it is found that he nowhere refers to the words which attach an atoning significance to the Servant's sufferings.[1] Nevertheless, it is clear that these two problems are closely related, and that the decision reached concerning the influence of Isa. 53 on the thought of Jesus and of the early Church is of great importance for the problem whether the Christian doctrine of Atonement derives from Jesus himself, or was evolved by his earliest followers.

CHAPTER 2

THE SERVANT PASSAGES: THEIR MEANING AND BACKGROUND

1. INTRODUCTION

In order to determine what influence, if any, the Servant figure exercised on the mind of Jesus, or on the writers of the New Testament, it is important to examine the interpretation of the Servant passages which was held in the time of Jesus. Too much study of our problem, as we have noted already, has been based on what is fundamentally a Christian interpretation of Deutero-Isaiah, unconsciously influenced by the traditional identification of Jesus with the Servant. It is therefore essential to discover, as far as is possible, the meaning which the concept held for the Jews of that period.

It is appropriate, however, before turning to this examination of the interpretation of the Servant in the first century A.D., to consider briefly the question of the original identity of the Servant. There is no need to attempt here any kind of summary of the various views which have been held on this subject, or a comparison of the evidence which has been brought to support them.[1] It may, however, prove of value to consider in this chapter the original place and meaning of the Servant passages in the whole context of Hebrew prophecy, and any theory as to the identity of the Servant which this may suggest, in so far as this may provide a valuable clue to later interpretation.

2. THE SONGS IN RELATION TO THEIR CONTEXT

Discussion of Deutero-Isaiah has inevitably centred around the problem of the Servant Songs, and this has resulted in a tendency to examine these so-called 'Songs' by themselves, with little regard either to their relation to the rest of Deutero-Isaiah, or to their place in Hebrew prophecy as a whole. Indeed, one of the most hotly debated questions concerning the Songs is whether they are in context; many scholars hold, either that they are not by Deutero-Isaiah, or that they were inserted out of place by the compiler. But the most careful examination of the language, style, metre and thought of the songs has not been able to disprove their genuineness.[1] In spite of this, ever since the Servant Songs were 'discovered', critics have tended to discuss them as a problem apart, an attitude which is undoubtedly a reaction against the older view which regarded Deutero-Isaiah—or even the whole of Isaiah—as an entity, a book written according to a predetermined plan.

In rejecting this earlier theory, however, it seems that modern criticism may have rejected with it a certain amount of truth which it contained. The desire to analyse prophetic material until it is reduced to a heap of fragments, each conforming to the critic's ideas of the pattern which the prophet should have adopted for his oracles, but bearing little relation to its context, should not be allowed to obscure the probability that behind the different utterances of one man there may lie some kind of common theme or motive. The sound recognition underlying this excessively analytical attitude, that the prophetic material is a collection of small complete units rather than a conscious attempt by the prophet to compose a polished literary work of art, must not cause us to forget that a prophet was a man with a vital message to proclaim, and that such a message is likely to recur throughout his oracles, however different the expression which it may receive in each. Unless there is evidence to the contrary, the supposition that a theme which appears to be common to the prophecy as a whole may be an important clue to the original intention of the author is at least worthy of serious consideration.[2]

The important question, therefore, is whether any such common theme can be traced throughout the individual poems which make up what we have of Deutero-Isaiah's work, and whether this pattern, if it exists, extends also to the Songs. If it does, then the latter form an integral part of his oracles; they may be a higher expression of his ideas, and they may introduce more profound concepts, but fundamentally they are at one with the rest of his thinking; they are not passages of an entirely different nature which belong to another period in his ministry when he was concerned with different ideas, and which have been inserted arbitrarily in totally irrelevant contexts.

A study of the text shows us that the great themes of Deutero-Isaiah are the power and glory of Yahweh, the election of Israel for his purposes, and her restoration to divine favour and consequent return to Jerusalem from Exile. These are but three parts to one whole; this is seen by examining the book and noting how these three strands are interwoven, recurring again and again throughout the oracles, and together forming the core of Deutero-Isaiah's message.

Examination of the Dominant Themes of Isa. 40–55

40. 1–8. The announcement of Israel's return from Exile, whereby Yahweh's glory will be revealed to the nations. Men are mortal, but the word of God endures.

40. 9–26. Introduction of her God to Israel, leading into a song of praise, in which God, the omnipotent Creator, is contrasted with men and with idols, who are as nothing before him.

40. 27–31. Promise of Yahweh's help for his people.

41. 1–7. Yahweh is at work through Cyrus: the nations are afraid.

41. 8–20. But Israel—Yahweh's chosen servant—need not fear, since Yahweh will help her. Her enemies will be wiped out. Yahweh will help Israel so that men may glorify him on her account.

41. 21–9. Idols can neither prophesy nor act, but Yahweh is at work through Cyrus.

42. 1–9. Yahweh's Servant is chosen to bring judgement to the nations, freedom and sight to the enslaved and the blind. He is called by God the Creator, who is jealous of his glory.

42. 10–13. Song of praise by the whole world to Yahweh, who is going out against his foes.

42. 14–17. Yahweh has held back, but now he will convulse Nature in order to bring Israel back from Exile. Contrast the idols!

42. 18–25. Israel's plight in captivity—the servant who is blind and deaf, robbed and spoiled. Yahweh sent Israel into captivity because of her sins.

43. 1–7. But Yahweh will redeem Israel and work miracles for her; he will bring back her children, because he created her for his glory.

43. 8–13. Israel is Yahweh's chosen servant and witness to the nations that he is the only God.

43. 14–21. Yahweh will overthrow Babylon and alter the course of Nature in order to bring back Israel, who was created to declare his praise.

43. 22–8. Israel sinned, and her downfall was the consequent punishment.

44. 1–5. Yahweh will help Israel, his chosen servant.

44. 6–20. Song of praise: there is no one like Yahweh—his people are his witnesses. Idols are made by men and are useless.

44. 21–8. Yahweh has forgiven the sins of Israel his servant. Songs of praise

to Yahweh, Redeemer of his people, Creator of the world, who is working through men to bring about the Return.

45. 1–8. Yahweh is working through Cyrus for the sake of Israel, his chosen servant, so that men may know that he, the Creator of the world, is the only God.

45. 9–13. Men must not question the purposes of Yahweh—he will use Cyrus as he chooses.

45. 14–25. The nations will bow to Israel, because her God is the only God. Yahweh is the Creator: the idols of other nations cannot save! He is the only Saviour—the nations will all bow to him, and in him Israel will glory.

46. 1–13. Idols are carried by their worshippers, but Yahweh carries his people: idols are powerless, but Yahweh is at work. He will deliver Israel for his glory.

47. 1–15. Taunt song over the fall of Babylon.

48. 1–11. Israel was obstinate; therefore Yahweh refined her in the Exile for the glory of his name.

48. 12–22. Yahweh is the Creator of the world; he has called Israel. Lament over her past failure, and promise of redemption from Babylon.

49. 1–6. The Servant is chosen by Yahweh for his glory: he is to restore Israel and bring salvation to the nations.

49. 7–21. Reversal of fortunes: the nations bow to Israel. The Exile is over—description of the Return, with Nature transformed for Israel's sake. The restoration of Israel's children; Yahweh has not forgotten her.

49. 22–6. The subjection of nations, so that all men acknowledge Yahweh.

50. 1–3. Israel's sin led to the Exile. Yahweh is the God of Nature and can deliver her.

50. 4–11. The Servant has suffered, but has learnt by his sufferings, and is now to be vindicated by Yahweh.

51. 1–8. The promise of the Return is confirmed by history. The endurance of Yahweh's salvation.

51. 9–16. Appeal to Yahweh—he is reminded of his past glories. Promise by Yahweh, the Maker of the world, to deliver his people.

51. 17–52. 2. Reversal of sufferings—now it is Babylon's turn.

52. 3–12. Yahweh's promise of Israel's restoration. The Return will manifest God's glory to the nations.

52. 13–53. 12. Reversal of the Servant's fortunes, and astonishment of the nations. Contrast between past sufferings—which, it is now recognized, were really deserved by others—and future exaltation.

54. 1–10. Restoration of Israel—the return of her children; Israel's sufferings are now more than made up, because she is called and restored by Yahweh, the Creator of the world. His everlasting covenant of peace with her.

54. 11–17. The prosperity of Jerusalem, which will be secure because Yahweh is almighty.

55. 1–13. The nations are invited to trust in Yahweh: Israel is the witness to them of his glory. Final song of joy and peace of Israel after the Return.

This examination of Deutero-Isaiah as a whole shows how consistent is his message throughout. It may be summed up as: 'Israel, who has been chosen by Yahweh as his servant, is to be restored from Exile and will manifest God's glory to all nations.' It is to be noted how strong is the emphasis on the greatness and omnipotence of God. Deutero-Isaiah hardly mentions the name of God without attaching some adjective of praise, and frequently breaks forth to sing spontaneously of his power; so everything which happens shows forth God's glory—his choice of Israel as his servant, the release from captivity, the raising of Cyrus to do this—these are all taking place in order to exhibit his might, and to enable Israel to manifest his glory to the whole world. Israel is to be restored because her God is the Creator of the universe, and the result of her restoration must be the acknowledgement of this fact by the other nations: Yahweh's honour is thus both the cause and the result of the Return.

When we turn to the Servant Songs we find that this threefold theme is still dominant: here it is the Servant who is to bring glory to Yahweh, and almost all that was predicated of Israel outside the Songs is attributed to the Servant within them. The Servant, like Israel, is the chosen one of Yahweh,[1] and his mission, like hers, is to bring glory to him;[2] this will be accomplished by the Return from Exile,[3] and by bringing other nations to acknowledge Yahweh.[4] The Servant has been taught by Yahweh through suffering,[5] but this suffering is now at an end, because Yahweh will vindicate him;[6] these past sufferings are described most poignantly in the fourth Song. Even more distressing than the actual physical pain, however, was the Servant's humiliation before others, who have treated him with the same contempt which was shown to Israel by her neighbours.[7] All, however, will be more than made up by the coming exaltation:[8] then the Servant will be rewarded by seeing the increase of his family, now accounted righteous because of his sufferings.[9]

This common possession of basic themes gives strong support to our claim that the songs should be studied, not simply in isolation, but against the background of Deutero-Isaiah's other oracles. Their unity is all the closer if we can identify the Servant of the Songs with Israel, who is herself often referred to elsewhere as the Servant.[1] Certainly the similarity between the fates of Israel and the Servant suggests such an identification, or at least a close relationship between the two.[2]

3. DEUTERO-ISAIAH IN RELATION TO HEBREW PROPHECY

There has long been a tendency to regard the problem of the Songs as one set apart from the rest of Old Testament study. Deutero-Isaiah has been proclaimed the greatest of the prophets, and Isa. 53 the culmination of prophetic thinking. But while he may represent the peak of Old Testament prophecy, he is, nevertheless, a son of the prophets, and stands in the same line of tradition with them, so that he can be fully understood only when he is considered against the background of those other prophets whom he surpasses, and on whose foundations he has built. It is, therefore, as important to study Deutero-Isaiah in relation to the oracles of other prophets, as it is to consider the Servant Songs in the context of his own.

Deutero-Isaiah stands at the junction of two themes in prophecy. Those who came before him were concerned primarily with proclaiming a message of judgement and doom: Amos, Hosea, Micah and Isaiah could see the inevitable catastrophe which must follow Israel's apostasy.[3] Those who were to follow him had a message of hope—there was a good time coming when Israel, under her Messianic King, would enjoy a Golden Age.[4] Deutero-Isaiah lived on what seemed to be the bridge between these two worlds—catastrophe had overtaken Israel, but now she had suffered more than enough for her sins, the end of her punishment was in sight, and her Restoration almost here—the Golden Age was just round the corner. To understand Deutero-Isaiah we must consider him in relation to both past and future, the aftermath of calamity and the hope of restoration.

With regard to the past, we find that Deutero-Isaiah, in common with the earlier prophets, denounces the sins of his people; the great difference is that whereas for his predecessors it was a prophecy of the punishment to come, for him it is an explanation of the present plight of Israel.[5] But Deutero-Isaiah, naturally, looks more to the future than to the past, and so his oracles present an expression of the typical Israelite hope of a good time to come, together with a vindication of this hope in view of the Exile. His picture of the Golden Age, however, is no vague hope of blessedness sometime in the future: for him, it takes the specific form of the Return from Exile, which is imminent; it is an event inside, not at the end of, history.[1] This hope is accompanied by an attitude to other nations which is characteristic of Hebrew prophecy as a whole—an attitude wavering between ardent nationalism and benevolent universalism.[2] It is not strange that Deutero-Isaiah, prophesying in captivity, should produce vindictive passages like 45. 14 and 49. 22–6, or the taunt song of 47; it is more remarkable, and a sign of his greatness, that he should be able to rise to feelings such as those expressed in 49. 5–6 and 45. 22–3.

Deutero-Isaiah was not alone, however, in standing between these two eras: some of the oracles attributed to Jeremiah and Ezekiel appear to come from the same period, and have a similar theme of restoration. It is, of course, characteristic of Hebrew prophecy that there should be a constant mingling of hope and despair; prophecies of doom are often followed by promises of final restoration.[3] This, however, is most likely due to the editors who compiled the books rather than a true indication of the original message of the prophet, and many scholars believe that in these cases the oracles of consolation belong to a later period than that of the prophets to whom they are attributed.[4] It seems, therefore, that there may be a considerable amount of material coming from the Exilic or post-Exilic period, although purporting to be the work of earlier times. As there can be no certainty about these various passages, however, it is best to concentrate here on those oracles which definitely belong in or near the Exilic period; a study of these should lead to a clearer understanding of the position of Deutero-Isaiah.

Jeremiah prophesied mainly before the destruction of Jerusalem in 586 B.C., but he himself survived the disaster, and chapters 30–1 probably belong to the period after the deportation. It is possible that the oracles of chapters 32–3 belong to the same period, but if not they are sufficiently near the Fall to reflect the early Exilic attitude. Whether all the oracles in these four chapters are genuine utterances of Jeremiah or were spoken by some unknown prophet of the Exile is not of vital importance for our purpose, since it is evident that in either case they come from the time of Jeremiah, and therefore provide valuable material for a comparison with Deutero-Isaiah.

A careful examination of these chapters from Jeremiah shows that there is a remarkable similarity between them and the oracles of Deutero-Isaiah. Their general theme is that Yahweh, because of the sins of Israel, has delivered her into the hands of Babylon; he has not, however, finally rejected his people, and when they have been purged he will restore them to their own land and enter into a permanent covenant with them. Although Babylon is mentioned as the oppressor there is no reference to the historical situation of the Return, as in Deutero-Isaiah; on the contrary, the background of chapters 32–3 is the Fall of Jerusalem, and disaster—whether it was still to come or had in fact already overwhelmed the people when the oracles were actually written—is much nearer than the Return, which is still a distant promise. Chapters 30 and 31, on the other hand, do not speak in historical terms of either the Fall or the Return; they are nearer in style, and seemingly in time, to the oracles of Deutero-Isaiah.

Examination of the Oracles of Restoration in Jer. 30–3, and Comparison with Deutero-Isaiah

JEREMIAH	DEUTERO-ISAIAH
30. 4–9. The present terror. Israel and Judah will be saved; they will be servants no longer, but will serve Yahweh their king.	49. 7. The servant of rulers will be honoured by past masters.
30. 10–11. Fear not, O servant Jacob—your offspring shall be gathered from captivity and the far corners of the earth, because Yahweh is with you.	41. 8–10. Fear not, O servant Jacob—Israel, whom Yahweh has gathered from the far corners of the earth; Yahweh is with you.[1]
30. 12–15. Israel is greatly wounded—she has no advocate or help. Yahweh has done this to her because of her sin.	51. 17–20. Israel's plight: there is no one to help. 50. 6–9; 53. 7–9. Her great sufferings, 50. 1–3; 43. 27–8, caused by her sin.
30. 16–17. But her foes shall go into captivity: the spoilers will be spoiled. Israel's wounds will be healed, although before she was an outcast.	47. Fall of Babylon. 51. 17–23. Reversal of sufferings. 49. 24–6. Spoilers spoiled. 53. 10. Israel restored, 53. 12, and given spoil, 49. 7, 53. 3, although previously she was an outcast.
30. 18–22. Restoration of tents and rebuilding of city—songs of thanksgiving. Children multiplied and oppressors punished. A ruler from among the people—Yahweh's people.	54. 1–3. Children multiplied and tents filled—sing! Cf. 44. 3–5; 49. 19–21. 49. 26. The fate of her oppressors.

THE SERVANT PASSAGES

JEREMIAH	DEUTERO-ISAIAH
30. 23–4. The anger of Yahweh will not return without accomplishing its task.	42. 13, 25. The anger of Yahweh. 55. 10–11. The Word of Yahweh will not return without accomplishing its task.
31. 1–3. Promise—appeal to the First Exodus.	51. 9–11. The Return—appeal to First Exodus.
31. 4–6. Israel adorned; she is to be rebuilt.	49. 18. Israel adorned, 44. 26, and rebuilt.
31. 7–9. Song of praise: the salvation of Yahweh. Restoration from farthest corners. Return of the blind and lame. Water and a path prepared, because Yahweh is Father to Israel.	49. 12–13. Restoration from far corners—Song of praise. Cf. 43. 5–7, 44. 23. 42. 16. The blind return, and paths prepared. 43. 19–20. Water and paths prepared. Cf. 40. 3–5, 41. 17–18.
31. 10–14. Oracle to nations and coastlands. Yahweh scattered Israel and gathers her again like a shepherd. Israel is redeemed from the strong. Israel exults in Yahweh's goodness.	41. 1; 43. 9. Oracles to the nations and coastlands. 49. 5. Israel gathered again. 40. 11. Yahweh is like a shepherd. 49. 24–5, Israel redeemed from the strong. 42. 10–12. Song of praise. Cf. 35. 10.
31. 15–19. Israel weeps for her children; but they will return. Israel repents—she bears the disgrace of her youth.	54. 1–8. Children for the barren one. Israel's sorrow—but she shall forget the shame of her youth.
31. 20. Israel is Yahweh's son—he yearns for him.	54. 8. Yahweh's anger is short-lived.
31. 21–2. The way back.	
31. 23–30. Restoration—instead of destruction.	40. 3–5; 35. The way back. 44. 3–4, 26. Restoration.
31. 31–4. The New Covenant between Yahweh and his people. He will forgive their sin.	51. 7. 'The people in whose heart is my law'; 52. 6, they know Yahweh; 40. 2, their sin is forgiven.
31. 35–7. Promise to Israel based on Yahweh's dominion over Nature. Mysteries of world cannot be understood by man.	51. 12–16. No need for Israel to fear—Yahweh is the Creator. 40. 12–14. Man cannot understand the creation.
31. 38–40. The city shall be rebuilt.	54. 11–12. Jerusalem to be rebuilt.
32. 36–44. Yahweh will gather Israel from far countries and establish her again. Covenant between God and people. Yahweh brought evil—so too he will bring good.	41. 9. Israel gathered from ends of earth. 49. 8, The Servant is the covenant of the people. 55. 3. The covenant.
33. 1–9. Yahweh, the Creator of the earth, will reveal hidden things. Destruction will be followed by restoration and prosperity. Israel to be purged and forgiven. Jerusalem will bring glory to Yahweh before the nations because of his goodness to her.	42. 5–9. Yahweh, the Creator, will reveal new things. 50. 4–11, 48. 10, Israel purged, 44. 22, and forgiven. 46. 12–13. Deliverance brings glory to Yahweh.
33. 10–18. Waste city inhabited: promises of joy, prosperity, and a Davidic ruler bringing justice and righteousness.	55. 12–13. Nature is changed, bringing prosperity. 42. 1–4. The Servant brings judgement, 49. 1–6, and salvation.

JEREMIAH	DEUTERO-ISAIAH
33. 19–22. Appeal to Yahweh's rule of Nature to confirm Davidic promises.	51. 12–16. The power of Yahweh over Nature.
33. 23–6. Israel is despised by other nations, who regard her as rejected by Yahweh. But Yahweh, the Ruler of Nature, will restore her again and give her a Davidic ruler.	53. 3; 49. 7. The Servant is despised by the nations. 40. 27; 49. 14, Israel thought she was forsaken by Yahweh; 40. 28–31, but he, the Ruler of Nature, will help her.

In the book of Ezekiel the oracles of Restoration are found in chapters 33–7. Here the theme is again the scattering and regathering of Israel. The people have been punished because of their sins, but this has brought about the profanation of Yahweh's holy name; therefore he will restore them to their own country and bless them with prosperity, so that the nations may acknowledge his power. The motive for Yahweh's action—his desire to vindicate his holy name—is typical of Ezekiel; with it we may compare Deutero-Isaiah's insistence that Yahweh is restoring Israel for his glorification. The similarity in the general theme can again be observed by examining and comparing the oracles.

Examination of the Themes of Ezek. 34–7, and Comparison with Deutero-Isaiah

EZEKIEL	DEUTERO-ISAIAH
34. 1–6. The failure of Israel's shepherds led to the scattering of the sheep.	
34. 7–16. Yahweh will seek for his sheep like a shepherd, and bring them back to their own land: he gives them good pasture, on the hills.	40. 11. Yahweh will lead Israel like a shepherd. 49. 9–13. Yahweh leads his people; they feed on hills and by springs. He gathers them from the nations. Cf. 43. 5–7.
34. 17–24. Judgement of the sheep. Yahweh will be their God and David their prince.	
34. 25–31. A covenant is to be made with the people, banishing wild beasts and oppressors from the land. The prosperity of nature. The yoke of captivity is to be broken, so that Israel is no longer a prey to the nations, nor a reproach. Yahweh will be her God, and Israel his people.	55. 3. A covenant. 35. 9. No wild beasts. 44. 3; 35. 6–7. Prosperity. (Jer. 30. 8.)
35. 1–15. Oracle against Edom.	47. 1–15. The Fall of Babylon.
36. 1–15. Israel has been mocked by the other nations because she was desolate. Therefore the other nations will in their turn suffer reproach. But Israel will become fertile; her waste places will be rebuilt and her people multiplied. She will no longer be reproached.	43. 28; 49. 7; 51. 7–8; 52. 13–15. Israel mocked. 49. 22–6; 51. 21–3. Her sufferings are reversed. 49. 19–21. Israel's prosperity.

THE SERVANT PASSAGES

EZEKIEL

36. 16-32. Israel was scattered because of her sin: Yahweh's name was thus profaned among the nations. For the sake of his holy name, therefore, in order that the nations may know that Yahweh is God, he will gather Israel and bring her back. He will cleanse her, and they will be God and people. The prosperity of the land: Israel's disgrace will be removed.

36. 33-8. Restoration of the land and its prosperity; the cities repeopled; increase of men. Purpose—that the nations may acknowledge Yahweh.

37. 1-14. Vision of bones: Israel is without hope and appears dead, but Yahweh will renew her life and the people will return to their own land.

37. 15-28. Israel is to be gathered and united into one nation instead of two, and to be given one king. There will be an everlasting covenant of peace, and they will be God and people. Purpose —that the nations may acknowledge Yahweh.

DEUTERO-ISAIAH

50. 1-2. Israel was exiled because of her sin. 42. 24-5. Yahweh's anger poured out upon her. 48. 11. Yahweh saves Israel for his own sake, lest his name be profaned. 43. 5-7. Yahweh will gather Israel and bring back the people created for his glory. 48. 10. Yahweh has refined Israel. 51. 3. The prosperity of the land.

41. 18-19. The renewal of the land's fertility, 41. 20, in order that men may acknowledge Yahweh.

53. 1-12. The Servant is apparently dead, but he will see his descendants.

55. 3-5. Covenant with Israel: result—the nations will flock to her because of Yahweh who glorifies her.

From this brief examination it is evident that the three sets of oracles have much in common in their general theme of Restoration. They agree in attributing the cause of Israel's sufferings to her sin: in Jeremiah this is specified as the worship of Baal and Molech;[1] Deutero-Isaiah, prophesying later, is concerned with the present temptations of worshipping the Babylonian idols, and his attack takes the form of ridiculing these useless objects. It is clear that the Return is thought of as necessary to prove the power of Yahweh: the prestige of a god depended upon the prosperity of his people, and so the plight of Israel brought dishonour to her God as well as to herself. Ezekiel stressed the fact that God will restore Israel, not for her own sake, but for the sake of his own name. Although Deutero-Isaiah comes much nearer to an understanding of the love which Yahweh bears for his people, he also follows the same line of thought, expressed in his constant insistence on the glory which will be brought to Yahweh by the Return.[2]

This interdependence of God and people is seen further in the promise of the everlasting covenant which Yahweh is to make with

Israel. Jeremiah is the first to speak of this new covenant,[1] and he says of it:

> Behold, the days are coming, says the Lord, when I will make a new covenant with the house of Israel and the house of Judah, not like the covenant which I made with their fathers when I took them by the hand to bring them out of the land of Egypt, my covenant which they broke, though I was their husband, says the Lord. But this is the covenant which I will make with the house of Israel after those days, says the Lord: I will put my law within them, and I will write it upon their hearts; and I will be their God, and they shall be my people. And no longer shall each man teach his neighbour and each his brother, saying 'Know the Lord', for they shall all know me, from the least of them to the greatest, says the Lord; for I will forgive their iniquity, and I will remember their sin no more (Jer. 31. 31–4).

The new covenant is thus to include the following points:

(*a*) The covenant will not this time be broken, because it will be written upon the hearts of the people.[2]

(*b*) Yahweh is to give the people his law.

(*c*) Yahweh will be Israel's God, and they will be his people.

(*d*) The people will all know Yahweh.

(*e*) Their iniquity will be forgiven.

In Jer. 32. 40 the covenant is mentioned again. Here it is said that:

(*a*) The covenant is to be everlasting.

(*b*) Yahweh will not turn away from doing good to his people.

(*c*) They are to have the fear of Yahweh in their hearts, and will not turn from him.

In Jer. 33. 20–1 the covenant is with David and the Levitical priests, promising them descendants.

This same promise of a covenant reappears in Ezekiel.[3] In 37. 26–7 it is promised that:

(*a*) It will be a covenant of peace.

(*b*) It will be everlasting.

(*c*) It will include Israel's blessing and multiplication.

(*d*) Yahweh will dwell with them for evermore.

(*e*) They will be God and people.

This is very similar to the promise of 34. 25–31, which says that:

(*a*) It is a covenant of peace.

(*b*) Enemies are to be driven out, and Israel delivered.

(c) Israel will enjoy prosperity and security.
(d) Israel is to be reproached by the nations no longer.
(e) The people will know that Yahweh is their God, and that they are his people.

It is clear that the promise of a covenant is important for both Jeremiah and Ezekiel—or whoever is responsible for these oracles—in their thought about the Restoration. Israel's failure and suffering naturally led them to seek a promise of a relationship between Yahweh and his people which could not be broken, unlike the earlier covenant. Apart from these actual references to the covenant, there is constant insistence that Yahweh is to be their God, and they are to be his people.[1]

Both Ezekiel and Jeremiah speak of a ruler who is to govern Israel after the Return. It is interesting to note that almost all the references to this figure appear in passages which are closely associated with the covenant promises. The first reference is in Jer. 30. 8-9, an oracle promising the end of oppression, where it is said that Israel will no longer be the servant of strangers, but will serve Yahweh, and David their king. In the same chapter, in *vv.* 21-2, a description of the renewed fortunes of the people includes the promise that their prince shall be one of them; this is closely linked with the typical phrase 'You shall be my people, and I will be your God'. The final reference in these chapters from Jeremiah is in 33. 14-26, where Yahweh declares that he will fulfil the promise he made to give his people a Davidic ruler who shall bring justice and righteousness to the people. Yahweh has not broken the covenant which he made with David; his family have been mocked and regarded as rejected by Yahweh, but he will restore them.

In Ezekiel the ruler is called David in 34. 23-4, where his rule is closely identified with that of Yahweh himself; this passage comes immediately before the description of the covenant of peace which Yahweh is to make with his people. The other reference to David occurs in a similar position; after promising the reunification of Israel under one king in 37. 15-23, Yahweh declares that his Servant David is to rule as king over the people for ever, and they shall dwell in their own land for ever; this promise is then followed immediately by a description of the covenant which Yahweh will make with his people.

It is evident from these passages that the idea of a Davidic ruler is closely linked in the minds of these prophets with the promise of Restoration and the making of a new covenant. God, king and people are to enter into some new relationship in which each has a vital part to play.[1]

When we turn from these chapters to Deutero-Isaiah, we find that the whole tempo of expectation has quickened: what was a hope has now become a present reality. Restoration no longer belongs to 'those days', but is an event which has already come upon them. The message is no longer 'At that time, says the Lord, I will be the God of all the families of Israel, and they shall be my people'; the promise is now fulfilled and the proclamation is 'Behold your God!'; Yahweh declares 'I am the Lord, your Holy One, the Creator of Israel, your king'.[2] The tone of the prophecy suggests that the promises are now all being fulfilled. By his action Yahweh is proving his good faith: the Return involves the establishment of the covenant.

The covenant itself is mentioned only four times. In 55. 3–4 Yahweh says:

> Incline your ear, and come to me;
>   hear, that your soul may live;
> and I will make with you an everlasting covenant,
>   my steadfast, sure love for David.
> Behold, I made him a witness to the peoples,
>   a leader and commander for the peoples.

This passage, combining the establishment of a covenant with the promise to David, is very similar to those in Jeremiah and Ezekiel. But here the covenant is to be established in the immediate, not the remote, future; it is made when the people accept the invitation to come to Yahweh: like the Restoration, the covenant is an event belonging to the present epoch, not to 'those days'. A similar expression is given in the previous chapter, 54, where in *vv.* 9–10 Yahweh says that he has already sworn not to be angry with Israel, nor to rebuke her:

> For the mountains may depart and the hills be removed,
>   but my steadfast love shall not depart from you,
>   and my covenant of peace shall not be removed,
>   says the LORD, who has compassion on you.

The other references to the covenant are found in 42. 6 and 49. 8, although as the phrases are identical in the two passages some scholars omit one or other of them as a gloss.¹ In both cases, however, it is important to note that the phrase 'I have given you as a covenant to the people' is either part of, or closely associated with, one of the Servant Songs. Again, in both cases, the task of the one who is given as a covenant is to bring out the prisoners, the blind and the desolate. Whoever this figure may be, he is, in some way, connected with the Restoration; through this figure it appears that God is establishing his promised covenant with the people. There may well be a connection here with the thought of Jeremiah and Ezekiel, where at the Return Yahweh is to make a covenant with his people, which includes the re-establishment of a ruler of the Davidic line.

If Deutero-Isaiah's message is indeed a proclamation that the promises are now being fulfilled and the covenant being established we expect to find that the details foretold will again receive emphasis. Summarizing the various references to the covenant in Jeremiah and Ezekiel we find the following features:

(a) The covenant is everlasting. Jer. 32. 40; Ezek. 37. 26. This means that:
  (i) Yahweh will not turn from doing good to his people. Jer. 32. 40.
  (ii) The people will not turn from Yahweh, or break the covenant. Jer. 31. 32; 32. 40.
(b) The relationship involved in the covenant: Yahweh and Israel are to be God and people. Jer. 31. 33; Ezek. 37. 27; 34. 30. This means that:
  (i) Yahweh will send out his law. Jer. 31. 33.
  (ii) Yahweh will forgive Israel's sin. Jer. 31. 34.
  (iii) Yahweh will dwell with his people. Ezek. 37. 26-7.
  (iv) The people will know Yahweh. Jer. 31. 34.
(c) The results of the covenant:
  (i) It is a covenant of peace. Ezek. 37. 26; 34. 25.
  (ii) Israel's enemies will be driven out. Ezek. 34. 25-28.
  (iii) The people will be blessed and multiplied. Ezek. 37. 26.
  (iv) Israel will enjoy prosperity and security. Ezek. 34. 25-9.
(d) The Davidic covenant will be fulfilled: there will be a successor for David. Jer. 33. 20 f.

An examination of Deutero-Isaiah shows that these are, in fact, the very themes which receive emphasis throughout the whole prophecy. Although the word 'covenant' itself is seldom used, its features, as foretold by Jeremiah and Ezekiel, are now being fulfilled: Yahweh is Israel's God, and they are his people; their sin has been forgiven, and he is redeeming them from their enemies; they will in future live in happiness and prosperity. This is not to suggest that Deutero-Isaiah had a copy of the oracles of Jeremiah and Ezekiel before him and deliberately tried to show how all the details of the promises were about to be fulfilled. It does, however, suggest that he is not, as is sometimes supposed, a completely isolated figure: the ideas which lie behind Jer. 30–3 and Ezek. 34–7 were well known to Deutero-Isaiah, whether or not he was acquainted with the oracles themselves.[1] Although he may have been the first to believe that the end of the Exile was in sight, and although he may have been alone in seeing Cyrus as Yahweh's instrument of deliverance, the things which he proclaimed were not unknown. *The events which he depicts are the signs which were commonly recognized to be those which would accompany the New Age.* The new factor in his message was that these things are happening—now!

Most of these themes run continuously throughout the prophecy, but they may be illustrated by the following passages:

(*a*) The covenant is everlasting. 55. 3. This means that:
  (i) Yahweh will not turn from doing good to his people. 54. 9–10.
  (ii) The people will not turn from Yahweh, or break the covenant. This point alone does not find explicit expression in the words of Deutero-Isaiah, although it is implied in the fact that the covenant is to be everlasting (55. 3). Its absence is probably due to his emphasis on the activity of Yahweh, who is redeeming Israel for his own sake.

(*b*) The relationship involved in the new covenant: Yahweh and Israel are to be God and people. 40. 9; 51. 4, 15–16. This means that:
  (i) Yahweh will send out his law. 51. 4, 7.
  (ii) Yahweh will forgive Israel's sin. 40. 2; 43. 25.
  (iii) Yahweh will dwell with his people. 52. 8.
  (iv) The people will know Yahweh. 52. 6.

(*c*) The results of the covenant:
  (i) It is a covenant of peace. 54. 10.
  (ii) Israel's enemies will be driven out. 49. 24–6.
  (iii) The people will be blessed and multiplied. 44. 3–5.
  (iv) Israel will enjoy prosperity and security. 54. 11–17.
  (v) She will no longer be reproached by the other nations. 49. 7.

(*d*) The Davidic covenant will be fulfilled: there will be a successor for David. 55. 3–5.

4. THE SERVANT

In the light of this study of Deutero-Isaiah and his contemporaries we may now turn to a consideration of the identity of the Servant. The great problem of the Songs is that they contain material which may be summoned as evidence to support many and varying views: individual, collective, Messianic and mythological theories have all been substantiated to some extent from the Songs, some not at all convincingly, others quite strongly, but none in so conclusive a manner as to command universal support. The result is a bewildering mass of theories which leads us to despair of the correct one ever being found; indeed, the debate has continued for so long that it appears very unlikely that any overwhelming evidence will ever be brought forward to prove any one single theory.

This very problem, however, may itself prove to be a clue to the solution: the fact that all theories can claim some evidence to support them suggests that they may all contain some truth, although none presents the final answer. In seeking a basis for their own theories, critics have naturally, albeit unconsciously, selected a part of the evidence available and concentrated on that alone, ignoring or explaining away the rest. But the very fact that so many interpretations have been suggested points to the existence, side by side, of many strands of evidence. If these are closely interwoven, as seems probable, we are more likely to understand the prophet's meaning by studying them together, and seeking a synthesis, than by trying to unravel what is essentially a unity, thereby giving undue emphasis to what is but one part of the whole, and so selecting only partial truth. It may be that an exclusive interpretation, which sees the problem as a stark Either/Or, is the wrong approach to the question, and that opposing theories represent, not incompatible opinions, but different facets of one truth.[1]

This co-existence of various concepts is confirmed by the work of those scholars who support the theory that the Servant represents a changing concept:[2] they find a different element predominant in each Song and name the Servant accordingly. But the fact that there is disagreement even here as to the interpretation in each Song illustrates that it is not a question of one concept being in mind in each passage, but rather that the different concepts are completely interwoven throughout the whole. Now one strand and now another may come to the fore, and these are seized upon and 'labelled' according to the mind of the interpreter; but this method is surely an attempt to analyse by mathematics what is, essentially, the work of a poet. It may be that the prophet could hold together in his mind varying and contrasting ideas which, when he tried to express them in words, proved too great for the medium of speech.[1] If so, then we must attempt to understand this interweaving of concepts before we can interpret the figure of the Servant.

As our starting-point we may take the examination which we made above of the themes of Deutero-Isaiah. The correspondence between the Songs and the other oracles clearly pointed to so close a relationship between Israel and the Servant as to suggest identity. If, then, this evidence leads us to support the collective interpretation as an essential part of the concept of the Servant, how are we to explain the strong individual characteristics of the figure?

A possible solution to this question is offered in the idea of corporate personality, which has been found to underlie much Hebrew thought. The principle exponent of this view, H. Wheeler Robinson,[2] has shown the importance which the group played in the life of the Hebrew people. In contrast to modern thought it was the community, not the individual, which was of primary consequence, and the individual had significance only as a member of the group. This concept was presupposed in the basis of Hebrew religion, the idea of election and covenant; so fundamental was it that it continued at the heart of that religion, even after the rise of individualism in the time of Jeremiah and Ezekiel. Each society, whether family or nation, included both past and future members, so that the history of the community possessed a concrete unity, and events which occurred in the past could be spoken of as though they had happened to the present society.[3]

The idea of corporate personality is thus far more than a mere 'personification'; it is not a figure of speech, but a fundamental of life. It involves three primary factors, all of which are relevant to our study: first, the group can be spoken of as an individual; secondly, an individual member of the group can represent the whole society; thirdly, because the group includes the individual, and the individual represents the group, there is a fluidity in the concept which makes it possible to pass from an individual to the group of which he is a member and back again without any straining of the idea.

In seeking a solution to the problem of the Servant, we have to remember, not only that the nation could be spoken of in highly individualized terms, but also that the whole community could be represented in the figure of one man. This, of course, was especially true of the king, who was, in some supreme way, the Representative of his people. The great importance which was attached to the ritual surrounding the king in the Ancient East arose from the fact that the life, health and prosperity of the nation depended on his: everything which happened to the king affected also the well-being of his people. Although the Hebrews did not accept the kingly ritual in its entirety, there is sufficient evidence to show that they did attach great significance to the figure of the king.[1] This factor explains to a large extent the rise of the Messianic hope in Judaism, for the Messiah was the projection into the future of the king of the past.[2] This new Son of David was to be to his people all that his great ancestor had been in the past: as the people's fortunes had been symbolized in the figure of the king, so they were to share in the triumphs of the Messiah's victory, and his glory would be theirs.

The third corollary of the concept of corporate personality, the fluidity which attached to it, is well illustrated in the Old Testament. In Num. 20. 14–21 there is continual change between the use of 'I' and 'we'; the people are regarded as a unit.[3] Many examples are to be found in the familiar problem of the 'I' of the Psalms: to the question 'Who is this "I"? Are the Psalms "collective" or "individual"?' the answer is probably that they are both; the individual's experience was bound up with that of the community, and even when the psalmist was being most intensely personal, his words remained true for others.[4] Even in modern thought this fluidity is possible to some extent: the words which sum up the heart of Christian belief begin 'I believe', and whoever joins in reciting the Creed is not making merely an individual affirmation of faith, but is at that moment supremely a member of the Christian community.

How far, then, do these different factors play their part in the making of the Servant Songs? This study of Hebrew thought, brief as it is, should show clearly that it is impossible to sort out the many ideas which the poet has woven together. The view which recognizes the fluidity in the poet's conception is surely the only one which can do justice to them all. This fluidity, however, is not, as many scholars maintain, a 'linear' development, which moves from one idea to another, rejecting one figure and choosing a new one: there is, on the contrary, a continual oscillation between one concept and another,[1] so that various images may be in the poet's mind at one time, and we cannot point to one song and say 'Here it is Israel', and to another, and say 'Here the Messiah, or the prophet, is meant': rather the Servant is at once Israel and the prophet and the Messiah, so that although one concept may be primary, we cannot deny the presence of the others.[2]

While individual traits are present in the Songs, however, it is the corporate concept which is dominant above all others.[3] Although the examination of contemporary oracles revealed the expectation of a 'Messianic' figure,[4] it must be emphasized that both there, and in the rest of Deutero-Isaiah, the king is never an active partaker in the actual Restoration: the re-establishment of the Davidic line is not a means to the Return, but one of the results.[5] For if the king was the symbol of his people, it was inevitable that any Restoration to divine favour must include the reinstitution of the king, and the fulfilment of the promise which was made to David. It must be remembered, however, that the monarchy was to a certain extent foreign to prophetic belief, since there was a danger of its undermining the supreme authority of Yahweh. It is not surprising, therefore, that the oracles of Jeremiah and Ezekiel never speak of the new Davidic king as the Restorer of Israel's fortunes: it was Yahweh, and he alone, who was to bring again the captivity of his people, and it was Yahweh who would restore to Israel their king, as a symbol of his favour. How much more true was this of Deutero-Isaiah, to whom Yahweh was the only God, the Creator of the world and the Saviour of his people: it was Yahweh himself whom the prophet proclaimed unceasingly to be Israel's Redeemer; great men were but tools in his hands for the accomplishment of his purposes. It is extremely unlikely that Deutero-Isaiah could conceive of any king as playing an important role in the actual Restoration: his part in the Return would be only as the symbol of his people, for the great relationship which is emphasized throughout Deutero-Isaiah is that between Yahweh and his people.¹ Only after the Return will the king, as leader of his people, be important as Yahweh's witness to the Gentiles.

It is unlikely, therefore, that Deutero-Isaiah had any particular king in mind, except the present one, whoever he might be: he was important, not as an individual in his own right, but as the symbol of his people, the sign of the covenant between Israel and Yahweh. For it was only later that the truly Messianic figure developed, the result, like the eschatological hope, of disappointment with actual events. Deutero-Isaiah is no prophet of despair and distant hope, however, but of eager expectancy: the individual in the Servant is more than the king of the Old Israel, and he is not yet the Messiah of Judaism. For here past and future meet in the present, and the Servant is both the summing up of the old and the foreshadowing of the new. Israel, so Deutero-Isaiah believes, is at the turning-point of her history: her sufferings are over, her exaltation is imminent; the figure of the Servant thus stands between two eras of Jewish thought: the old kingdom has gone, but the birth-pangs of the new are almost over, and everything is concentrated in expectant hope for the future.²

5. THE PROBLEM OF ISA. 53

The correspondence in general theme between the Songs and the rest of Deutero-Isaiah's work, and between this and other Hebrew prophecy, suggests that they should not be regarded as something entirely apart, but studied in relation to one another. There is, however, one idea in the Songs, so puzzling in its expression and apparently so foreign to all other Deutero-Isaianic thought, that it is the primary cause for regarding the Songs as 'unique'; this is, of course, the idea of vicarious suffering and the promise of resurrection in Isa. 53. In considering this concept, however, it is more than ever important to try to understand it against such background of contemporary thought as we have; is Isa. 53 indeed something totally foreign and unexpected, or is it the prophetic—if not logical—outcome of the themes already studied, the crowning apex of Deutero-Isaiah's faith that Israel will receive 'joy for mourning, the garment of praise for the spirit of heaviness'?³

If we interpret the fifty-third chapter in accordance with the themes examined above, we find that it may be understood as one of the Old Testament attempts to deal with the problem of suffering. The particular form in which this author considered it was similar to that which confronted Habakkuk—why does Yahweh allow Israel to suffer more than she deserves? Obviously she deserved punishment for her disobedience and obstinacy, but she has suffered 'double for all her sins' —why? This is the moral problem of the Exile which confronted Deutero-Isaiah. His answer, given in the fifty-third chapter, is that what Israel has suffered over and above what she deserved, she has suffered on behalf of other nations.[1]

The influence of Christian interpretation of Isa. 53 as a Messianic prophecy fulfilled in Jesus has obscured the fact that Deutero-Isaiah nowhere says that his 'Servant' is a willing sufferer. Although the Servant may have suffered in silence, this does not mean that he offered himself voluntarily as a vicarious sacrifice; while he submitted to the torture which was laid upon him, it is nowhere said that he consciously accepted the path of pain for the express purpose of saving others.[2] The sufferings which he endured may have brought salvation to his fellows, but this is a judgement made after the event by those whose deliverance his sufferings have obtained. This picture is fully consistent with the interpretation of the Servant as Israel: she, certainly, did not suffer willingly. Deutero-Isaiah has offered the portrait of the Suffering Servant as a theodicy, an attempt to justify Israel's suffering during the Exile: his greatness lies in the fact that he does even more than this, and is able, while the sufferings are still present, to see the transformation which future exaltation will make to past humiliation.

This identification of the Servant as Israel removes the difficulty of the idea of resurrection in chapter 53. This concept is quite foreign to Hebrew thought, but it was perfectly permissible to use it as a metaphor. Israel had been subjected to terrible humiliation; she was oppressed and afflicted, taken from her own country and led like a lamb to the slaughter: but now her sufferings are over, and she is to return; she will be exalted and know prosperity again, and rejoice in the return of her children. It is not surprising if the description of these joys sounds like a return to life from death, for that is, in fact, what is happening to Israel: she is returning from death in a strange country to her own land —the land of the living, the land of Yahweh. The fact that the Servant is spoken of in this passage as an individual does not invalidate this theory: the personification is no more acute than the descriptions of

Israel elsewhere in Deutero-Isaiah, or in passages such as Ezek. 16.[1] The idea of 'resurrection' is expressed in language very similar to that which in other oracles describes the return of Israel to her own land,[2] and is applied to Israel even more explicitly in Ezek. 37.[3]

Unless Deutero-Isaiah is moving in a world which is quite unknown to us, it is difficult to see how he could have had in mind any one single individual in this chapter. For if he were speaking of the sufferings of some person now dead, who had borne unprecedented sufferings, it is strange that we hear nothing of him elsewhere;[4] if he were thinking of himself, as some have claimed, he had a most strange and unprophetic conceit of himself;[5] but if, on the other hand, he were thinking of some figure in the future,[6] it is above all difficult to conceive why he should imagine a person who would have to suffer so supremely, or should find it necessary to create such a figure. A prophet's task was to resolve difficulties, not to invent them: to interpret present events and point to their consequences, rather than to foretell future events unrelated to the existing situation. While we may expect to find Deutero-Isaiah in advance of contemporary thought, we do not expect him to introduce ideas which are completely contrary to Hebrew thinking, such as the necessity for atonement by one man and the resurrection of an individual: such ideas, moreover, would be in conflict with his fundamental conception of the omnipotence and uniqueness of God, a belief which was the consummation of all that was best in prophetic religion.

We expect the prophet to offer an answer to the present problem, and we are not disappointed. Deutero-Isaiah's message is not that Israel still has sin for which atonement must be made, but that her sin has already been forgiven: he is sent to tell Israel that her sufferings are over, that they have been more than sufficient, and that she is to be restored—now. Yahweh has no need to make a righteous man suffer for her sins sometime in the future: Israel herself has been punished, and Yahweh is now redeeming her, without money, and without price, not because some individual has atoned for her sin, but because he is Yahweh and she is his people, and in order that his name may be glorified throughout the earth. There is no need to search for a way in which Yahweh can forgive his people: he has already done that, because he is Yahweh, and for the sake of his own reputation. The message is glorious, not only because Israel will exchange degradation for exaltation, but because the change will be so profound that other nations will be forced to admit that their attitude to her must have been wrong: so her very sufferings will be transformed into a means of bringing other nations to worship her God.

Some scholars have claimed that the influence of the Babylonian ritual of the dying and rising god can be seen in this chapter.[1] This was, however, the very feature of Babylonian ritual which was most unacceptable to the mind of the Hebrew, for whom Yahweh was the ever-living One, and while it is possible that there may have been mythological elements in the background of Deutero-Isaiah's thought, it is extremely unlikely that the prophet to whom the Babylonian idols were anathema should have chosen such a concept for the centre of his message.[2] It should, indeed, be noted that he never actually speaks of a 'resurrection'; although a return to life is implied, the language suggests a figurative idea of deliverance, such as we find in the Psalms, rather than the idea of the physical resuscitation of an individual body.[3]

If we accept this interpretation of the fourth Servant Song there is no difficulty in seeing it as a part of Deutero-Isaiah's general theme of the choice of Israel by Yahweh and the end of her sufferings through her restoration. It is, of course, the climax to his thought: any attempt to understand the mystery of suffering must always be obscure, and this is no exception. But the vision which the poet had of the glory which was to result from suffering is not contrary to his attempt elsewhere to explain the purpose of both the Exile and the Return, but is rather its most supreme and inspired expression.

6. OBJECTIONS TO THE COLLECTIVE THEORY

Since the interpretation of the Servant which has been supported here is, primarily, a collective one, some of the arguments which have been brought against that theory must now be considered briefly. These difficulties have been listed by C. R. North as follows:[4]

(a) 'The Servant in the Songs is anonymous; outside the Songs he is equated with Jacob–Israel.' This is not entirely a fair representation of the facts, as North himself allows;[5] the Servant is actually mentioned, without identification, in the following passages outside the Songs—42. 19; 43. 10; 44. 26; 50. 10—although he is equated with Jacob–Israel in 41. 8f.; 44. 1f., 21; 45. 4; 48. 20. In the Songs the Servant is unidentified in 42. 1; 49. 5f. and 52. 13, but in 49. 3 he is named as Israel. Although the proportion of references to Israel is higher outside the Songs, this is not in itself sufficient evidence to indicate that there are two different Servants; the real question is whether the character of the Servant is consistent inside and outside the Songs, and this problem will be taken up below.

(*b*) 'The anonymity of the Servant in the Songs is accompanied by a heightened individualization in the portrait of the Servant.' While it is possible to explain the individualization in the Songs merely by the 'personification' which, as we have seen, was one part of the concept of corporate personality, it is important also to remember the oscillation which took place between the group and the individual. In passages which are obviously of greater intensity it is not surprising if the personal note is more dominant, for the prophet can speak for the nation only in terms of his own experience; in matters which touch his sensitivity most closely, therefore, his words are of necessity most personal. Certainly we may expect the prophet to be sensitive about the sufferings of his nation, and about her call to mission. It is probable that this oscillation is in part the reason for the anonymity of the Songs. This is not a phenomenon which belongs only to them, however: the portrait of Zion in Isa. 54. 1–10 is intensely personal, but that, too, is 'anonymous'.

(*c*) 'The character of the Servant in the Songs is different from that of the Servant Israel in the rest of the prophecy.' While it is true that the Servant is portrayed in various characters, there is no sharp distinction between the Songs and the other oracles, since many of the different guises cut right across the divisions which are drawn between them. Thus we find the Servant given a mission both inside and outside the Songs,[1] just as he suffers within and without. It is true that in Isa. 40 Israel suffers for her own sins, and in the fourth Song the Servant is recognized to have suffered for the sins of others, but these two things, as we have seen, are by no means incompatible. While a poet's general themes may, as has been argued above, be consistent, we do not expect every verse he writes to be a mere repetition, with no new thought ever added. In these chapters we see a man struggling with great ideas and with moral problems, seeking for a solution to offer to his fellow-countrymen; his answer is not given all at once, but takes shape as his faith and insight grow. Isa. 53 is the pinnacle of Deutero-Isaiah's work, and the beauty of its language is matched by a climax in his thought. While Isa. 40 declares the original reason for Israel's punishment, Isa. 53 goes on to try to understand why she has suffered 'double for all her sins', and in doing so discovers that the coming glory will be because, not in spite of, Israel's suffering. There is no inconsistency between the picture drawn of Israel in 42. 18–25 and 48. 1–19 as blind and helpless, and the triumphant and vindicated Servant of Isa. 52. 13–53. 12. Both are very true pictures of Israel—the sinful nation of the past, her plight in captivity and her slowness to learn, and the role which now in faith Deutero-Isaiah visualizes for her in the Return.[1]

(*d*) 'The Servant of the Songs has an active mission; the Servant Israel outside the Songs is the passive recipient of salvation.' This, again, is not entirely a true distinction, since even outside the Songs Israel is entrusted with the mission of witnessing of the glory of God to other nations. Quite apart from this, however, there is no difficulty in understanding all the passages as referring to Israel. It is very true that Israel has been 'passive', and that the Return is worked by Yahweh and not by Israel herself; this, indeed, is one of the lessons of the Exile. But no one, whether individual or nation, can ever undertake an 'active mission' until he has been the 'passive recipient of salvation'; it is only when Israel has herself been saved that she can be the witness to others:[2] these are not incompatibilities, but two essential and complementary parts of one truth. While Israel has been 'passive' in the past, nothing can alter the fact that Yahweh has chosen her for something more than this, and the time is now ripe for this to be declared: Israel is to be no longer blind and dumb, but is to become alive to her mission, and active in working for Yahweh; but the result, as in her 'passive' role of being saved, will still be to bring glory to God.

(*e*) 'On the collective theory all the disappointments, the uncomelinesses, the sicknesses, sufferings, and death of the Servant are so many allegorical representations of the Exile. There is no real progress from the situation depicted in one Song to that depicted in the next. Everything is, so to speak, presented on a flat surface. Instead of a drama moving steadily to a climax, we have a series of tableaux all representing the same situation.' It is, indeed, the same basic situation which is represented throughout the oracles—the fact of deliverance: but there is nothing flat about this! No suggestion could be farther from the truth. The fact that Deutero-Isaiah is consistent does not mean that he is monotonous, and to interpret the Servant as Israel is not to deny development in his thought. There is, on the contrary, the most vital progress in the situations he depicts, as he unfolds the whole drama of Israel's deliverance. Reading through the chapters, one is conscious of a mounting tension which increases until the climax is reached in chapter 53, and which is sustained throughout the final chapters: the arrangement, in fact, suggests far more of conscious planning than most modern critics are ready to admit; this is no haphazard collection of oracles. From the first announcement of deliverance in chapter 40, the poet moves through the scenes of Cyrus' victories and Babylon's fall, the release of the captives and the journey across the transformed desert, the re-establishment of Jerusalem and her subsequent exaltation, which results in the vindication of her past shame in the eyes of the whole world, until the final picture of prosperity is reached, with the nations flocking to worship Israel's God. There is no 'flat surface' here, but the most moving development of a glorious theme, which is matched by the poet's growing realization of the part which Israel is to play in bringing to Yahweh the glory which is the uniting theme of the whole story.[1]

(*f*) 'The Servant appears to have a mission to Israel.'[2] The second Servant Song speaks of a mission to Israel, as well as to the other nations; significantly, it is this same passage which identifies the Servant as Israel. Is it possible for Israel to have a mission to herself? Here again, we see an oscillation between the group and the individual, although the sense of 'Israel' is by no means excluded. It may well be the leader of the nation who is in mind here; he will be at the head of the returning exiles, and summon the Israelites who are scattered among the other nations to join them. The people also are still included, however, for their first duty is to themselves, to return to Jerusalem and to rebuild the nation. But this alone is not the whole purpose of the Return; Deutero-Isaiah has realized that there is still more in store, and that Yahweh is to be glorified, not by the Return of his own people alone, but by the worship of other nations: the ultimate task, therefore, of his Servant, nation and leader together, will be to proclaim his salvation to the whole world.

The objections which have been brought against the collective theory, therefore, are not of sufficient strength to undermine the soundness of the interpretation to which the evidence has pointed us. It is the vocation of a nation which is revealed to us in the Servant Songs: but that vocation is expressed for us through the personal experience of the individual who was most aware of it, and it was only through the response of individuals that the vocation would ever be obeyed.

CHAPTER 3

JEWISH INTERPRETATION OF THE SERVANT

1. THE SERVANT IN JEWISH LITERATURE

A consideration of the Jewish understanding of the Servant concept at the time of Christ is obviously of the greatest importance in any attempt to discover the meaning which the concept would have held for Jesus and his followers, and hence for an estimate of the influence which it is likely to have had upon their thought. There is, however, very little evidence regarding the interpretation of the Servant during this period; references in contemporary literature are few and uncertain, and even where they may exist they are often obscure. Our sources for this study will be the Old Testament, Old Testament Apocrypha and Pseudepigrapha, the gospel narrative in so far as it reflects the mind of the common people, the versions and the Targum, other contemporary Jewish literature, and Rabbinic writings.

(a) The Old Testament

In the Old Testament itself there are no certain references to the Servant passages. It is possible that the description of the lowly king of Zech. 9. 9 may have been influenced by Isa. 50 and 53, but if so we may note that no use has been made of the idea of suffering. In chapter 12 of the same book there is perhaps a reminiscence of Isa. 53 in the one who was pierced (*v.* 10), although this is doubtful.

Some scholars have maintained that the Servant concept lies behind Dan. 12. 3, which speaks of the wise who turn many to righteousness.[1] Again, however, there is no connection with the thought of suffering.

(b) The Old Testament Apocrypha and Pseudepigrapha

A close parallel to the ideas of Isa. 53 is to be found in Wisd. 5. 1–5, in the description of the suffering which there falls to the lot of the righteous man; there are also possible echoes of the same chapter in

2. 12–20 and 3. 1–9. The author of these passages, which probably date from the end of the second century B.C.,[1] may be merely borrowing from Deutero-Isaiah's phraseology, or he may have consciously identified the community of the righteous with the Servant of the Songs: in either case, however, there is no use of the idea of vicarious suffering.

In Ecclesiasticus, which was written about 180 B.C.,[2] a phrase from Isa. 49. 6 is combined with Mal. 3. 24 and referred to Elijah in 48. 10, but the concept of vicarious suffering is again missing. The prayer of the seventh son in 2 Macc. 7. 37 asks that God may have mercy on the nation, and refrain from further punishment, but does not carry the idea of the innocent suffering instead of the guilty: rather the martyrs die as representatives of their sinful race. It is, in fact, only in 4 Maccabees, a book dating from the beginning of the last century B.C.,[3] that the idea of vicarious suffering recurs; here, in 6. 27–9 and 17. 20–2, it is suggested that the sufferings of Eleazar and his fellow-martyrs may atone for the sins of the whole nation. This concept may perhaps derive from Isa. 53, although there are no linguistic echoes of that passage; if this is so, then it suggests a collective interpretation of the fourth Song among the Jews at that time. In 4 Maccabees, the atonement is effective for Israel, not for the other nations: a distinction is made between the righteous, whose sufferings are described, and the rest of the nation, who are recognized as being sinful. This is the interpretation we should expect, for in the first century B.C. the trial fell most heavily on those Jews who were trying to remain faithful to the Law in the face of bitter opposition, not only from Gentiles, but also from members of their own nation.

Some scholars have maintained that the Son of Man in the Parables of Enoch[4] has been influenced by the figure of the Servant:[5] numerous phrases which are used of him are reminiscent of the words of Deutero-Isaiah, and also of the Messianic oracles of Isa. 9 and 11. While it is possible that the author may have been drawing on these two concepts of 'Servant' and 'Messiah', however, he nowhere speaks of the Son of Man as suffering in any way. If some of the attributes of the Son of Man have in fact been taken from the Servant, therefore, the absence in Enoch of the idea of suffering, which is the most distinctive feature of the Servant, is the more remarkable.[6]

(c) The Gospels

For our present purpose we are concerned with the gospels, not as evidence for the origin of the use of the Servant concept by the early Church, but as testimony to Jewish thought of the first century A.D. Now it is quite clear from the gospel narrative that the idea of a Messiah who was destined to suffer was alien to at least the majority of the people; for if such a concept had been in keeping with normal Jewish belief, it would be impossible to explain the inability of the disciples to grasp the necessity for Jesus' sufferings, the failure of the people to recognize him as the Messiah, and the way in which the Cross became the great 'stumbling-block' to the Jewish nation.[1] However much the apostles—and possibly Jesus himself—may have endeavoured to show that the Messiah's sufferings were implicit in the Old Testament scriptures, the fact was certainly not self-evident, even to Jesus' most intimate followers, until after the event.

If no doctrine of a suffering Messiah was known at the time of Jesus' ministry, however, it follows that the third and fourth Servant Songs, unless they were already accorded the cavalier treatment which was later given them by the Targum, could not yet have been interpreted Messianically.

(d) The Greek Translations, Peshitta and Targum of Jonathan

An attempt has recently been made by H. Hegermann[2] to trace a Messianic interpretation of the Servant in the later Greek translations, in the Peshitta and in the Targum. He maintains that these all contain hints that official Judaism understood the Servant as the Messiah. The evidence which he adduces is, however, extremely doubtful: the Christian origin of the translation by Symmachus, and Christian influence on the Peshitta, make it impossible to accept them as witnesses to Jewish exegesis, while the scanty and ambiguous nature of the evidence for a Messianic interpretation in Aquila and Theodotion makes Hegermann's argument totally unconvincing.

The present form of the Targum of Jonathan dates, in all probability, from about the fifth century A.D.,[3] although it reflects tradition from a much earlier period. In its extraordinary interpretation of Isa. 52. 13–53. 12 the Targum identifies the Servant with the Messiah,[4] but transfers all the phrases about suffering to either Israel or the Gentiles.[1] While it witnesses to a Messianic interpretation of this passage, therefore, it is evident that, in the circle in which the Targum originated, the two concepts of suffering and of Messianism were still incompatible.[2]

(e) *Other Jewish Writings*

Phrases from Deutero-Isaiah have been used both in the Zadokite fragments and in the non-biblical manuscripts of the Dead Sea Scrolls, for example, in the 'War of the Sons of Light against the Sons of Darkness',[3] but in neither case has any use been made of the actual Servant concept.[4] No use seems to have been made of the Servant passages by either Philo or Josephus.[5]

(f) *Rabbinic Literature*

The concept of the vicarious atoning power of suffering and of death, first found in Isa. 52-3, reappears in the Rabbinic literature, where there are many examples of the idea that the death of the righteous atones, or helps to atone, for the sins of the community.[6] While it is well established by the time of the Talmud and the Midrash, however, it seems doubtful whether the doctrine was prevalent as early as the time of Jesus. Thus in the very full investigation which is made by A. Büchler[7] in his study of Jewish ideas of sin and atonement in the first century A.D., there is no hint of the idea: on the contrary, when a righteous man was martyred or suffered in any way the explanation was sought in some trivial sin which he might have committed, perhaps unwittingly, and the suffering was regarded as a purging which saved him from direr consequences in the life to come.[8] The absence of the concept of vicarious suffering and atonement from the literature of this period suggests that it was developed only with the Fall of the Temple, when the cessation of the sacrificial system naturally caused other means of atonement to become increasingly important.[9]

(g) *Conclusion*

The evidence which we have examined thus points to the conclusion that there was no pre-Christian doctrine of a suffering Messiah based upon Deutero-Isaiah. Nowhere in Jewish literature before the time of

Christ, or in the tradition of the earliest centuries A.D., is there any reference to the Servant concept which combines the idea of suffering with the dignity of Messiahship: the two concepts appear to be mutually exclusive. Thus we find, on the one hand, that those passages which speak of a 'Messiah' all avoid the concept of suffering; this is most clearly evident in the Targum of Jonathan, but is true also of Zech. 9. 9 and the Parables of Enoch.[1] Those references, on the other hand, which do include the concept of suffering are never found in a Messianic context; this is seen in Zech. 12. 10,[2] Wisd. 5. 1–5, 2. 12–20 and 3. 1–9, and in 4 Macc. 6. 27–9 and 17. 20–2.[3]

There is, indeed, no suggestion anywhere in Jewish literature until long after the time of Christ, of a coming Messiah who should suffer. In spite of this fact, there have been many attempts to prove that the concepts of Servant and of Messiah were combined in the pre-Christian era. The only evidence for such a theory, however, is either of a post-Christian date, or based upon a common predication to the two figures of various attributes: it is quite insufficient to prove that any such identification was made before the time of Christ.[4]

We may note here the views of those scholars who find in the Servant Songs an expression of a whole complex of ideas which appears in various forms throughout the Old Testament: those who, like I. Engnell and A. Bentzen,[5] trace the 'Servant' figure, together with the Messiah and the Son of Man, back to a common origin in either primitive kingship ideology, or the figure of 'First Man'. Upon this interpretation, Jesus reunited the three figures of Messiah, Son of Man and Servant, and thus brought together three strands of what had once been a common theme, but which had become divided in Judaism. It is not necessary to discuss the truth of this view, since it is concerned with the origin of the concepts, and not their interpretation in Judaism, but it must be recognized that the absence of any evidence in Jewish exegesis of the pre-Christian era for an association of these three figures shows that it cannot provide any basis for our interpretation of Jesus' understanding of his own person. Whether or not these three figures had a common origin, there is no evidence that this was in any way recognized in Jewish thought, so that even if Jesus did bring together prophetic, political and apocalyptic interpretations of what had once been one figure, there is nothing to indicate that he was conscious of this fact, or knew that he was thereby reuniting 'all aspects of the idea of Primeval Man and Primitive King in His own person'.[1]

What, then, was the Jewish interpretation of the Servant Songs in the pre-Christian era? The evidence is, as we have seen, very scanty, but such as it is, it points to two possible solutions to the problem. First, the 'partial Messianic' interpretation of the Targum may possibly reflect a tradition stretching back as far as the first century A.D.[2] Secondly, passages such as those which we have examined in Wisdom, 4 Maccabees, and possibly also Dan. 12. 3, suggest that the Songs were interpreted collectively, either of Israel, or of the righteous within Israel.[3] This second solution receives some support from the fact of the nation's continued sufferings.

2. THE NEGLECT OF THE SERVANT CONCEPT

The paucity of references to the Servant concept is in striking contrast to the importance which is attached to it today, and suggests, not only that the idea must have remained something of an enigma to the Jews of the period, but also that it was largely ignored. This judgement is confirmed by a study of three apocryphal books, 1 Baruch, 2 Esdras and 2 Baruch (The Syriac Apocalypse). These three books are all written against the background of the Babylonian Exile, although in fact the first probably dates from the second century B.C., and the others from the first century A.D.[4] Their importance for our present study lies in the fact that they all pre-suppose the same basic situation as is found in Deutero-Isaiah, and attempt to deal with the same problem, that of Israel's sin and suffering.

1 Baruch, purporting to be written by Jeremiah's scribe, is half prose and half poetry. The first part consists of an historical introduction (1. 1–14), and a confession that Israel has sinned and is therefore suffering, together with a prayer for forgiveness (1. 15–3. 8); the second is made up of a 'Wisdom' poem, which blames Israel's neglect of God's laws as the cause of her calamities (3. 9–4. 4), and a final song of comfort, promising restoration (4. 5–5. 9). This last poem is quite clearly based on Deutero-Isaiah; the language and ideas are unmistakably his, and like Isa. 40–55 it consists on the one hand of a lament over the present desolation, and on the other of promises of deliverance by Yahweh himself, and of future glory.[5]

2 Esdras and 2 Baruch are closely related, and the latter book is probably a revision of the former.[1] In 2 Esdras we are concerned with the Apocalypse of Shealtiel, which forms chapters 3-10. Here the author is described as pleading the cause of Israel before Yahweh: his problem is the same as that which appears to lie behind Isa. 53—why is Israel suffering so much more than she deserves? Granted that Israel has been disobedient, she is yet no worse than the Gentile nations who are now prospering at her expense; can this be reconciled with divine justice? The answer he receives, unfolded in a series of visions, is that God's ways are inscrutable and that man, whose intelligence is limited, cannot hope to comprehend them; the course of the world has been predetermined, and evil must have its way until the appointed time, but in spite of appearances to the contrary Yahweh still loves Israel. While there is no definite literary connection with Deutero-Isaiah, there are phrases in chapter 4 which are reminiscent of the passage in Isa. 40. 12-31 on the same theme, while the description of Jerusalem in 9. 38-10. 28 as a barren woman who bears a son, is then bereaved, and finally is transformed into a beautiful city, may well be dependent upon such passages as Isa. 49. 14-23; 51. 17-52. 2 and chapter 54.

The same themes are found again in 2 Baruch. Thus chapter 14 speaks of the incomprehensibility of God's ways; in *v.* 8 Baruch suggests that Zion should not have been overwhelmed, but forgiven on account of the good works of the righteous: this argument is rejected by Yahweh in chapter 15, but the righteous are promised glory in the coming world to make up for their present suffering. In chapter 85 the righteous intercede for their fellows, who are forgiven by Yahweh for their sake; this, however, is not dependent upon the sufferings of the interceders, but upon their good works.

In these three books, therefore, where we would most expect to find use made of the Servant figure, there is no trace of the concept: the authors have completely ignored Deutero-Isaiah's answer to the problem of suffering. 1 Baruch quite definitely borrows from Deutero-Isaiah, but finds Israel's sin an adequate explanation of her suffering: the two apocalypses are not satisfied with this solution, and both seek a further reason; their only answer, however, is that God's ways are past searching out, and that the coming Judgement will set things right. Thus the comfort which all three offer is the promise of future happiness for Israel and the punishment of her enemies; as in Deutero-Isaiah, the roles are to be reversed, but the great feature of that prophet, his universalism, is lacking.

The continued urgency of the problem of Israel's suffering is evident enough. It had not, as Deutero-Isaiah expected, been solved by the Return: Israel was still under domination, persecuted and oppressed. It is therefore the more remarkable that the solution which he had offered was never developed. Only, possibly, in 4 Maccabees was the vicarious element in his message remembered: elsewhere, it was the picture of suffering and exaltation alone that was used. Thus Isa. 53 was influential only in so far as it contained the contrast between degradation and glory which is found throughout Deutero-Isaiah's oracles: the unique feature of the chapter, the concept of vicarious suffering, is missing in later writings.

What is the explanation of this failure by the Jews to appreciate Isa. 53? The answer would appear to lie, in part, in the religious outlook of this period. The historical deliverance which was expected by Deutero-Isaiah, and is hoped for even in 1 Baruch, had failed to fulfil expectations; there seemed to be no chance of salvation in any kind of historical terms, and Judaism therefore took refuge in apocalyptic speculation about the approaching End, such as is found in Daniel, Enoch, 2 Esdras and 2 Baruch. One of the characteristics of this apocalyptic literature was its nationalism;[1] the Jewish religion had always been essentially nationalistic, and the years of bitter subjection in the last centuries B.C. and the first century A.D. could only intensify this feature. It is not surprising, therefore, that there are many passages in the literature of this period which gloat over the destruction of Israel's enemies; this attitude is found even in Deutero-Isaiah,[2] making his universalistic vision all the more impressive. It is very largely true to say that even Jewish universalism comes, ultimately, from the race's nationalism, since it is based on the conviction that Israel's God, Yahweh, is the only God.[3]

If our interpretation of the fourth Servant Song is correct, then Deutero-Isaiah depicts there the sufferings of Israel as becoming effective in bringing other nations to worship Yahweh. Such a concept must have been dependent upon his universalism, for while Israel is to be exalted high above the other nations, they are yet given a place in the worship of Yahweh. Few of his successors, however, were able to rise to such heights of forgiveness; with a few exceptions, such as Mal. 1. 11, and the books of Ruth and Jonah, later writers, and especially the apocalyptists, were content to hand the Gentiles over to destruction. It is significant that, as we have seen, the one use of the idea of vicarious suffering in this period, in 4 Maccabees, concerns atonement within Israel herself. Thus while the authors of 1 and 2 Baruch and 2 Esdras visualize, like Deutero-Isaiah, the future exaltation of Israel over her enemies, while they speak, like him, of Israel's sin and suffering, and the incomprehensibility of the ways of Yahweh, and while they may even express these ideas in language borrowed from his poems, the one idea which they nevertheless failed to use was that of Israel as the Servant of Yahweh, whose sufferings are powerful to convert the nations; for them the future exaltation will compensate for past sufferings, but it will not transform them into a saving power.

The continued absence of the Servant theme from Jewish literature points to two conclusions: first, that the figure of the Servant, as such, was not a living concept at the time of Jesus; secondly, that the idea of vicarious suffering, found in Isa. 53, had fallen into the background of Jewish thought. Indeed, not only Isa. 53, but all the Servant Songs were neglected, since their essential feature, the idea of active mission, is very largely missing in this period of Judaism. The general themes of the book, however, developed and eschatologized, continued to be important, while phrases from the Songs themselves were used in various other writings.

CHAPTER 4

THE SERVANT IN THE SYNOPTIC GOSPELS

I. BASIS OF STUDY

In considering the subject of the Servant in the Synoptics, it is important to establish first of all the criteria upon which our judgement of the evidence is to be based. An examination of those passages in the gospels which are claimed as proof of the influence of the Servant concept upon the mind of Jesus shows that they fall roughly into two classes: these are, first, those which have some linguistic affinity to one of the Servant Songs or related passages, and secondly, those which express the necessity for Jesus to undergo suffering. Some passages, of course, may be found on examination to fall into both these groups.

Now in studying those sayings which belong solely to the former of these groups, it is clear that no attempt to resolve the dilemma on linguistic grounds alone can be successful if the evidence is only probable. To claim that there is verbal similarity between a New Testament passage and an Old Testament one cannot be taken as conclusive evidence of direct influence unless it can be shown that the language and ideas found in the New Testament reference have come from, *and could only have come from*, that particular Old Testament passage. Unless the New Testament passage is an actual quotation from the Old Testament, or contains an idea found uniquely in that Old Testament reference, then the claim remains only as subsidiary evidence, and cannot be accepted as proof of any identification. Furthermore, even if such a connection is established, it still cannot be accepted as proof of any identification of Jesus with the Servant, unless the words are found to apply in both cases to the person or mission of the central figure.

Such references, if established, will show that Jesus—or his disciples —did apply some of the Servant characteristics to his life. They cannot, however, be taken as proof that he saw himself as the *Suffering* Servant, unless passages from this first group fall also into the second. For if he is found to apply to himself various characteristics of the Servant, but yet omits those which speak of his suffering and death (as the Targum interprets the Servant's attributes of the Messiah, but relegates the suffering to others), then he is not drawing on the significant features of the prophecy. Unless, therefore, we can find within the early strata of the New Testament any claim by Jesus to fulfil the essential and unique function of the Servant, the verbal similarities with Deutero-Isaiah can offer no conclusive proof that this identification was made either by Jesus himself, or by the early Church, or that Jesus attributed any vicarious significance to his death such as that described in Isa. 53.

With regard to the second group of sayings, we are faced with the problem of Jesus' attitude to his death. To dismiss the passages as *vaticinia ex eventu* is no solution unless we can find some other evidence of the way in which he regarded his passion, for he must have foreseen its probability. No such evidence can be produced, however. If, on the other hand, we accept as genuine the fact of these prophecies, if not their details, then we have to consider what was the origin of this realization by Jesus of the necessity for his death. Did the conviction that he must suffer come upon him gradually, or in a moment? Was it the result of his own thinking only, or did it arise from a perusal of Scripture?

It is often stated that Jesus' conviction that he must suffer could only have come from the application of Isa. 53 to himself.[1] This judgement, however, may be based on an over-emphasis of the importance of the Suffering Servant passages, due, on the one hand, to the failure of a later age to recognize the possible existence of other sources which could have influenced Jesus, and on the other, to a Christian interpretation of Isa. 53 in terms of a subjective experience of forgiveness centring round the death of Christ, which has magnified the vicarious teaching originally contained in the passage.

If Jesus did indeed find the key to the understanding of his own suffering and death in the figure of the Servant, then we may expect to find some points of contact between the first group of sayings and the second. If there is a complete exclusion of linguistic references to Deutero-Isaiah from Jesus' own words about his death then this must point to the conclusion that there was no connection in his own mind between the destiny of the Servant and the purpose of his own suffering and death. If, however, such references are interwoven, then the further problem remains, whether the Servant references are primary in the sense that Jesus' fundamental conception of himself was as the Servant, or whether they are present because Jesus saw himself, not primarily as the Servant, but as one greater than the Servant who included in himself the attributes of that figure.

2. PASSAGES FOR CONSIDERATION

The following is a list of the references which must now be examined; the first group has been further subdivided into those passages which speak of Jesus and his mission, and those which give details in the Passion narrative. In each section the Marcan passages are in general given first, followed by those which appear only in Matthew and Luke.

Group 1. Linguistic references to Deutero-Isaiah

(a) *Words or phrases from Deutero-Isaiah used of the person or work of Jesus*
 (i) Mark 1. 1, etc. Εὐαγγέλιον.
 (ii) Mark 1. 2–3 (Matt. 3. 3; Luke 3. 4). John, the forerunner of Jesus.
 (iii) Mark 1. 8, 10 (Matt. 3. 11, 16; Luke 3. 16, 21f.). The gift of the Spirit.
 (iv) Mark 1. 11 (Matt. 3. 17; Luke 3. 22). 'My beloved Son.'
 (v) Mark 9. 7 (Matt. 17. 5; Luke 9. 35). 'My beloved Son.'
 (vi) Mark 3. 27 (Matt. 12. 29). The strong man spoiled.
 (vii) Mark 10. 45 (Matt. 20. 28). 'A ransom for many.'
 (viii) Mark 13. 27 (Matt. 24. 31). The gathering of the Elect.
 (ix) Mark 13. 31 (Matt. 24. 35; Luke 21. 33). 'My words will not pass away.'
 (x) Mark 14. 18, 21 (Matt. 26. 21, 24; Luke 22. 22). Παραδώσει...παραδίδοται.
 (xi) Mark 14. 24 (Matt. 26. 28; Luke 22. 20). The new covenant.
 (xii) Matt. 8. 16f. Quotation of Isa. 53. 4.
 (xiii) Matt. 12. 18–21. Quotation of Isa. 42. 1–4.
 (xiv) Luke 2. 32. A light for the Gentiles.
 (xv) Luke 4. 16–21. Quotation by Jesus of Isa. 61. 1f.
 (xvi) Luke 7. 22. Message of Jesus to John.
 (xvii) Luke 22. 37. Jesus quotes from Isa. 53. 12.

(b) *Details in the Passion Narrative*
 (i) Mark 14. 61 (Matt. 26. 63). Jesus silent before Caiaphas.
 (ii) Mark 15. 5 (Matt. 27. 12, 14). Jesus silent before Pilate.
 (iii) Luke 23. 9. Jesus silent before Herod.

(iv) Mark 14. 65 (Matt. 26. 67f.; Luke 22. 63f.). Jesus ridiculed by Caiaphas' men.
(v) Mark 15. 15–20 (Matt. 27. 26–31). Jesus ridiculed by Pilate's men.
(vi) Luke 23. 11. Jesus ridiculed by Herod's men.
(vii) Mark 15. 27 (Matt. 27. 38; Luke 23. 33). Jesus crucified between two thieves.

Group 2. Predictions of suffering in the mouth of Jesus

(i) Mark 2. 19f. (Matt. 9. 15; Luke 5. 34f.). The bridegroom will be taken away.
(ii) Mark 8. 31 (Matt. 16. 21; Luke 9. 22). The Son of Man must suffer.
(iii) Mark 9. 31 (Matt. 17. 22f.; Luke 9. 44). The Son of Man must suffer.
(iv) Mark 10. 33f. (Matt. 20. 18f.; Luke 18. 31–3). The Son of Man must suffer.
(v) Mark 9. 12b (Matt. 17. 12). What is written of the Son of Man.
(vi) Mark 10. 38 (Matt. 20. 22). The cup and baptism.
(vii) Mark 12. 10 (Matt. 21. 42; Luke 20. 17). The rejected stone.
(viii) Mark 14. 8 (Matt. 26. 12). 'She has anointed my body.'
(ix) Mark 14. 21 (Matt. 26. 24; Luke 22. 22). 'The Son of Man goeth.'
(x) Mark 14. 27 (Matt. 26. 31). The shepherd will be smitten.
(xi) Mark 14. 49 (Matt. 26. 56). The fulfilment of prophecy.
(xii) Luke 12. 49f. Fire and baptism.
(xiii) Luke 13. 32f. A prophet perishes only in Jerusalem.
(xiv) Luke 17. 25. The suffering of the Son of Man.
(xv) Luke 24. 25ff. The sufferings of Christ in the scriptures.

These various passages must now be examined carefully with a view to establishing in each case whether the suggested reference to Deutero-Isaiah may be regarded as being either certain or probable, or whether, on account of insufficient or opposing evidence, the claim cannot be upheld.

3. GROUP I (a): WORDS OR PHRASES USED OF THE PERSON OR WORK OF JESUS

(i) Mark 1. 1.

Εὐαγγέλιον. Cf. the use of the cognate verb in the LXX to translate the Hebrew root בשׂר in Isa. 40. 9; 52. 7.

This noun occurs in Mark at 1. 1, 14, 15; 8. 35; 10. 29; 13. 10; 14. 9; (16. 15), and in Matthew at 4. 23; 9. 35; 24. 14 and 26. 13. The cognate verb, εὐαγγελίζομαι, is found in Matt. 11. 5, and in Luke 1. 19; 2. 10; 3. 18; 4. 18; 7. 22; 8. 1; 9. 6; 16. 16 and 20. 1. Neither the verb nor the noun is used in John.

It is clear that εὐαγγέλιον is closely associated with the person of Jesus. This is made plain at the very beginning by Mark, who heads his work 'the beginning of the gospel of Jesus Christ'; twice in Mark we find the phrase 'for my sake and the gospel's' (Mark 8. 35; 10. 29). In most cases the gospel is identified with the preaching of Jesus (Mark 1. 1, 14, 15; Matt. 4. 23; 9. 35; 11. 5; Luke 4. 18; 7. 22; 8. 1; 16. 16 and 20. 1). In Luke we find the verb used before the ministry of Jesus, twice of the news of his birth (Luke 1. 19; 2.10), and once of the words of John the Baptist (Luke 3. 18). In Luke 9. 6 the disciples, sent by Jesus, preach the gospel throughout the land, and in the remaining cases the noun is used of the message which the disciples are to spread after Jesus' death (Mark 13. 10; 14. 9; 16. 15; Matt. 24. 14; 26. 13).

In the LXX the noun is used only in the plural, at 2 Sam. 4. 10 and 18. 22, 25. The form ἡ εὐαγγελία is used at 2 Sam. 18. 20, 27 and 2 Kings 7. 9. The meaning is 'tidings' of any nature, not necessarily good. The verb is used more frequently, and translates the Hebrew root בשר; there are two senses in which the word is used—the 'profane' for any good news, and the 'religious', for the good news of Yahweh's salvation.

(a) *Profane.* 1 Sam. 31. 9; 2 Sam. 1. 20; 4. 10; 18. 19, 20, 26, 31; 1 Kings 1. 42; 1 Chron. 10. 9; Ps. 67 (68). 11 and Jer. 20. 15.

(b) *Religious.* Ps. 39 (40). 9; 95 (96). 2; Nahum 1. 15; Isa. 40. 9; 52. 7; 60. 6; 61. 1.[1]

It seems clear that it is this religious use of the verb which lies behind the New Testament usage of the root; it is here alone that a background is found with significance sufficient to explain the sense in which the New Testament writers understand the word; this background is the proclamation of the salvation which is being wrought by Yahweh for his people. The fact that Luke returns to the use of the verb instead of the noun confirms that this is so, especially as in at least one passage he is actually quoting from Trito-Isaiah.[2]

We may conclude, then, that the words εὐαγγέλιον and εὐαγγελίζομαι are taken from a group of passages centring on Deutero- and Trito-Isaiah. The fact that they are closely connected with the person of Jesus suggests that his message is a renewed proclamation of the era announced by Deutero-Isaiah.[3] This interpretation is confirmed by the

Old Testament usage of the root בשׂר, which similarly associates the bearer of news with his message, and indeed almost identifies them: thus Jesus himself would be the bearer of the salvation which he proclaims.[1] There is as yet no indication, however, that Jesus is to be identified in any way with the figure of the Servant.

(ii) Mark 1. 2–3 (Matt. 3. 3; Luke 3. 4; cf. John 1. 23).

As it is written in Isaiah the prophet (in the prophets),
'Behold, I send my messenger before thy face,
who shall prepare thy way;
the voice of one crying in the wilderness:
Prepare the way of the Lord,
make his paths straight.'

This direct quotation combines Mal. 3. 1 with Isa. 40. 3, and the Greek is almost identical with the LXX text.[2] In Mark it follows immediately upon the words 'the beginning of the gospel of Jesus Christ'. This 'gospel', as we have seen, is the message that the salvation of God is at hand—or perhaps rather it is the salvation itself, in the figure of Jesus. In the Old Testament the words from Isa. 40 introduce the chapters of Deutero- and Trito-Isaiah which announce the coming of this salvation; so it is appropriate that Mark should describe 'the beginning of the gospel of Jesus Christ' by quoting them, for the preaching of John the Baptist is the beginning of Christ's work. He who preaches the 'baptism of repentance for the forgiveness of sins' is successor to the prophet who proclaimed to Jerusalem that her iniquity was now forgiven. These words confirm the conclusion that εὐαγγέλιον is taken from Isa. 40–65, and show that the evangelist in some way identified the coming of Jesus with the deliverance promised in these chapters. This, however, still does not imply that Jesus is seen as the Servant.

(iii) Mark 1. 8–10 (Matt. 3. 11, 16; Luke 3. 16, 21 f.; cf. John 1. 32 f.).

I have baptized you with water; but he will baptize you with the Holy Spirit.... And when he came up out of the water, immediately he saw the heavens opened and the Spirit descending upon him like a dove.

In the Old Testament the Spirit of God is the hallmark of the man of God. The Spirit may rest upon anyone—for example, on a craftsman (Exod. 31. 3), or on a leader of Israel (Judg. 6. 34), but above all upon the prophet (Mic. 3. 8). It follows, therefore, that the Spirit will rest upon the Messiah (Isa. 11. 2–4) and on the Servant of Yahweh (Isa. 42. 1; cf. 61. 1). In later times it became part of the message of the New Age that *all* Israel would possess the gift of the Spirit (Joel 2. 28; Isa. 32. 15; 44. 3; 59. 21). The descent of the Spirit upon Jesus is therefore the sign that he is appointed for some task by God—he is the first to receive the gift of the Spirit which he will in turn hand on to others; the fire, which is mentioned by Matthew and Luke, is the reverse side of this baptism with Spirit—the fire of judgement and purification.[1] These ideas are part of Old Testament belief, and do not necessarily derive from Deutero-Isaiah.

The figurative description of the opening of the heavens is used in the Old Testament of the participation of Yahweh in an act of deliverance. It is found in Isa. 64. 1; Ps. 18. 9 and 144. 5; of these the first is the closest to Mark 1. 10, although Mark uses a different verb; Matthew and Luke, however, revert to the ἀνοίγω of Isaiah. There is again no proof that it is the last chapters of Isaiah which are primarily in Jesus' mind, although the fact that so many of the ideas in this verse are found in them does suggest that this is so. This, however, proves no more than that Jesus did in some way see in his work the fulfilment of the New Exodus proclaimed by Deutero-Isaiah.

There is little agreement concerning the significance which should be attached to the figure of the dove, although evidence has been brought forward to support the views, both that it is a symbol for the Spirit, and that it represents Israel.[2] In either case, there is no direct link with Deutero-Isaiah.

(iv) Mark 1. 11 (Matt. 3. 17; Luke 3. 22; cf. John 1. 34).

Σὺ εἶ ὁ υἱός μου ὁ ἀγαπητός, ἐν σοὶ εὐδόκησα.

(v) Mark 9. 7 (Matt. 17. 5; Luke 9. 35).

Οὗτός ἐστιν ὁ υἱός μου ὁ ἀγαπητός.

Cf. Isa. 42. 1: בְּחִירִי רָצְתָה נַפְשִׁי; LXX: Ἰσραὴλ ὁ ἐκλεκτός μου, προσεδέξατο αὐτὸν ἡ ψυχή μου.

Since these two passages have both been traced to Isa. 42. 1, they may be considered together. There seems to be no reason to doubt that the Marcan readings represent the most primitive tradition of the sayings: a comparison of the various Synoptic accounts reveals evidence in both cases of assimilation in Matthew, and of textual variants in Luke. Our study will therefore be based primarily on the Marcan version.

Σὺ εἶ ὁ υἱός μου. This phrase in Mark 1. 11 is very similar to the LXX version of Ps. 2. 7, which reads Υἱός μου εἶ σύ. Either Luke or an early editor of Luke recognized this fact and changed the words into a definite quotation from the psalm. The problem thus arises whether he was right in interpreting the phrase as a reference to that passage.

Commentators usually presume that Luke's interpretation is correct, and explain the incident as the recognition by Jesus of the fact that he was the Messiah, although they find evidence in the words ὁ ἀγαπητός, ἐν σοὶ εὐδόκησα that his conception of Messiahship was considerably qualified, and conveyed few of the characteristics which were generally associated with it.[1] It must, however, be remembered that there is no evidence that the phrase 'son of God' was ever a recognized Messianic title in pre-Christian Judaism.[2] The concept of physical relationship between God and man, even between God and the king, was quite alien to Hebrew thought: its presence in Ps. 2. 7 is due to foreign influence on the kingly ritual, of which this psalm was a part. This influence can also be traced in Ps. 89. 27. In 2 Sam. 7. 14 and 1 Chron. 28. 6, Solomon is spoken of as Yahweh's son: this is only metaphorical, however, as the use of the preposition ל shows, together with the reminder in 1 Chron. 29. 1 that Solomon is David's son and has been chosen by Yahweh. In non-canonical books the concept of the Messiah as son of God is found only in Enoch 105. 2, a fragment of uncertain date and origin, and in 4 Ezra, which probably dates from the end of the first century A.D.[3]

It is therefore invalid to argue, as so many have done, that Jesus took the title from this psalm, but qualified it with concepts drawn from Deutero-Isaiah, thus reinterpreting the idea of Messiahship. For the title 'Son of God' is meaningless as a Messianic designation apart from the context of this psalm. Moreover, the political character of this passage, which is the very epitome of all that Jesus did *not* consider his mission to be, makes it incredible that he should have found confirmation of his Messiahship here.[4] It is easy, however, to understand how the Lucan interpretation arose, when the early Church sought for proofs of Jesus' Messiahship in the Old Testament.

This part of the verse has also been traced, not to Ps. 2, but to Isa. 42. 1.[1] This depends upon the suggestion that the original tradition used the ambiguous παῖς, and that this was clarified by Mark as υἱός. This assumption is justified only if the remainder of the verse is found to come from Isa. 42. 1, since we have no evidence elsewhere that Mark reinterpreted παῖς in this way: indeed, the use of παῖς in the early chapters of Acts speaks against it, since we should expect to find a similar change in the writing of Luke.

Ὁ ἀγαπητός. This expression used in both Mark 1.11 and 9.7,[2] does not appear in any of the Greek versions of Isa. 42. 1 which are known to us, nor is it ever used in the LXX to translate the Hebrew root בחר which is used there, and which always has the meaning of 'choice'. The LXX keeps to this meaning by translating בְּחִירִי as ὁ ἐκλεκτός. It is significant, however, that in the version of this passage which is quoted in Matt. 12. 18–21 ἀγαπητός is used; the great differences between this version and that of the LXX suggest that the evangelist was using a Greek translation unknown to us; if so, then this unknown version may lie behind Mark 9. 7 also. We may note, too, that the original reading in Luke 9. 35 was probably ὁ ἐκλελεγμένος.

Ἀγαπητός is not common in the LXX version of the Old Testament, but where it does occur it translates primarily[3] the following Hebrew roots:

(a) יחיד Only:
  (i) Gen. 22. 2, 12, 16, of Isaac: Λάβε τὸν υἱόν σου τὸν ἀγαπητὸν ὃν ἠγάπησας, τὸν Ἰσαάκ.
  οὐκ ἐφείσω τοῦ υἱοῦ σου τοῦ ἀγαπητοῦ δι' ἐμέ. (bis)
  (ii) Amos 8. 10, in simile: θήσομαι αὐτὸν ὡς πένθος ἀγαπητοῦ.
  (iii) Jer. 6. 26, in simile: πένθος ἀγαπητοῦ ποίησαι.
  (iv) Judg. 11. 34, of Jephthah's daughter: καὶ ἦν αὕτη μονογενής (A + αὐτῷ ἀγαπητή).
  (v) Zech. 12. 10, in simile: κοπετὸν ὡς ἐπ' ἀγαπητῷ.

(b) ידיד (poetical) Beloved:
  (i) Ps. 59. 7 (60. 5); 107. 7 (108. 6); 126 (127). 2, of Israel: ὅπως ἂν ῥυσθῶσιν οἱ ἀγαπητοί σου. (bis)
  ὅταν δῷ τοῖς ἀγαπητοῖς αὐτοῦ ὕπνον.
  (ii) Isa. 5. 1, of Yahweh: Ἄσω δὴ τῷ ἠγαπημένῳ ᾆσμα τοῦ ἀγαπητοῦ μου.
  (iii) Ps. 44. 1 (45), song title: ᾠδὴ ὑπὲρ τοῦ ἀγαπητοῦ.

(iv) Ps. 83. 2 (84. 1), of the dwelling of Yahweh: Ὡς ἀγαπητὰ τὰ σκηνώματά σου.

(c) יָקִיר Dear: Jer. 38 (31). 20, of Ephraim: υἱὸς ἀγαπητὸς Ἐφράιμ.

It is noteworthy that in all the uses of the word under (a) and (c), ἀγαπητός is used of an only son (or daughter). It is almost identical in meaning with μονογενής,[1] which suggests that the use of this word in John 1. 18 may be a further echo of the Marcan verse. This Old Testament usage shows that there is very possibly a closer relationship between the two phrases σὺ εἶ ὁ υἱός μου and ὁ ἀγαπητός, ἐν σοὶ εὐδόκησα than is sometimes supposed. Jesus' sonship, announced in Mark 1. 11 and 9. 7, is immediately defined by the emphatic ἀγαπητός as being a unique relationship. This suggests that the origin of the word is to be found in the Old Testament concept of the only Son, rather than in that of the Servant.

Ἐν σοὶ εὐδόκησα. This phrase has been referred to the words in Isa. 42. 1 which are translated in the LXX as προσεδέξατο αὐτὸν ἡ ψυχή μου, but in the version of Theodotion as ὃν εὐδόκησεν ἡ ψυχή μου.[2]

The verb εὐδοκέω is used in the LXX to translate the following Hebrew expressions:

רָצָה with בְּ or the accusative;

חָפֵץ בְּ;

צָלַח in the Hiph'il.

The following are the occasions when it is used of God taking pleasure in a person or in people:

Ps. 43. 4 (44. 3), of Israel: ὅτι εὐδόκησας ἐν αὐτοῖς—רצה.
Ps. 149. 4, of Israel: ὅτι εὐδοκεῖ Κύριος ἐν λαῷ αὐτοῦ—רצה.
Isa. 62. 4, of Israel: ὅτι εὐδόκησε Κύριος ἐν σοί—חפץ ב.
2 Sam. 22. 20, of David: ὅτι εὐδόκησεν ἐν ἐμοί—חפץ ב.
Ps. 146 (147). 11, of those who fear God: εὐδοκεῖ Κύριος ἐν τοῖς φοβουμένοις αὐτόν—רצה.
Mal. 2. 17, of the good in God's eyes: ἐν αὐτοῖς αὐτὸς εὐδόκησεν—חפץ ב.
Jer. 14. 10, of Israel: ὁ Θεὸς οὐκ εὐδώσεν (Α—εὐδόκησεν) ἐν αὐτοῖς—רצה.

In all these cases the construction used is εὐδοκέω ἐν, as in Mark 1. 11. In four cases this represents a use of the Hebrew particle בְּ, in two of a suffix, and in one an accusative particle. The LXX version of Isa. 42. 2, on the other hand, reads προσδέχομαι with the accusative; similarly, both Theodotion and Matt. 12. 18 have ὃν εὐδόκησεν ἡ ψυχή μου. The

Hebrew construction behind these translations is defective, the text reading simply רָצְתָה נַפְשִׁי.[1]

It is therefore clear that if these two verses do refer to Isa. 42. 1, they are by no means a quotation of that passage. On the contrary, the three key-words in Mark, υἱός, ἀγαπητός and εὐδόκησα, are all different from the normal translations of the verse. Moreover, if Matthew understood the words as a reference to Isaiah, then it is strange that he did not make them agree with his other citation of the passage in Matt. 12. 18. The question therefore arises whether there lies behind these passages a tradition that Jesus was identified as the Servant at his Baptism, which has already by the time of Mark become so obscured that none of the key-words has remained unchanged.

Our answer to this question, since we have no evidence for the pre-Marcan tradition itself, must depend upon an examination of both the Old Testament background of the concepts which are used, and their context in the New Testament. The general similarity in thought between Mark 1. 11 and 9. 7 and Isa. 42. 1 can be no proof that Jesus is thought of in terms of the Servant, if it is found that these passages all belong to a wider pattern of ideas.

We have already noted that the concept of an individual as the son of God is abhorrent to Hebrew thought. Nevertheless, the idea of sonship is present in the Old Testament, since Israel as a nation could be spoken of as the son of God. Although the term 'son' itself is not often applied to Israel directly, probably because of hesitancy lest the term be taken too literally, there is no doubt that the concept of Yahweh as the Father of Israel was a very real one in prophetic thought. This relationship of Israel to her God never takes the crude form of physical sonship found in neighbouring countries. In Hebrew religion man is created by God, not begotten of him; so the Fatherhood of Yahweh is expressed in the redemptive acts which he performs, and Israel's dependency upon him.[2] In later Jewish use we find the idea of sonship narrowed down to those who thought of themselves as the true Israel, the righteous members of the nation.[3]

The concept which is conveyed by the words ὁ ἀγαπητός is clearly applicable to Israel. In Jer. 31. 20 Israel is described as Yahweh's beloved son, and the unique position of Israel in God's sight is a commonplace of Hebrew religion. It was unnecessary for the prophets to stress that Israel was loved by Yahweh: rather they had to remind the people that this love did not exempt them from responsibility. Similarly, εὐδοκέω was used of God's attitude to his chosen people: of the seven passages noted above which speak of God taking delight in someone, five refer to Israel.

Thus the three words which have been traced, somewhat dubiously, to Isa. 42. 1, together form a concept which in the Old Testament is applied only to Israel. The fact that so many commentators have understood them as a reference to that passage in particular is understandable if, as seems probable, the first Servant Song was meant originally to depict Israel. Finally, we may note that this wider background of the Old Testament concept of sonship is in keeping with the context of Mark 1. 11, which is the Johannine baptism. For in submitting to this rite of baptism Jesus was associating himself with those who, in response to the preaching of John, were joining themselves to the righteous Remnant of Israel. John, in accordance with the words of the later prophets, not only foretold judgement, but demanded repentance, and promised the gifts of the New Age, principally the descent of the Holy Spirit through the Coming One, to the True Israel.[1] Thus the words of the voice are connected with the gift of the Spirit, not only in the Old Testament hope of the End, but also in the preaching of John.

(vi) Mark 3. 27 (Matt. 12. 29; cf. Luke 11. 21 f.).

But no one can enter a strong man's house and plunder his goods, unless he first binds the strong man; then indeed he may plunder his house.

Although there is no verbal correspondence between the Greek text and the LXX version of Isa. 49. 24 f., the similarity in meaning is so great that there is little doubt that Jesus had this passage in mind when he spoke these words;[2] nor is there any comparable picture elsewhere in the Old Testament. Jesus describes his work of saving from the grasp of Satan those who are in the power of demons, in terms which were originally applied to Yahweh's redemption of Israel from her captors. Again, this passage is an indication that Jesus was familiar with Deutero-Isaiah, but it sheds no light on the problem of his identification with the Servant, since it is not the Servant in this passage who defeats the strong man but Yahweh himself, so that Jesus' activity fulfils the redemptive work of God. It is true that in Isa. 53. 12 the Servant is to 'divide the spoil with the strong', but there is no indication in the New Testament passage that this verse was present in Jesus' mind.[1]

(vii) Mark 10. 45 (Matt. 20. 28; cf. Luke 22. 27).

καὶ γὰρ ὁ υἱὸς τοῦ ἀνθρώπου οὐκ ἦλθε διακονηθῆναι, ἀλλὰ διακονῆσαι, καὶ δοῦναι τὴν ψυχὴν αὐτοῦ λύτρον ἀντὶ πολλῶν.

Cf. Isa. 53. 11: לָרַבִּים; LXX: δουλεύοντα πολλοῖς.

Isa. 53. 10: אִם־תָּשִׂים אָשָׁם נַפְשׁוֹ; LXX: ἐὰν δῶτε περὶ ἁμαρτίας, ἡ ψυχὴ ἡμῶν ὄψεται σπέρμα μακρόβιον.

The influence of the Servant Songs has been traced here in the concepts of service, the ransom and the giving of life, and in the word 'many'.[2] This is the first of the passages so far examined to fall also into the second group of sayings, which are concerned with suffering.

The idea of service is expressed by the use of the word διακονέω: this verb, which is unknown in the LXX, is used in the New Testament and in Classical Greek with the sense of domestic service.[3] The word δοῦλος, which occurs in *v.* 44, is used in the LXX, together with its cognate verb δουλεύω, and with λατρεύω, to translate the Hebrew root עבד. In Deutero-Isaiah, δοῦλος and δουλεύω are used frequently, although παῖς is preferred for the passages which actually speak of Yahweh's Servant.[4] In 53. 11, however, the words δουλεύοντα πολλοῖς occur together, and this fact supports the claim that the concept of the Suffering Servant may lie behind Mark 10. 45. It is important, however, to examine the thought lying behind the two passages.

In Mark 10. 44 f. we have presented the idea of lowly service, rendered by one member of the community, and supremely by Jesus himself, to the others: the suggestion that this saying may be linked with the Johannine narrative of the feet-washing[5] is important in this connection, since that is the kind of service which is implied by the language here used. In the Isaian passages, however, the terms δοῦλος and παῖς are used only of the relationship between the Servant and Yahweh.[6] The fact that the central figure of Deutero-Isaiah is commonly known as 'The Servant' has tended to obscure the fact that he is primarily *Yahweh's* Servant, and is indicated as such by the use of the pronominal suffix. In the passages known as the Servant Songs he is portrayed as one who is above all else submissive to the will of Yahweh, and this picture of obedience reaches its climax in the final Song; there the Servant is shown as submissive to the pains inflicted upon him by men, but always it is as the Servant of Yahweh, not as a servant of men, that he endures the suffering. We may compare the use of the phrase 'My Servant' with other occasions in the Old Testament where individuals are described as the Servant of Yahweh: the phrase is used in particular of Moses,[1] but also of the Patriarchs, Joshua, Job, David, Daniel, Isaiah and even Nebuchadrezzar.[2] The term is one of special honour, and is used of the individual's relationship to Yahweh, not to his fellow-men.

The saying of Mark 10. 45 must be read in the context of the verses in which it is set, and not be taken in isolation: in *v.* 42 Jesus has described the rule of Gentile leaders; then, saying 'It shall not be so among you', he goes on to depict what must be the attitude of the disciple who would be 'first' among his brethren.[3] The whole passage takes the common form of antithesis, contrasting the rule exercised among the Gentiles and in the flock of Jesus. The verbs used of the Gentiles are κατακυριεύω and κατεξουσιάζω: these are both compounded with the preposition κατά, here meaning 'under', and they carry respectively the senses of 'to hold in subjection' and 'to wield power over'.[4] It is the very opposite of this attitude which is portrayed in *vv.* 43 f. in the behaviour of one who is willing to serve those of whom, technically, he is the head;[5] this is the character which is epitomized in the One who is the head of all men, the Son of Man himself.

Although the Christian may believe that this attitude is possible only for one who has, like the Servant of Isa. 53, learnt to be perfectly submissive to the will of God, the connection is not made in this particular passage. The picture drawn here is one of willing service by those whom the world would expect to be served; there is no apparent connection with the figure of Isa. 53, one whom the world ridiculed and who had no social standing whatever, and who of necessity rather than of choice endured the pains inflicted upon him.[6]

The concept of suffering enters only into the second half of the verse. Many scholars reject these words as being alien to the context,[7] and the fact that they are not represented in the Lucan account of the incident supports this opinion. For the purposes of this examination, however, they will be treated as genuine. The important words are λύτρον and πολύς.

Λύτρον is a term which is found, in the LXX, only in the technical sense of 'purchase money', never as a sacrificial term; it implies the idea of a payment which is the equivalent of what is redeemed, whether this be a man's life, or a slave's freedom, or land previously sold and now to be rebought.[1] The cognate verb λυτρόω is used far more frequently, and while it translates several Hebrew roots, in the overwhelming majority of cases it stands for גאל or פדה. Although the verb is often found in the Pentateuch in the same sense as the noun, it is also used there in a more figurative sense of the redemption by Yahweh of his people from the bondage of Egypt.[2]

This figurative use is continued in the prophetic writings—and especially in Deutero-Isaiah—where the roots גאל and פדה, translated in the LXX by λυτρόω or ῥύομαι are used of the work which Yahweh is to accomplish for his people.[3] Whereas the Pentateuch references look back to the redemption from Egypt, these references look forward, generally to the redemption from Exile. The use of גאל or פדה in several passages in Deutero-Isaiah where the Return is depicted in terms of the Exodus makes it probable that the conception of the Return as a Second Exodus lies behind the usage of these two words in the prophetic writings.[4] In any case, there is no doubt that they represent what is one of the most important concepts of Hebrew religion—the belief in Yahweh as the Redeemer and Deliverer of his people. The vital nature of this idea is seen in the central place given to the covenant, which was made on the basis of God's deliverance of the people from Egypt, and in the frequent references which are made back to this event by the prophets, who in referring to it speak on the one hand of Yahweh's continued faithfulness to his people, and on the other of Israel's apostasy. It should be noted that the primary thought in this conception of God as Redeemer is one of historical activity by Yahweh, either in the past, at the Exodus, or in the future, at the Return; it may be used, too, of the deliverance of some individual from distress: if the forgiveness of sins is sometimes involved, then it is secondary to this main theme. Nor is there any emphasis on the payment of an equivalent, the original meaning of ransom: it is enough that Yahweh acts decisively; the result, not the method of his action, is what is important.[5]

This concept of redemption is, naturally, a dominant one in Deutero-Isaiah, who finds in the root גאל the most adequate description of the relationship of Yahweh to Israel. Again and again he describes Yahweh as the Redeemer, or as the One who redeems Israel. The same is true also of those chapters which are most closely associated with Deutero-Isaiah, Isa. 35 and 56–66.[1] פדה, although not so common, seems to have been used with the same meaning.[2]

It has already been noted that Jesus drew from the language of Deutero-Isaiah in his teaching, and apparently understood a connection between his own mission and the New Era announced by that prophet. If, then, he associated his own person so closely with the promised redemption of Israel by Yahweh, it seems most probable that he would have connected his death also with that event, and that the term λύτρον, which he applies to his death, is derived from the same source. This is, in fact, what is claimed by many scholars who hold that λύτρον refers to the אָשָׁם spoken of in connection with the Servant.[3] There is, however, not the slightest evidence to show that these two terms were ever connected: the λύτρον, as we have seen, was the redemption of a person or thing by purchase; the אָשָׁם was the repayment of something wrongfully withheld, together with a guilt-offering by means of expiation: the one is a business transaction; the other involves a sacrifice for sin. Some scholars have stressed the substitutionary element implied by the word ἀντί in Mark 10. 45.[4] The אָשָׁם, however, was never a substitute: it was repayment, together with compensation and a guilt-offering. The concept of substitution belongs more to the λύτρον, where an equivalent price was paid: it is interesting to note that the only place where ἀντί is used in connection with λύτρον in the LXX is in Num. 3. 12, where the Greek has the phrase, not represented in the Hebrew text, λύτρα αὐτῶν ἔσονται. This is also the only occasion where the λύτρον really was fully substitutionary: here each Israelite is redeemed, man for man, by a Levite; elsewhere the redemption is always monetary, or paid in different kind.

There is, however, considerable evidence to justify the linking of λύτρον with the general theme of Deutero-Isaiah, which is the expected redemption of Israel by Yahweh. If Jesus were indeed thinking in terms of Deutero-Isaiah when he said that the Son of Man came to give his life as a ransom for many, then he was linking this action with the decisive event which should redeem Israel. This event was, in fact, what his disciples had expected Jesus to accomplish, although not in this way:

for they 'had hoped that he was the one who should redeem Israel'.[1] But it is always Yahweh himself who redeems his people: it follows, therefore, that the Son of Man is the instrument of God's purpose.

Our interpretation of this passage depends ultimately upon our understanding of the term 'Son of Man'.[2] Whether, however, Jesus was speaking only of his own death, or whether he was thinking also of the probable fate of his followers, the significance of the action lies in the redemption by God of his people: there is no emphasis on the question of sin. This, of course, is not to deny that sin is involved; on the contrary, it is the nation's sin which both makes the redemption necessary, and causes the death of the Son of Man. Nevertheless, as in the Old Testament, it is the result of the redemption which is of importance, not its reason or method.

This, then, is a concept much wider than the Servant theme, although it may indeed include the Servant. The emphasis is upon death and deliverance rather than upon sin and suffering. The words are thus in keeping with the spirit of the first half of the first century A.D., which, as we have seen, was still concerned with deliverance from foreign oppression, rather than with theories of atonement as such.[3] It is true that the idea of atonement does appear in 4 Macc. 6. 27 ff.; 17. 20 ff., in connection with the death of the martyrs: the word which is used there, however, is ἀντίψυχον, not λύτρον.

The phrase 'to give his life a ransom for many' is also in harmony with the first half of the verse; it does not, as some have claimed, introduce a 'sacrificial' concept into what was merely an exhortation to serve others. For the willingness to give one's life is not only the supreme example of service for others, but is in this case the culmination which gives meaning to the whole of that service. So Jesus, who has spent his whole life in the lowly service of others, now gives that life itself in the supreme act which, he believes, will complete the act of redemption.

Πολύς occurs three times in Isa. 53. 11 f., each time as translation of the Hebrew רַב. Here we are told, first, that by his knowledge Yahweh's righteous Servant shall justify many, and bear their iniquities; next, that the many will be given to him as his portion; finally, that he bore the sin of many. Nowhere here, apart from the use of the word πολύς, is there any connection, either in thought or in language, with Mark 10. 45.

Although the Greek πολύς is an exclusive term, its equivalent in both

Hebrew and Aramaic could be used in an inclusive sense, since neither had a word for 'all' in the plural. It is thus very probable that the word πολλῶν in this verse is a 'Semitism', and reflects an earlier Aramaic tradition. Such an interpretation, however, is in no way dependent upon the possibility of a reference to Isa. 53. 11f.[1] While Jesus may have in mind the prophetic theme of universalism, which is found in Deutero-Isaiah, there is no justification, in the absence of supporting evidence, for assuming that he was thinking also of the Servant when he used this word.

(viii) Mark 13. 27 (Matt. 24. 31).

[The Son of Man] will send out the angels, and gather his elect from the four winds, from the ends of the earth to the ends of heaven.

C. H. Dodd traces this passage to the gathering of God's people through the Servant in Isa. 49. 5 f.[2] The gathering together of Israel was, however, a traditional idea which appears repeatedly in the post-Exilic prophets. There is no reason for supposing that in this passage Deutero-Isaiah is in mind; indeed, there is more similarity with some of the other Old Testament references to the same idea.[3]

(ix) Mark 13. 31 (Matt. 24. 35; Luke 21. 33).

Heaven and earth will pass away, but my words will not pass away.

These words echo the thought of Isa. 51. 6, where Yahweh says that the heavens will vanish, the earth wear away and its inhabitants die, but his salvation and deliverance will endure. Similarly, in Ps. 102. 25f., it is Yahweh himself who endures, in contrast to both earth and heaven. It seems very probable that the Old Testament passages were in Jesus' mind at this point; if so, then we again find an instance of the connection between Jesus and Yahweh's work of redemption: Jesus' words of proclamation, like God's salvation, will endure. There is no connection, however, with the figure of the Servant.

(x) Mark 14. 18, 21 (Matt. 26. 21, 24; Luke 22. 22).

'Ἀμὴν λέγω ὑμῖν ὅτι εἶς ἐξ ὑμῶν παραδώσει με...οὐαὶ δὲ τῷ ἀνθρώπῳ ἐκείνῳ δι' οὗ ὁ υἱὸς τοῦ ἀνθρώπου παραδίδοται.

Cf. Isa. 53. 6, 12: וַיהוָה הִפְגִּיעַ בּוֹ ··· תַּחַת אֲשֶׁר הֶעֱרָה; LXX: καὶ Κύριος παρέδωκεν αὐτόν...ἀνθ' ὧν παρεδόθη εἰς θάνατον ἡ ψυχὴ αὐτοῦ...καὶ διὰ τὰς ἀνομίας αὐτῶν παρεδόθη.

This passage is cited by Jackson and Lake as being one where a connection with Isa. 53 has been found in the use of the word παραδίδωμι.[1] They do not, however, state who has upheld this view, and certainly this exegesis is not common. Even A. E. Abbott,[2] who maintained that in predicting his Passion Jesus always used this word in the sense of 'deliver up'—that is by God—and not of 'betray', and that in using it he had in mind the words of Isa. 53. 12, agreed that the word in Mark 14. 18 'refers to the treachery of Judas and to nothing else'. In v. 21, however, Abbott believed that the words do refer primarily to 'a divine act, though wrought through human agency'.[3]

Although the verb is used three times in the LXX version of Isa. 53, however, it seems reasonable to agree with Jackson and Lake that 'it is hard to see what other word the writers could naturally have used. It seems far more likely that παραδίδωμι was used as the most natural word, though probably it afterwards did much to strengthen the Christian interpretation of Isaiah when the coincidence in language was noted.'[4] Abbott adds to the difficulties of his exposition by maintaining that while παραδίδωμι is linked with the LXX version of Isaiah, Jesus himself was thinking in terms of the original meaning in the Hebrew, which is not 'he was delivered up for the transgressors', but 'he shall make intercession for the transgressors'.[5]

(xi) Mark 14. 24 (Matt. 26. 28; Luke 22. 20).

Τοῦτό ἐστι τὸ αἷμά μου τῆς (καινῆς) διαθήκης τὸ ὑπὲρ πολλῶν ἐκχυνόμενον.

The parallel accounts in Matthew and Luke are as follows:

Matthew: Τοῦτο γάρ ἐστι τὸ αἷμά μου, τὸ τῆς (καινῆς) διαθήκης, τὸ περὶ πολλῶν ἐκχυνόμενον εἰς ἄφεσιν ἁμαρτιῶν.

Luke: Τοῦτο τὸ ποτήριον ἡ καινὴ διαθήκη ἐν τῷ αἵματί μου, τὸ ὑπὲρ ὑμῶν ἐκχυνόμενον.

The verse is missing from Luke in some Western texts, and it is possible that the words are an insertion from the Pauline version in 1 Cor. 11. 23–5, where the equivalent passage reads

Τοῦτο τὸ ποτήριον ἡ καινὴ διαθήκη ἐστὶν ἐν τῷ ἐμῷ αἵματι.

Cf. Isa. 42. 6 and 49. 8: וְאֶתֶּנְךָ לִבְרִית עָם; LXX, 42. 6 and 49. 6, 8: ἔδωκά σε εἰς διαθήκην γένους/ἐθνῶν.

Isa. 53. 12: תַּחַת אֲשֶׁר הֶעֱרָה לַמָּוֶת נַפְשׁוֹ; LXX: ἀνθ' ὧν παρεδόθη εἰς θάνατον ἡ ψυχὴ αὐτοῦ.

Isa. 53. 11f.: רַבִּים...בָּרַבִּים...לָרַבִּים; LXX: δουλεύοντα πολλοῖς... διὰ τοῦτο αὐτὸς κληρονομήσει πολλούς...καὶ αὐτὸς ἁμαρτίας πολλῶν ἀνήνεγκεν.

Influence by the Servant concept has been traced in the Marcan account in the words διαθήκης, ἐκχυνόμενον and πολλῶν.[1]

Διαθήκη. In the LXX διαθήκη translates a word which expresses what is perhaps the most important concept in Hebrew religion—בְּרִית, 'covenant'. In the great majority of places where this word occurs in the Old Testament, it is used of the covenant between Yahweh and his people—the covenant upon which the whole relationship between God and Israel was based: this might be the old covenant, made at Sinai with Moses, or it might refer to the new covenant which was promised by the prophets. The word was used in the phrase 'ark of the covenant' —the visible representation of the agreement into which God and people had entered. Mention is also made of a covenant between God and some part of the nation, or between God and a representative of the nation, for example, God's covenant with the Remnant, the priests, Abraham, Noah, or David and his kingdom; there is also the threefold agreement between God, king and people, and the covenants made between king and people in the sight of Yahweh.[2]

The word is also found in a 'secular' usage, although even here the idea that the agreement is one which is entered into in the presence of Yahweh is probably involved; in these cases the covenant may be one made between Israel and other nations, or it may be between individuals.[3]

'Covenant', however, must be considered in the context of the phrase of which, in this passage, it is an integral part; and not simply in isolation. The phrase 'blood of the covenant' would appear to have been taken directly from the old ritual of Mount Sinai,[4] although its new significance has been made clear by the addition of the pronoun μου, and possibly also of καινή. J. Jeremias[5] has pointed out the impossibility of the construction Τοῦτό ἐστι τὸ αἷμά μου τῆς διαθήκης in Aramaic, since it would involve the use of a pronominal suffix with a noun in the construct case. He accordingly omits the words τῆς διαθήκης as being a later gloss. An alternative solution to this linguistic problem, however, would be to retain these two words and to omit the word μου: it is highly probable that the original phrase was τὸ αἷμά τῆς διαθήκης, and that the possessive was added at the Greek stage of the tradition, as a parallel to the words τοῦτό ἐστι τὸ σῶμά μου in *v*. 22. Alternatively, it is possible that the original phrase was 'the blood of my covenant', in exact parallel to the words 'the blood of thy covenant' in Zech. 9. 11, and that the possessive has become misplaced in translation.[1]

If we may take this phrase as representing the genuine words of Jesus, it seems probable that he was deliberately contrasting the new covenant, which he himself was sealing, with the covenant of Sinai. Whether it is original, however, or whether his words were simply τοῦτό ἐστι τὸ αἷμά μου, it is improbable that the phrase owes anything to Deutero-Isaiah. The greatest similarity between the verse in Mark and the thought of the prophet is the use of the word διαθήκη, which is used by the LXX to translate בְּרִית in Isa. 42. 6 and 49. 8. In those two passages, however, the word is used of the promised leader; if Jesus did see himself as the leader who was to be a covenant to his people, that concept is clearly only a secondary one in this passage. Finally, the complete absence of the idea of blood-shedding from both Isa. 42. 6 and 49. 8, as well as from the Servant Songs themselves, makes any connection between these passages and the words of Jesus, in whichever form we regard as being the original, extremely unlikely.

Ἐκχύνω (more correctly ἐκ-χέω) is used in the LXX to translate שָׁפַךְ —to pour out.[2] In the New Testament the phrase αἷμα ἐκχεῖν is used frequently of bloodshed, and is the equivalent of the Hebrew שָׁפַךְ דָּם.[3] This phrase appears to have no connection with the concept of Isa. 53. 12, where it is said that the Servant is laid bare to death.

Πολύς. This word has already been examined in connection with Mark 10. 45. Here again there is no justification for associating it with Isa. 53 unless it can be shown that other words or concepts in the verse are derived from the same source. The only echo from that chapter is found in Matthew, who has added the words εἰς ἄφεσιν ἁμαρτιῶν. The absence of this phrase from all the other accounts shows plainly that this is a gloss expressing the meaning which the early community had found in the death of Christ.[4] It is possible that this interpretation was made only after Jesus had been identified by his followers as the Suffering Servant. In any case, Matthew's addition detracts from the main point of the original *logion*, as given by Mark, which is that Jesus, by his death, is establishing a new covenant between God and the 'many'. Any exegesis which sees a fundamental connection with Isa. 53

can only arise from reading Mark 14. 24 in the light of an already accepted doctrine of Atonement.

(xii) Matt. 8. 16–17.

That evening they brought to him many who were possessed with demons; and he cast out the spirits with a word, and healed all who were sick. This was to fulfil what was spoken by the prophet Isaiah, 'He took our infirmities and bore our diseases'.

In this passage we find a direct quotation from the fourth Servant Song, from Isa. 53. 4: the translation is not that of the LXX. The words are not attributed to Jesus, and are clearly a reflection of the author, so that they cannot be accepted as evidence for Jesus' own self-consciousness. They are important, however, in considering whether the Church has distorted the facts for apologetic reasons.

The author applies the words to the healing of the sick by Jesus: they are understood, not in any figurative way of mental grief, but of the actual physical ailments of those he cured. This passage is of the greatest significance: far from proving that Jesus was thought of as One who suffered because of the sins of others, directly bearing their guilt, it will, unless other passages are found to be used with this meaning, point to exactly the opposite conclusion. For if the very quotations which would, used in certain contexts, make abundantly evident the identification of Jesus with the Servant who by his suffering expiates the sins of others are instead used only of his work in other spheres, then this is strong evidence that such an identification was never made, either by Jesus or by his earliest followers. There is no thought in this verse of any expiation of sin; the meaning is certainly not that the guilt which caused the suffering was transferred in some way to Jesus. It is important, too, to notice that the words are applied only in a very loose sense to Jesus: for while he cured those who suffered, he did not transfer their ailments to himself. If the early Christians were able to use Old Testament texts in this way we must be very wary of assuming that vague references imply that all the details of a prophecy are taken over and applied literally to Jesus: Matthew's purpose here is to show that Jesus' work was foreordained by God, and foreshadowed in the Old Testament, not to derive evidence from the Old Testament for any doctrine concerning the meaning of that work.

(xiii) Matt. 12. 18–21, quotation from Isa. 42. 1–4.

The quotation here has little in common with the LXX, and appears to be an independent translation from the Hebrew, either made by the evangelist or known to him. The words are again a comment by the evangelist on his narrative.

The context of this passage is the healing on the Sabbath of a man with a withered hand, and the consequent dispute with the Pharisees, who then plot to kill Jesus. He withdraws from them, and although he continues to cure all who come to him, he enjoins those he heals 'not to make him known'; this would appear to be the Matthaean version of the account in Mark 3. 7–12, where it is the demons who are charged with secrecy, since they know him to be the Son of God. These actions are seen by Matthew as a direct fulfilment of the Old Testament prophecy: in refusing to quarrel with the Pharisees or to allow the open acknowledgement of his Messiahship he is the one who 'will neither wrangle nor cry aloud'. Whether, in quoting these verses, Matthew was consciously identifying Jesus with the Servant, or whether he was merely concerned with showing that these few phrases were fulfilled in him, is a problem in which our judgement will depend largely upon our understanding of the methods of scriptural exegesis of the period. In either case, there is no link with the Songs of the *Suffering* Servant, or any indication that Matthew had the idea of suffering in mind when he quoted these words.

(xiv) Luke 2. 32.

φῶς εἰς ἀποκάλυψιν ἐθνῶν.

Cf. Isa. 42. 6; 49. 6: לְאוֹר גּוֹיִם; LXX (some MSS. only in 42. 6): εἰς φῶς ἐθνῶν.

The words 'a light for revelation to the Gentiles' seem to echo the 'light for the Gentiles' in Isa. 42. 6 and 49. 6. They prove, however, nothing more than that whoever is responsible for this verse in Luke was familiar with the Jewish hopes and ideas of the day: the metaphor of light and the attitude of universalism are by no means confined to Deutero-Isaiah in the Old Testament.[1] There is nothing here which is unique to the Servant, and certainly nothing which is connected with the Suffering Servant.

(xv) Luke 4. 16–21.

Jesus reads Isa. 61. 1–2 in the synagogue at Nazareth, and declares 'Today this scripture has been fulfilled in your hearing'. The translation is once again not that of the LXX.

This passage is frequently appealed to by those who hold that Jesus believed himself to be the Servant of Deutero-Isaiah.[1] Although Isa. 61. 1f. is not one of the Servant Songs, it is very similar in both theme and style, and was probably interpreted in connection with them. If the Lucan passage is a genuine report of the words of Jesus, then he is here associating himself with the mission which was no doubt understood as that of the Servant.

The context of the incident makes it clear that Jesus is referring the words to his own mission and work; furthermore, this work is something already present and in progress—it has been fulfilled 'σήμερον', and in the hearing of those in the synagogue: Jesus has proclaimed the good news to the poor, the message of release from captivity and recovery of sight. The conclusion seems to be inevitable that Jesus is again interpreting his mission in connection with the news of redemption originally proclaimed by Deutero-Isaiah; he himself is in some way associated with God's act of deliverance. But there is no suggestion that because he connected himself with this redemptive activity of God, he also applied to himself the prophecy of Isa. 52–3: Jesus' words apply here only to his preaching and healing; there is no mention of his death.[2]

(xvi) Luke 7. 22.

Τυφλοὶ ἀναβλέπουσι, χωλοὶ περιπατοῦσι, λεπροὶ καθαρίζονται, καὶ κωφοὶ ἀκούουσι, νεκροὶ ἐγείρονται, πτωχοὶ εὐαγγελίζονται.
Cf. Isa. 61. 1 f.; LXX: εὐαγγελίσασθαι πτωχοῖς ἀπέσταλκέν με....κηρῦξαι αἰχμαλώτοις ἄφεσιν καὶ τυφλοῖς ἀνάβλεψιν.
Isa. 35. 5 f.: אָז תִּפָּקַחְנָה עֵינֵי עִוְרִים וְאָזְנֵי חֵרְשִׁים תִּפָּתַחְנָה: אָז יְדַלֵּג כָּאַיָּל פִּסֵּחַ וְתָרֹן לְשׁוֹן אִלֵּם; LXX: τότε ἀνοιχθήσονται ὀφθαλμοὶ τυφλῶν, καὶ ὦτα κωφῶν ἀκούσονται. τότε ἁλεῖται ὡς ἔλαφος χωλός, τρανὴ δὲ ἔσται γλῶσσα μογιλάλων.

In this verse we find the practical application of the quotation in Luke 4. 18f. Jesus' answer to John the Baptist's question 'Are you the Coming One?' is to appeal to the things which he is doing. Here is clear evidence of the close relationship which Jesus understood to exist between his person and his work of preaching and healing. It is reasonable to suppose that he has Isa. 61 in mind at this point, still more so that he is thinking of Isa. 35; this verse confirms his use, noted in our examination of the last passage, of concepts from Deutero-Isaiah and the allied chapters.[1]

(xvii) Luke 22. 37.
For I tell you that this scripture must be fulfilled in me, 'And he was reckoned with transgressors'.
Luke: καὶ μετὰ ἀνόμων ἐλογίσθη. LXX: καὶ ἐν τοῖς ἀνόμοις ἐλογίσθη.

Here, for the first and only time in the Synoptic gospels, we have a clear quotation of Isa. 53 in the words of Jesus. Unfortunately it occurs in a very obscure passage, of which both the meaning and genuineness are extremely doubtful. The intention of the passage appears to be to show that Jesus' rejection fulfils the purpose of God: possibly it implies also that his disciples must expect to share a similar fate.[2] Jackson and Lake claim this verse as support for their[3] view that the identification of Jesus with the Suffering Servant appears first in the Lucan writings. On the other hand, as Cadbury[4] points out, there is no reference here to the essential function of the Suffering Servant, the vicarious bearing of sin, or even directly to the concept of suffering and death. Whether these ideas are in fact implied by the words which are quoted here depends once again on the method of using scripture which was adopted by the author. In view of the context, however, it seems extremely unlikely that the thought of vicarious atonement was in mind. If this is true, then the use of Isa. 53 here does not, as so many maintain,[5] support the traditional view. On the contrary, its use in this context throws into sharper relief the absence of any reference to the chapter in the words of Jesus about the meaning of his death.

4. GROUP I(b): DETAILS IN THE PASSION NARRATIVE

It has been maintained by various scholars that many of the details given in the Passion narrative are influenced by, and may even have been derived from, passages in the Old Testament, including the Servant Songs.[6] Obviously any such influence can tell us nothing, directly, about the light in which Jesus himself viewed his death.

Nevertheless, these passages are of importance for our study, since if it is found that details from Deutero-Isaiah have seriously affected the Passion narrative, this will throw grave doubt upon the historical reliability of any references to the Servant Songs elsewhere in the gospels. For if the evangelists have fashioned the Passion narrative to conform with the details of the Servant's sufferings, then they have allowed a certain interpretation of the events which they describe not only to colour their account of those events, but to interfere with its accuracy. If, then, they have been influenced to this extent by their desire to make clear the fulfilment of the Servant Songs in the person of Jesus, we may expect to find the same process at work in other passages, and we may suspect that all their references to the Songs are due to the same motive: if details were added to the historical narrative in order to make the identification of Jesus with the Servant clear, then we may believe that the words of Jesus would have been expanded with a similar intention.

(i) Mark 14. 61 (Matt. 26. 63).

ὁ δὲ ἐσιώπα, καὶ οὐκ ἀπεκρίνατο οὐδέν.

With this verse may be considered also (ii) and (iii):

(ii) Mark 15. 5 (Matt. 27. 12, 14; cf. John 19. 9).

ὁ δὲ Ἰησοῦς οὐκέτι οὐδὲν ἀπεκρίθη.

(iii) Luke 23. 9.

αὐτὸς δὲ οὐδὲν ἀπεκρίνατο αὐτῷ.

There are three possible explanations of these sayings about the silence of Jesus before his judges. It may be decided that they are quite unconnected with Isa. 53: if, on the other hand, they are found to be influenced by this chapter, then this may be due either to the conscious imitation of the Servant's attitude by Jesus himself, or to the desire of the evangelists to show that he was the Servant.

The fact that Jesus did refuse to answer certain accusations is firmly established in all the accounts: Mark and Matthew record two such incidents, Luke and John one each. An examination of the various accounts reveals an interesting pattern which can best be set out in tabular form on the following page.

JESUS AND THE SERVANT

Mark	Matthew	Luke	John
	I. *Trial before Sanhedrin*		
14. 61. To false witnesses. No reply	26. 63. To false witnesses. No reply		
14. 62. To Caiaphas. 'Are you the Messiah, the Son of the Blessed?' Reply	26. 64. To Caiaphas. 'Tell us if you are the Messiah the Son of God.' Reply	22. 70. To priests. 'Are you the Son of God?' Reply	
	II. *Trial before Pilate*		
15. 2. To Pilate 'Are you the King of the Jews?' Reply	27. 11. To Pilate. 'Are you the King of the Jews?' Reply	23. 3. To Pilate. 'Are you the King of the Jews?' Reply	18. 33–8. To Pilate. 'Are you the King of the Jews?' Reply
15. 5. To accusations by the Jews. No reply	27. 12. To accusations by the Jews. No reply		19. 9. To accusations by the Jews. No reply
	III. *Trial before Herod*		
		23. 9. To Herod. No reply	

This examination reveals clearly the following points:

(1) The Synoptists are all agreed that when Jesus was directly asked by the High Priest whether he was the Messiah, and by Pilate whether he was the King of the Jews, in each case he replied; furthermore, the replies were, to some extent at least, affirmative.

(2) Mark and Matthew are agreed that Jesus refused to answer the false accusations which were made by the Jews, both before his reply to Caiaphas, and after his reply to Pilate. The contrast between this refusal to speak and his previous reply to Pilate is drawn out by Mark's use of the word οὐκέτι in 15. 5.

(3) Luke has replaced the accusations at the first trial by an indirect question about Jesus' Messiahship, to which he makes an indirect reply (22. 66–9); the accusations at the trial before Pilate are replaced by questions from Herod, who receives no answer.

(4) John has no account of questions before the Sanhedrin, except that Jesus was asked concerning his teaching, and made an indirect reply. Before Pilate, Jesus is twice asked whether he is a king; on the

first occasion, when he suspects that this is a question suggested by the Jews' accusations, his reply is indirect; when Pilate repeats the question, however, Jesus' answer is the same as in the other gospels: Σὺ λέγεις. Later, when Pilate has learnt from the Jews that Jesus has claimed to be the Son of God, Jesus refuses to answer him.

The Synoptic evangelists are agreed, then, that Jesus' refusal to answer was confined to the false accusations of the Jews: he did not refuse to reply to the direct questions of the High Priest or of Pilate concerning his person. Memory of this fact seems to lie behind even the developed account of the fourth gospel. This being so, it seems certain that behind the accounts of Jesus' silence there lies a genuine recollection of the original events. There is no indication that the evangelists were in any way influenced by the picture in Isa. 53. 7 of the 'lamb led to the slaughter'; in fact the language is totally different. If they had in any way introduced the silence of Jesus solely in order to agree with Isa. 53, it is incredible that they would have failed to make the reference clearer, or even that they would have recorded any replies at all.

There remains the question whether Jesus himself had the words of Deutero-Isaiah in mind. There is, of course, no way of reaching a certain conclusion to this problem. While, however, it is quite possible that the sufferings of the Servant may have been present in his thoughts, there is no indication that Jesus was consciously acting in accordance with that picture, or that he understood his sufferings to be fulfilling the same purpose as those of the Servant.[1] His silence regarding the false and conflicting accusations made against him is consistent with his attitude to the authorities at all times: he is prepared to answer an honest question but ignores partisan assertions. It is inconceivable that the one who withdrew himself rather than quarrel with the Pharisees, and who refused to perform signs to prove his Messiahship, should now wrangle with his accusers, who had already determined to condemn him.[2]

(iv) Mark 14. 65 (Matt. 26. 67f.; Luke 22. 63f.; cf. John 18. 22).

Mark: And some began to spit on him, and to cover his face, and to strike him, saying to him, 'Prophesy!' And the guards received him with blows.

Matt.: Then they spat in his face, and struck him; and some slapped him, saying, 'Prophesy to us, you Christ! Who is it that struck you?'

Luke: Now the men who were holding Jesus mocked him and beat him; they also blindfolded him and asked him 'Prophesy! Who is it that struck you?' And they spoke many other words against him, reviling him.

With these passages we may compare (v) and (vi).

(v) Mark 15. 15–20 (Matt. 27. 26–31; cf. John 19. 1–3).

Mark: Pilate...having scourged Jesus...the soldiers... clothed him in a purple cloak, and plaiting a crown of thorns they put it on him. And they began to salute him, 'Hail, King of the Jews!' And they struck his head with a reed, and spat upon him, and they knelt down in homage to him. And when they had mocked him....

Matt.: ...having scourged Jesus...the soldiers...stripped him and put a scarlet robe upon him, and plaiting a crown of thorns they put it on his head, and put a reed in his right hand. And kneeling before him they mocked him, saying, 'Hail, King of the Jews!' And they spat upon him, and took the reed and struck him on the head. And when they had mocked him....

(vi) Luke 23. 11.

And Herod with his soldiers treated him with contempt and mocked him then, arraying him in gorgeous apparel, he sent him back to Pilate.

Several words in these passages quite evidently echo words in the LXX version of Isa. 50. 6, which reads as follows:

τὸν νῶτόν μου ἔδωκα εἰς μάστιγας, τὰς δὲ σιαγόνας μου εἰς ῥαπίσματα, τὸ δὲ πρόσωπόν μου οὐκ ἀπέστρεψα ἀπὸ αἰσχύνης ἐμπτυσμάτων.[1]

Are these echoes intentional? The significant words are found as follows:

Mark 14. 65. ἐμπτύειν, πρόσωπον, ῥαπίσμασιν.
Matt. 26. 67. ἐνέπτυσαν εἰς τὸ πρόσωπον, ἐρράπισαν.
John 18. 22. ῥάπισμα.
Mark 15. 15–20. ἐνέπτυον.
Matt. 27. 26–31. ἐμπτύσαντες.
John 19. 1–3. ἐμαστίγωσε, ῥαπίσματα.

The general agreement of the gospels that Jesus was subjected to the kind of treatment described in these passages confirms their historicity: the only question is whether in their descriptions the evangelists have deliberately used words or introduced details from Isa. 50. 6. If so, it will be noted that the tradition goes right back to Mark, and, far from being introduced by Luke, all the words reminiscent of the Servant have been dropped by him.[1] Apart from the use of individual words, there is only one phrase in the gospels which is reminiscent of Isa. 50. 6: this occurs in Matt. 26. 67—τότε ἐνέπτυσαν εἰς τὸ πρόσωπον αὐτοῦ. The construction, however, is totally different from the LXX. We may note also that the four words which echo Deutero-Isaiah, ἐμπτύω, πρόσωπον, ῥάπισμα and μαστιγόω, are all the most obvious in the context.

It is, of course, impossible to prove whether or not the writers were thinking of Isa. 50, but it should be noted that they have by no means made their accounts conform exactly to the picture given there: if their aim had been to show clearly that Jesus was the Servant they would surely have kept more closely to the original. In fact, if they were influenced by Deutero-Isaiah, it seems to be only in order to explain the scandal of the Cross, to represent the events which they knew to have happened as being foretold in the Old Testament: they have not invented further details in order to prove that Jesus is the Servant. This conclusion is further borne out by the complete absence of any theological interpretation in the account; if the evangelists have been influenced by Isa. 50 they have used it, as they have used other Old Testament passages, to justify the extraordinary events of Jesus' life. There is no evidence whatever for assuming that if they saw in Jesus the fulfilment of Isa. 50—the sufferer who trusted in his vindication by God—they therefore identified him further with the Servant of Isa. 53 who made expiation for the sins of others.

(vii) Mark 15. 27 (Matt. 27. 38; Luke 23. 33; cf. John 19. 18).

Mark: And with him they crucified two robbers, one on his right hand and one on his left. (And the scripture was fulfilled which says, 'He was reckoned with the transgressors'.)
Matt.: Then two robbers were crucified with him, one on the right and one on the left.
Luke: They crucified him, and the criminals, one on the right and one on the left.

The gloss (given in brackets in the citation above) which is found in some manuscripts of Mark shows that at an early time the fact that Jesus was crucified between two evil-doers was regarded as a fulfilment of the words of Isa. 53. 12. Both Bousset and Bultmann[1] have suggested that the detail is derived from that passage, but they are not dogmatic on the subject. There is no reason to suppose that it is anything but a genuine recollection of an actual event, since it is found in all four gospels. The fact that the reference to Isaiah in Mark is missing in all the best texts indicates that the event suggested the prophecy, and not *vice versa*.[2]

5. GROUP 2: REFERENCES BY JESUS TO HIS SUFFERING

(i) Mark 2. 19f. (Matt. 9. 15; Luke 5. 34f.).

Can the wedding guests fast, while the bridegroom is with them? As long as they have the bridegroom with them, they cannot fast. The days will come, when the bridegroom is taken away from them, and then they will fast in that day.

The authenticity of this passage is, of course, hotly contested by many scholars who dismiss all Jesus' predictions of his death as *vaticinia ex eventu*;[3] even some who believe it to be genuine hold that Mark has misplaced it in placing it so early in his narrative, since all the other sayings of this nature occur after Peter's Confession at Caesarea Philippi.[4] Its relevance to our problem lies only in its witness to the belief of the Church that Jesus did foretell his death, since there is no connection with the Servant passages.

(ii) Mark 8. 31 (Matt. 16. 21; Luke 9. 22).

And he began to teach them that the Son of man must suffer many things, and be rejected by the elders and the chief priests and the scribes, and be killed, and after three days rise again.

With this we shall consider also passages (iii), (iv) and (v):

(iii) Mark 9. 31 (Matt. 17. 22f.; Luke 9. 44).

The Son of man will be delivered into the hands of men, and they will kill him; and when he is killed, after three days he will rise.

(iv) Mark 10. 33f. (Matt. 20. 18f.; Luke 18. 31–3).

Behold we are going up to Jerusalem; and the Son of man will be delivered to the chief priests and the scribes, and they will condemn him to death, and deliver him to the Gentiles; and they will mock him, and spit upon him, and scourge him, and kill him; and after three days he will rise.

(v) Mark 9. 12b (Matt. 17. 12).
And how is it written of the Son of man, that he should suffer many things and be treated with contempt?

These four passages are again and again referred to by those who maintain the traditional view. The problem is here made extremely complex by the great divergence in views as to the authenticity of the sayings; while some accept the passages as they stand as genuine words of Jesus, and others reject them *in toto* as the later interpretation of the Church, the majority of scholars regard the substance of the sayings as genuine, rejecting various details as later additions.[1] If we accept the view of the radical scholars, then we reject at the same time the idea that Jesus spoke about the meaning of his death at all. If, on the other hand, we accept the tradition that he did speak about it—and this, as we have seen,[2] seems the more reasonable assumption—then we have to consider the problem whether the sayings show the influence of the Servant concept. If the more doubtful parts of these predictions are not genuine, then they are clearly influenced by the events of the Passion itself, rather than by Deutero-Isaiah, for there is no verbal similarity with the Servant Songs in these details. The problem, therefore, assuming as we may that the tradition goes back to Jesus, is in what way he interpreted the meaning of his sufferings, and whether he had the Servant in mind.

Many argue that Jesus could not have come to this belief in the necessity for his sufferings except through studying Deutero-Isaiah: they hold that the word 'must', which is used so emphatically in all three gospels on the first occasion,[3] and the sense of which is echoed in the later passages, shows a conviction in the mind of Jesus of the necessity for his death which could have been derived only from scripture; further, in the Old Testament the only passage which could give rise to such a conviction is Isa. 53.[4]

This position is set out most clearly by R. H. Fuller, who, as we have seen,[5] maintains that the basis of these four sayings, together with Mark 10. 45, forms, when the details which could be due to later knowledge have been removed, 'a clear description of the Suffering Servant of Isa. 53'.[6] This description Fuller interprets as follows: '[The Son of Man] must suffer many things, and be rejected and set at nought, and delivered up into the hands of men and they shall kill him. [For he came] not to be ministered unto, but to minister (= be the Servant of Yahweh), and to give his life a ransom for many.' Now we have already found reason to reject the second sentence in this summary —a paraphrase of Mark 10. 45—as pointing to the Servant.[1] Furthermore, it is questionable whether it is permissible to combine the various sayings in this way. For while it can be seen that the main purpose of the first four passages is the same in each case—i.e. to proclaim that Jesus must suffer and be killed—the last saying introduces an entirely new element: in none of the other passages does Jesus say anything about the *purpose* of his Passion; he merely stresses its necessity.[2]

We are left, then, with the record of four separate occasions on which Jesus is reputed to have instructed his disciples that he is about to suffer. Do these statements echo the fourth Servant Song? Linguistically there is little evidence that they do. Fuller finds a connection between the Hebrew text of Isa. 53. 3 and the use of ἀποδοκιμασθῆναι in 8. 31 and ἐξουδενωθῇ in 9. 12. While neither of these words occurs in the LXX version of this verse, it is true that ἐξουδενόω is the usual rendering of בָּזָה, as can be seen in Ps. 22. 6.[3] The connection is doubtful, however, and certainly not conclusive: Ps. 22. 6 itself has as good a claim to be the original for ἐξουδενόω, especially in view of the use made of this psalm elsewhere in the Passion story, and a likely source for ἀποδοκιμάζω, if one is needed, is found in Ps. 118. 22, a verse which the early Church, or possibly Jesus himself, understood of his rejection.[4] L. S. Thornton claims that the verb παραδίδωμι, which is used both in Mark 9. 31 and parallels, and in Mark 10. 33 and parallels, has been taken from Isa. 53. 12.[5] There is, however, no connection in meaning with the double use of παραδίδωμι in that verse: as in Mark 14. 21, it seems to be the natural word to use in the context. In the LXX, παραδίδωμι is used well over 250 times, and in the overwhelming majority of cases where it is a translation from the Hebrew the one who performs the 'handing over' is Yahweh: when a nation defeats, or is defeated by Israel, the event is attributed to the activity of God, who has 'handed over' the one nation into the power of the other. It is only on about twenty occasions that the word is used of human agency. In the apocryphal books, while the verb is still sometimes used with the idea of God's activity, the more general use is found much oftener than in the Old Testament. It seems probable that the biblical usage of παραδίδωμι lies behind its use in the Synoptic passages: the word would thus imply that the Passion is part of the predetermined will of God, and that he is still master of the situation.

As a general summary, however, the predictions do correspond broadly with the picture of Isa. 53. The problem, therefore, really turns on the question whether Jesus' conviction could indeed have come only from studying that passage, or whether he could have derived it elsewhere. If he did have Deutero-Isaiah in mind, then it is significant that he refers only to the *fact* of the Servant's sufferings, and not to their result, which is the significant feature of the fourth Song.

In the consideration of this problem is it very important to note that on each of these four occasions Jesus speaks, not directly of his own sufferings, but of those of the Son of Man. This tradition is followed in ten out of the eleven accounts in the Synoptic gospels, the exception being Matt. 16. 21. We have, therefore, a firmly established tradition that Jesus spoke of suffering with reference to the Son of Man: accordingly, the whole problem of the meaning of this title is raised.

Now the outstanding characteristics of all these sayings are as follows: (1) They all (with the exception noted above) speak of the Son of Man. (2) They all speak of future suffering and rejection; on three occasions out of four Jesus speaks of death. (3) There is a note of necessity, not merely of certainty, about the sayings. This last point is seen in the use of certain words and tenses in the various accounts. We have already noted the significance of the word παραδίδωμι. To this we may add:

	Mark	Matthew	Luke
(ii)	δεῖ	δεῖ	δεῖ
(iii)	Pres.	μέλλει	μέλλει
(iv)	Fut.	Fut.	Fut.
(v)	γέγραπται	μέλλει	

The note of necessity in the Marcan version of (ii) is followed exactly by the other two evangelists in the use of the same word, δεῖ; in (iii) they prefer μέλλει to his 'prophetic' present, but the sense is the same;[1] particularly important is the use of γέγραπται in Mark's version of (v), which is echoed in Matthew's use of μέλλει, and by Luke's πάντα τὰ γεγραμμένα διὰ τῶν προφητῶν in (iv). It is only in (iv) that the sufferings are spoken of in the simple future; but here the events are already so imminent that their inevitability is implied in the circumstances, rather than the language, of the sayings: Jesus is already 'in the way, going up to Jerusalem': he has taken the irrevocable step leading to suffering and death.[1]

In examining any explanation of this conviction of Jesus we may ask whether these three strands—Son of Man, suffering and divine necessity —are all represented. Those who support the view that its source was Isa. 52–3 emphasize that here is the supreme picture of suffering, and that its Old Testament authority is the most likely explanation of Jesus' conviction that he was ordained to suffer. To explain its relevance to the first point, however, they are forced to argue that Jesus had so fused the two concepts of Son of Man and Servant in his own mind that he could select the title of an apocalyptic figure and join to it the sufferings of a prophetic one. There is no justification for this elaborate theory if a more simple and natural explanation of the facts can be found. There is, in fact, little evidence for this 'fusion' apart from the sayings which are at present under consideration. Do these point to the Servant Songs? All that the fourth Song has in common with these sayings of Jesus is the actual suffering and rejection. For while the Song speaks of the suffering of the *Servant*, and the things which he accomplishes through his sufferings, the Synoptic passages speak of the suffering of the *Son of Man*, and are silent as to the result of his rejection. Even if we admit a fusion of these two concepts in the mind of Jesus, it seems unlikely that he would have spoken of one figure in terms of another without some word of explanation; for while the sayings are admittedly enigmatic, he would hardly have appealed to his hearers concerning the things which are written of the Son of Man if he were referring primarily to passages which they connected with a totally different concept.

Further discussion of this problem must be deferred until we come to examine in more detail the most probable significance of the term 'Son of Man' in the gospel sayings. In the meantime, however, it is clear that there is insufficient evidence to claim with any certainty that Jesus had the Servant concept in mind when he spoke on these four occasions of the rejection and sufferings of the Son of Man. All that has been shown so far is that he did find his destiny set forth in the Old Testament scriptures: his major predictions of his suffering and death, as recorded in the Synoptics, make no reference to the Servant passages in particular. These predictions, therefore, could only be taken as evidence of the influence of the Servant concept upon the mind of Jesus, if the Servant Songs were the only passages in the Old Testament which could be applied to his Passion: as we shall see, however, there are other passages in the Jewish scriptures which speak of suffering and some of these were, in fact, referred to Jesus' sufferings by the early Church.[1]

Finally, we may note that even if further examination should lead us to the conclusion that Isa. 53 has been influential in the formulation of Jesus' statements about himself, this will not necessarily lead us to think of a fusion of the Servant concept with the figure of the Son of Man, or to a belief that Jesus interpreted the *meaning* of his death in the light of Isa. 53 or thought of himself as primarily 'Servant': his conception of the Son of Man may prove to be inclusive of many truths, one of which may be the necessity for suffering, which, although reflected in Isa. 53, is also to be found elsewhere.

(vi) Mark 10. 38 (Matt. 20. 22; cf. Luke 12. 50).

Are you able to drink the cup that I drink, or to be baptized with the baptism with which I am baptized?

This passage is further evidence for the belief that Jesus spoke about his suffering and death. Here again it has been argued that his words about the nature of his destiny show a conviction which must be derived from the Old Testament.[2] There is no evidence, however, for associating this passage with Isa. 53 in particular. The 'cup' is a common Old Testament metaphor, used always of a fate sent by God, whether evil or good.[3] It is certainly found in Deutero-Isaiah (Isa. 51. 17ff.), where it is used of 'the cup of Yahweh's wrath', but this fact is not enough to make probable any connection between the Marcan passage and Isa. 53.

(vii) Mark 12. 10f. (Matt. 21. 42; Luke 20. 17).

Have you not read this scripture: 'The very stone which the builders rejected has become the head of the corner; this was the Lord's doing, and it is marvellous in our eyes'?

It is probable that this verse, which quotes Ps. 118. 22f., has been added to the Parable of the Wicked Husbandmen by the early Church, who interpreted the story allegorically of Christ,[1] although it is possible that the words were applied to himself by Jesus on some occasion. Whether they are genuine, however, or were added during the very earliest stage of the tradition,[2] it is significant that it is this passage, rather than Isa. 53, which was chosen: the direct citation here is also in notable contrast to the possible allusions to that chapter which, it is claimed, exist elsewhere.

(viii) Mark 14. 8 (Matt. 26. 12; cf. John 12. 7).
She has anointed my body beforehand for burying.

If these words are genuine, they are further evidence for Jesus' prophecy of his death. There is no direct connection, however, with the Servant-concept.

(ix) Mark 14. 21 (Matt. 26. 24; Luke 22. 22).
For the Son of man goes as it is written of him.

This saying is linked by its position to the words about the Betrayal in *vv.* 18 and 21, which have already been examined under Group 1 (*a*) (x); by the title 'Son of Man' to the prophecies of the Passion; and by its reference to scripture to the saying in Mark 9. 12.

The phrase 'as it is written of him' is still further evidence for the belief that Jesus was in some way fulfilling the Old Testament prophecies: there is again no reference to any particular passage. While V. Taylor admits that 'no citation is made, or indeed is possible', he yet claims:

> Behind this utterance lies His identification of the Son of Man with the Suffering Servant; it is so firmly established in His thought that He can say of the Son of Man what, so far as the text of Scripture is concerned, is true only of the Servant. Each successive example of this identification reveals how deep-rooted it is in the Markan tradition.[3]

For such a judgement there is no evidence whatever. The fact that is 'deep-rooted in the Markan tradition' is that Jesus understood the destiny of the Son of Man to be one of suffering, and that he understood the Old Testament scriptures as pointing to this destiny. To claim that such a destiny is described only in the Servant Songs of Deutero-Isaiah is to ignore, not only the other Old Testament passages which speak of suffering, but also the deeper understanding of the history of Israel:

the fate of the Son of Man is to be found, not simply in one passage of scripture, but in the whole course of the Hebrew people.[1]

(x) Mark 14. 27 (Matt. 26. 31).

You will all fall away; for it is written, 'I will strike the shepherd, and the sheep will be scattered'.

If this passage is genuine, we again have evidence that Jesus spoke about his death. Again, as in (vii), we should note the direct quotation of a prophecy other than Isa. 53: this is the more significant in that the words are used in a sense which is probably not in accordance with the original context.[2] If Jesus had, indeed, thought of himself in terms of the 'Servant', or if the early Church had considered Isa. 53 as of unique importance, then they would surely have turned to that chapter here for the supreme example of the scandalizing of a man's companions.

(xi) Mark 14. 49 (Matt. 26. 56; cf. Matt. 26. 54).

Day after day I was with you in the temple teaching, and you did not seize me. But let the scriptures be fulfilled.

There is no reason to associate these words with Isa. 53 in particular: it is most probable that the phrase 'the scriptures' refers to an understanding of the Old Testament as a whole, rather than to any particular passage.[3]

(xii) Luke 12. 49f.

I came to cast fire upon the earth; and would that it were already kindled! I have a baptism to be baptized with; and how I am constrained until it is accomplished!

Most commentators understand this passage as a metaphorical reference to the suffering and death which Jesus knows await him. If genuine, this passage exemplifies once again Jesus' full awareness of the nature and significance of his destiny.[4]

(xiii) Luke 13. 32f.

Go and tell that fox, 'Behold, I cast out demons and perform cures today and tomorrow, and the third day I finish my course. Nevertheless I must go on my way today and tomorrow and the day following; for it cannot be that a prophet should perish away from Jerusalem.'

Both the meaning and authenticity of this passage are extremely doubtful.[1] Whether or not, however, the saying represents the original words of Jesus, it reflects an early belief that his death was in some measure in succession to the treatment accorded to the prophets; the idea that he must die in Jerusalem clearly owes nothing to Deutero-Isaiah.

(xiv) Luke 17. 25.

But first [the Son of Man] must suffer many things and be rejected by this generation.

Here a saying very similar to the three great predictions of the Son of Man's sufferings is found in the middle of an apocalyptic discourse concerning the day of the Son of Man. The strangeness of the context has caused many to regard the verse as an interpolation.[2] The authenticity of the verse in itself, however, has been defended on the grounds that it is free from the theological bias of the other three predictions.[3]

While the verse certainly interrupts the continuity of the passage, the tradition that Jesus taught that the Son of Man would suffer before he was exalted is important. This passage is not alone in associating these two concepts of suffering and exaltation. Thus Mark 8. 31 is followed by the promise that Jesus' followers must share in his sufferings, and then by a saying concerning the coming of the Son of Man; Mark 10. 33 is followed by the request of the sons of Zebedee that they may share in his glory when he enters into his Kingdom, and by the promise that they will share his sufferings; Mark 9. 12 follows immediately after the Transfiguration, a preview of Jesus and his glory. This association of suffering, which must be endured, with subsequent vindication is not confined to Isa. 53 in the Old Testament, but is a continual theme.

(xv) Luke 24. 25–7.

And he said to them, 'O foolish men, and slow of heart to believe all that the prophets have spoken! Was it not necessary that the Christ should suffer these things and enter into his glory?' And beginning with Moses and all the prophets, he interpreted to them in all the scriptures the things concerning himself.

These words, attributed to the Risen Christ, demonstrate the faith of the early Church that the sufferings he endured were the fulfilment of prophecy, and are probably a faithful reflection of the belief of Jesus himself. The attitude they reveal is extremely important to our investigation: far from concentrating attention on any particular Old Testament passages, they refer to all the prophets, starting with Moses. What is in mind is not the fulfilment of any particular details in the events of the Crucifixion; rather all history, as understood in the prophetic writings, has been leading up to the events of these days. The prophets are now fulfilled, because the events foreshadowed in the Old Testament are completed in the sufferings and resurrection of Christ. This passage confirms the suggestion that other sayings which speak of 'the scriptures' or 'the prophets' are to be understood in the sense of an interpretation of the sufferings of Christ as part of the prophetic pattern; fulfilment is something much wider than the mere repetition of particular details; it is the 'completion', in the death and resurrection of Christ, of a pattern of humiliation and exaltation which appears throughout the whole of Old Testament history.

6. CONCLUSION

We have now examined all the passages in the Synoptic gospels which are relevant to our study, and must consider whether or not they have supplied sufficient evidence for a solution to our problem.

It will be remembered that, with regard to the first group of passages, the criteria of judgement were stated to be first, proof that the reference was exclusively to Deutero-Isaiah, and secondly, the application of the Servant's sufferings to Jesus. We found that a considerable number of passages fulfilled the first of these conditions, but of those that did so only one, Luke 22. 37, fulfilled the second. Of the other passages in this group which speak of suffering, none could be proved to have the Servant Songs definitely and exclusively in mind.

In those passages in this first group which fell within the Passion narrative, there was nothing to suggest that the authors had deliberately altered the details of the events which they described in order to demonstrate that Jesus was to be identified with the Servant.

Regarding the second group of passages, where Jesus speaks of his approaching sufferings and death, we may again ask whether there is any indication that the ideas expressed there are derived from, and could only be derived from, the relevant passages in Deutero-Isaiah.

Here again, we found nothing to suggest that this was the case: in all these passages Jesus speaks in a general way of the fact that his death was foretold in the prophets, and there is nothing to indicate that he thought that these prophecies were confined to two passages in the book of Isaiah: indeed, where particular passages are indicated, as happens twice (Mark 12. 10f. and 14. 27), there are quotations, not from Isaiah, but from quite different contexts.

There is, therefore, very little in the Synoptics to support the traditional view that Jesus identified his mission with that of the Servant of the Songs: certainly there is nothing which could be accepted as proof for this view. We are thus led to continue our search in the rest of the New Testament: it is possible that we may find there some evidence to show that it was among the primitive Christians that the identification of Jesus with the Servant was first made, or to suggest that the writers of the Gospels overlooked what had, in fact, been an important idea in the mind of Jesus.

CHAPTER 5

THE SERVANT IN THE EARLY CHURCH

1. INTRODUCTION

The passages which remain for consideration must be regarded primarily as evidence for the belief of the early Church. If, however, they point to any noticeable growth or decrease in the use of the Servant theme, this fact will have an important bearing also upon the question of Jesus' own use of the concept. The fourth gospel will be included in this section, apart from those passages which were noted in our study of the Synoptic gospels, since any references to the Servant theme which occur in the fourth gospel but have no parallel in the Synoptics are almost certainly due to the interpretation of the evangelist, and cannot be taken as direct evidence for the thought of Jesus.

2. THE FOURTH GOSPEL

The following passages may possibly reflect the Servant theme:

(i) 1. 29, 36. The Lamb of God.
(ii) 3. 14; 8. 28; 12. 32. The lifting up of the Son of Man.
(iii) 12. 37f.. Quotation of Isa. 53. 1.

(i) 1. 29, 36.

Ἴδε ὁ ἀμνὸς τοῦ Θεοῦ.
Cf. Isa. 53. 7: רָחֵל; LXX: ἀμνός.

The word ἀμνός is not used elsewhere as a title of Christ. It is, indeed, found only twice more in the whole of the New Testament: in Acts 8. 32 it occurs in the quotation from the LXX version of Isa. 53. 7f., and in 1 Pet. 1. 19 the blood of Christ is compared with that of 'a lamb without blemish or spot'. Nor was the title used by the early Fathers.[1] In the Apocalypse, however, the term ἀρνίον is used repeatedly of Christ.[2]

Various suggestions have been made as to the origin of the term used in these two verses, one of them being that it derives from Isa. 53. 7.[3]

Supporters of this theory have sought confirmation in the other two New Testament uses of the word. While, however, the verse in Acts is a quotation from the passage in Deutero-Isaiah, and the words in 1 Peter may possibly be connected with it,[1] these two passages both retain the element of comparison, which is found in the original. Thus in Isa. 53. 7 the Servant's submission is likened to that of a sacrificial sheep, or a lamb that is being shorn: he is nowhere said actually to be a lamb. In John 1, however, the word ἀμνός is used as a definite title, and not, as in Acts and 1 Peter, in a comparison. Since there is no evidence that this word was ever widely used as a title of Jesus, it seems extremely improbable that a term which was used only comparatively in the original could be transformed into a title, and thus become the equivalent of 'Servant'. This conviction is strengthened by the fact that the Baptist's words are definitely linked with sin-bearing, while in Isa. 53. 7 this concept is not mentioned, the whole point of the comparison being that of the humiliation and submission of the Servant.[2]

It has, however, been suggested that the reference was originally to the title 'Servant' itself, and not to the sheep of Isa. 53. 7. This theory rests on the supposition that ἀμνός is a mistranslation of the Aramaic טַלְיָא, a word which is really the equivalent of the Greek παῖς, but was here understood in the sense of the Hebrew טָלֶה, meaning 'lamb'.[3] The reference to the Servant was thus far more explicit in an earlier Aramaic tradition, or possibly an Aramaic original of the gospel, than in the version known to us. Although this theory has been accepted by some scholars,[4] it must be remembered that it rests on a supposition, and that it lacks any supporting evidence; as C. H. Dodd[5] has pointed out, the LXX never translates טָלֶה by ἀμνός, nor is there any known case of טַלְיָא being used for עֶבֶד.[6]

While it seems improbable that the primary reference of the word would be to Isa. 53. 7, however, it is quite likely that the evangelist, who elsewhere constantly interweaves Old Testament themes, would have been quick to see a secondary allusion to that passage in the term he used. Thus C. K. Barrett believes that the original figure in the mind of the Baptist was the Messianic lamb of apocalyptic, but that for the evangelist the primary significance of the term lay in a reference to the Paschal lamb, with which the lamb of Isa. 53, through the influence of the Christian Eucharist, had become fused.[7]

(ii) 3. 14; 8. 28; 12. 32.

As Moses lifted up the serpent in the wilderness, so must the Son of man be lifted up.

When you have lifted up the Son of man, then you will know that I am he, and that I do nothing on my own authority but speak thus as the Father taught me.

And I, when I am lifted up from the earth, will draw all men to myself.

Cf. Isa. 52. 13: יָרוּם וְנִשָּׂא וְגָבַהּ מְאֹד; LXX: καὶ ὑψωθήσεται καὶ δοξασθήσεται σφόδρα.

The use of the word ὑψόω, 'to lift up', in these three passages has been traced to Isa. 52. 13, although the verb is used fairly commonly in the LXX. Similarly, the theme of glory, which is linked so often with Christ's death in this gospel, may be associated with the same passage.[1]

In 3. 14 there is a direct reference to Num. 21. 9: as the Israelites looked on the brazen serpent set up by Moses, and thus lived, so those who believe on the exalted Son of Man will possess eternal life. The context of this passage suggests that the exaltation is considered in terms of the ascension, while the use of δεῖ indicates that the evangelist also has the manner of Christ's death in mind. The reference to the crucifixion is made plain in 8. 28 by the allusion to the part played by the Jews, and in 12. 38 by the evangelist's explanatory note. While it is the Jews, the enemies of Christ, who lift him up, however, John may be referring ironically to the fact that they were, in effect, also exalting him in a more profound sense.[2] This double significance of the verb ὑψόω is in harmony with the evangelist's tendency to identify the crucifixion with the exaltation which was, in historical terms, subsequent.

The same fusion of death with vindication is to be seen in the way in which John employs the concept of δόξα, since he finds the supreme manifestation of this glory in the Cross. His use of the term is in keeping with the Old Testament concept of כָּבוֹד; glory belongs to God. Thus the glory of Jesus himself always derives from God, and his actions glorify his Father. This reciprocal function is summed up in the prayer of Jesus in John 17. 1: 'Father, the hour has come; glorify thy Son that the Son may glorify thee.'[3]

It is possible that when the evangelist spoke of the glory of Christ he had in mind the theme of the fourth Servant Song. If so, however, he has identified the suffering of the Servant with his exaltation in the same way as he has presented the crucifixion in the light of the subsequent resurrection, and equated the earthly Jesus with the triumphant eschatological Son of Man of the Synoptics. He has thus rejected the contrast between humiliation and suffering on the one side, and exaltation and glory on the other, which forms the basis of the fourth Servant Song. Whereas in Deutero-Isaiah the Servant is glorified by his restoration, and Yahweh by the Return of Israel, in John both Father and Son are glorified already at the crucifixion. This may well be the result of John's consideration of Isa. 52. 13–53. 12, but this cannot be proved, since the theme is found elsewhere in the Old Testament.[1] Moreover, even if his concept is based on this passage, it reflects the meditation of a mystic on the meaning of the Cross, and can tell us nothing about the use of the Servant theme in the early Church. Finally, we may note that there is no suggestion that John had in mind the vicarious nature of the Servant's sufferings.

(iii) 12. 37f.

Though he had done so many signs before them, yet they did not believe in him; it was that the word spoken by the prophet Isaiah might be fulfilled: 'Lord, who has believed our report, and to whom has the arm of the Lord been revealed?'

This quotation from the fourth Servant Song—an exact transcript of the LXX text—is here applied to the failure of the Jews to believe the signs which had been performed by Jesus. It is significant that the passage is referred, not to the sign of Christ's death and resurrection, but to the sum of all the previous signs; here, as in Matt. 8. 17, we find words from Isa. 53 used, not of the Passion of Jesus, but of the works which he had done. The words which originally described the inability of the nations to grasp the fact of the Servant's exaltation are used by the evangelist to express the inability of the Jews to recognize the glory of God which was revealed in the signs performed by Jesus: but whereas in Isaiah the difficulty had been the Servant's suffering, in John the suffering of Jesus is still to come. There is no indication that the author intended any identification of Jesus with the Servant; the passage appears to have been used simply as an Old Testament proof-text of the incurable obduracy of Israel, and this is confirmed by its conjunction with Isa. 6. 10, which is quoted in *v*. 40.

3. THE ACTS OF THE APOSTLES

(i) 3. 13, 26; 4. 27, 30. παῖς as a title of Jesus.
(ii) 3. 14; 7. 52; 22. 14. ὁ δίκαιος as a title of Jesus.
(iii) 3. 18; 13. 27–9; 17. 2f.; 26. 22f. The sufferings of Christ foretold in Old Testament prophecy.
(iv) 8. 32–5. Isa. 53. 7f. quoted and applied to Jesus.
(v) 13. 46f.; 26. 16–18. Isa. 49. 6 and 42. 7 applied to Paul.

(i) 3. 13.

The God of Abraham and of Isaac and of Jacob, the God of our fathers, glorified his servant Jesus, whom you delivered up and denied in the presence of Pilate, when he had decided to release him.

3. 26.

God, having raised up his servant, sent him to you first, to bless you in turning every one of you from your wickedness.

4. 27–30.

For truly in this city there were gathered together against thy holy servant Jesus, whom thou didst anoint, both Herod and Pontius Pilate, with the Gentiles and the peoples of Israel, to do whatever thy hand and thy plan had predestined to take place. And now...signs and wonders are performed through the name of thy holy servant Jesus.
Cf. the LXX use of παῖς as a translation for עֶבֶד.

Many scholars find evidence for the early belief in Jesus as the Servant of Deutero-Isaiah in the use of the title παῖς in these two chapters.[1] The fact that it is found only here, in what appears to be an early source of Acts, certainly confirms the primitive character of the title.

Apart from these passages in Acts, the concept of 'servant of God' appears in the New Testament only in Matt. 12. 18; Luke 1. 54, 69 and Acts 4. 25. Thus except for the quotation of Isa. 42. 1 in Matt. 12. 18, the term is used with this special meaning only in Luke–Acts. Luke and Matthew also use the word παῖς occasionally in a general sense, meaning either child or servant, and John uses it once.[2]

In the Old Testament, the phrase 'my servant', as we have already noted,[3] is often used to describe outstanding men of God. It is, in fact, a thoroughly Hebraic expression. It is also to be found in certain

Jewish prayers of this period.[1] We should expect, therefore, to find that its use in early Christianity is derived from the Jewish usage. Such an interpretation seems to be confirmed by the character of the passages in the New Testament where the term is found. For an examination of the eight occasions in the New Testament where the phrase is used with the meaning 'παῖς Θεοῦ' shows that they all occur in passages of a Jewish colouring. Thus in Luke the word appears in the songs of Mary and Zacharias, the Jewish character of which is indisputable;[2] in Matt. 12. 18ff. it forms part of an actual quotation; in Acts, the phrase is found three times in an early Christian prayer, and twice in a sermon attributed to Peter, all within the framework of what appears to be very early traditional material from Jerusalem, in which we expect to find Jewish influence still very strong.[3]

There is no reason to doubt that the title παῖς, as applied to Jesus in Acts, has the meaning 'servant', and not that of 'child'.[4] This interpretation is supported, not only by the normal Jewish use of the phrase, but also by the fact that the title is also used of David in Acts 4. 25, and of Israel and David in Luke 1. 54, 69.

A consideration of the term παῖς in Acts must include also a brief examination of its use in other Christian writings of the first two centuries A.D. The following are the passages where the expression is applied to Jesus:

(a) 1 Clement 59. 2, 3, 4.
(b) Didache 9. 2, 3; 10. 2, 3.
(c) Epistle of Barnabas 6. 1; 9. 2.
(d) Martyrdom of Polycarp 14. 1, 3; 20. 2.
(e) Epistle to Diognetus 8. 9, 11; 9. 1.

It has frequently been noted that the majority of these passages are of a liturgical character:[5] those in 1 Clement, the Didache and the Martyrdom of Polycarp all appear in prayers, and those in the Epistle of Barnabas are quotations; only the Epistle to Diognetus uses the term in a straightforward context. The meaning of the term παῖς in these books is by no means consistent: thus the context of the phrase in the Martyrdom of Polycarp and the Epistle to Diognetus, and probably also in 1 Clement, shows that the translation must be 'child' or 'son', while that in the Didache and in the Epistle of Barnabas necessitates 'servant'.[6]

This restricted use of the term παῖς Θεοῦ confirms, not only that the title was an early one, but also that it soon died out. It has been suggested by F. C. Burkitt that it derives from the LXX version of the Servant Songs, and therefore belongs to Hellenistic, not to Palestinian Christianity. Burkitt supports this theory, as we have already seen,[1] by claiming that it would have been impossible for the early Christians to have thought of Jesus in terms of the Hebrew עֶבֶד, but quite possible that they should speak of him as παῖς. This argument is not supported, however, by the evidence which we have examined: for Jesus is never referred to in Acts as 'the servant' but as 'thy servant', thus emphasizing his special relationship to God, and forming an exact parallel to the Old Testament use of the concept עֶבֶד יהוה as a title of honour;[2] moreover, the unmistakably Jewish character of the passages in Acts where the term is used, suggests that its origin is to be sought in the Palestinian, not in the Hellenistic, community.[3]

The loss of the term παῖς in the general usage of the Church may be attributed, first, to the decrease of Jewish influence upon Christian thought before the ever-growing influx of Hellenistic concepts, and secondly, to the rise of a more considered Christology, which laid greater emphasis upon the divinity of Christ. For the phrase παῖς Θεοῦ, cut off from its Old Testament associations, inevitably conveys the idea of subordination, in whichever meaning παῖς is understood. Thus in the Greek Church the phrase would scarcely be considered fitting; to speak of Jesus as 'servant of God' would be to use what appeared a disparaging term, while to call him 'child of God' implies an element of subordination not found in the term υἱός, which soon replaced it.

The crucial question for our study is whether this term, when it occurs in Acts, was used in the general sense of the Old Testament concept, or implied an identification of Jesus with the Servant of Isa. 40–55. The fact that in Acts the title is used first of David, and then of Jesus, suggests that no particular reference is intended; it is true that the early Church proclaimed Jesus as far more than a servant of God, and as the Messiah himself, but she also emphasized that he stood in the succession of both David and the prophets. The title which had been given to Moses and to David would have been a fitting one for the early Church to apply to her Master: its use did not mean that she failed to recognize him as the Messiah, but, on the contrary, demonstrated her conviction that the judgement of the Jews who had condemned Jesus was wrong, and that he was the righteous and greater successor of the Old Testament leaders. Once again, the dignity of the title in its Jewish context must be emphasized. But the rapid growth in the Greek-speaking element of the Church would soon make the term inadequate.

It is thus highly probable that the title 'Servant' was used in the early Church with this general reference. We have to note, however, that in the first of the passages under discussion, Acts 3. 13, the word is associated with other reminiscences of the fourth Servant Song, namely the words ἐδόξασε, παρεδώκατε and δίκαιον.¹ Such a collection of ideas may reasonably lead us to suspect that the Servant concept of Deutero-Isaiah is in mind. But here it is vitally important to consider the question of order in time, and not to conclude, as so many have done, that the associations with the Servant concept here mean that the title παῖς is in all cases derived from Deutero-Isaiah.² In other words, we must consider whether the use of the title 'Servant' suggested the idea of the Servant Songs, or whether the identification of Jesus with the Servant of the Songs led to the use of the title 'Servant'. The evidence which we have examined, both here and in chapter 3, suggests that the first alternative is correct; the second would be proved, only if we found that the idea of the 'Servant of God', in the special sense of Isa. 53, was a living idea in Jewish thought of the period.³

Finally, we may note that even if we hold the view that the title 'Servant' in Acts is meant to have a primary reference to the special concept of Deutero-Isaiah, the only ideas which are adopted from Isa. 52–3 are those of 'delivering up' and of exaltation; no use is made of the two most distinctive characteristics of the third and fourth Songs, the nature of the Servant's sufferings, and their atoning value. These early chapters of Acts speak only of the historical fact of Christ's death; they do not dwell on his sufferings, or point out the parallel with the Servant Songs. Nor do they trace any connection between Christ's death and the forgiveness of sins, which we would expect if an identification of Jesus with the Servant were intended: for while the forgiveness of sins was proclaimed as part of the *kerygma* from the very beginning, it is not suggested that this forgiveness was dependent upon Christ's death; rather it is announced as a general consequence of the whole *kerygma* and of repentance.

(ii) 3. 14.

But you denied the Holy and Righteous One, and asked for a murderer to be granted to you.

7. 52.

Which of the prophets did not your fathers persecute? And they killed those who announced beforehand the coming of the Righteous One, whom you have now betrayed and murdered, you who received the law as delivered by angels and did not keep it.

22. 14.

The God of our fathers appointed you to know his will, to see the Just One and to hear a voice from his mouth.

With these we may compare also the following passages elsewhere in the New Testament where δίκαιος is used of Jesus:

Matt. 27. 19. Μηδέν σοι καὶ τῷ δικαίῳ ἐκείνῳ.[1]
Luke 23. 47. Ὄντως ὁ ἄνθρωπος οὗτος δίκαιος ἦν.
1 Pet. 3. 18. Χριστός...ἔπαθε, δίκαιος ὑπὲρ ἀδίκων.
1 John 2. 1. Ἰησοῦν Χριστὸν δίκαιον.
Cf. Isa. 53. 11: צַדִּיק; LXX: δίκαιον.

On the three occasions in Acts when δίκαιος is used of Jesus, it is found with the article and no noun, thus suggesting that it is to be understood as a title. It has been claimed[2] that this derives from the LXX version of Isa. 53. 11, which reads δικαιῶσαι δίκαιον εὖ δουλεύοντα πολλοῖς, 'to justify the just who serves many well', and has thus assumed a pointing different from that adopted by the Massoretes.

The concept of righteousness is a constant Old Testament theme, and although it is applied to individuals, to the Messiah, and to God himself, it is used most often in respect of those people who felt themselves to be righteous before God in contrast to the wickedness of their persecuting enemies.[3] It is significant that these same themes of contrast with the wicked and of unjust persecution are found in two of these passages in Acts, in the first of which Jesus is set over against a murderer, and in the second against the Jews, who had received the Law but failed to keep it; similarly, the two passages in the gospels emphasize the innocence of Jesus. There is certainly no indication in any of these passages that the idea of the justification of others was in mind; this thought is found only in the two passages in the epistles, where the word is no longer a title.

(iii) 3. 18.

But what God foretold by the mouth of all the prophets, that his Christ should suffer, he thus fulfilled.

13. 27–9.

For those who live in Jerusalem and their rulers, because they did not recognize him nor understand the utterances of the prophets which are read every sabbath, fulfilled these by condemning him. Though they could charge him with nothing deserving death, yet they asked Pilate to have him killed. And when they had fulfilled all that was written of him, they took him down from the tree, and laid him in a tomb.

17. 2–3.

And Paul went in, as was his custom, and for three weeks he argued with them from the scriptures, explaining and proving that it was necessary for the Christ to suffer and to rise from the dead, and saying, 'This Jesus, whom I proclaim to you, is the Christ'.

26. 22–3.

I stand here testifying both to small and great, saying nothing but what the prophets and Moses said would come to pass: that the Christ must suffer, and that, by being the first to rise from the dead, he would proclaim light both to the people and to the Gentiles.

These passages in the speeches of the apostles continue the theme found in the words attributed to Jesus in the gospels, that his sufferings were foretold in the scriptures; here again, the reference would seem to be the general theme and pattern of the prophets, rather than to any particular passage. Thus in 3. 18 Peter refers to 'the mouth of all the prophets'; Paul, in 13. 27, speaks of the prophets who are read 'every sabbath', thus suggesting the whole course of Old Testament history and prophecy, while in 17. 2[1] he uses the term 'the scriptures', which we have already discussed.[2] The general term 'the prophets and Moses' is used in the speech of Paul before Agrippa in 26. 23, again in connection with suffering, although the words 'light both to the people and to the Gentiles' echo Isa. 42. 6 and 49. 6.[3]

(iv) 8. 32-5.

Now the passage of the scripture which he was reading was this:
'As a sheep led to the slaughter
or a lamb before its shearer is dumb,
so he opens not his mouth.
In his humiliation justice was denied him.
Who can describe his generation?
For his life is taken up from the earth.'
And the eunuch said to Philip, 'About whom, pray, does the prophet say this, about himself or about some one else?' Then Philip opened his mouth, and beginning with this scripture he told him the good news of Jesus.

Here we have the first explicit use in Acts of a passage from the Servant Songs (quoted from the LXX) in connection with Jesus: the use of the definite ἡ περιοχή in v. 32, and of the singular ἡ γραφή in v. 35 should be noted. There is no reason to doubt the genuineness of the main outline of this story,[1] and it is clear evidence for the use of Isa. 53 in connection with Jesus' suffering by at least one of the earliest members of the Church. It is strange that this first quotation should be found in the mouth of an unconverted Gentile, and not a Christian preacher, or even a Jew. It cannot, therefore, be taken as evidence that this passage of scripture was central in the Christian preaching of the time. The story does, however, show how the early Church was ready to make use of any scripture which was presented to her, in order to show how Christ's work had been foreshadowed there. Thus Philip tells the eunuch the good news of Jesus, 'beginning with this scripture'; he clearly did not end there, and it may be that this passage was simply as good an introduction as any other to the subject of Christ's life and death. Thus, while it is clear that Philip was ready to interpret this chapter of Jesus, there is no proof that it was a passage of particular importance; behind this story there may lie a genuine recollection that this was the chapter which the eunuch happened to be reading.

It is significant that the passage quoted here consists of the last three lines of Isa. 53. 7, and the first three of v. 8; the dominant ideas are the deep humiliation of the Servant, his submission to suffering and injustice, and his death. The judgement of the onlookers that the Servant has suffered on account of their sins, expressed in the original in the verses immediately preceding this passage, and in the last line of v. 8, is strangely missing in Acts.¹ While it may be argued that the verses quoted are meant to convey the meaning of the whole passage, and while it is probable that the author of Acts, if questioned, would agree in referring it all to Christ, it is still remarkable that he has chosen these particular words. The exact verbal agreement with the LXX suggests that he was quoting from a written source, and not from memory, so that the choice is not a haphazard one. It seems that the significance of Isa. 53 lay, for the author of Acts at least, not in the connection between suffering and the sin of others, but in the picture of humiliation: thus yet again the chapter is used as a proof-text of the necessity for Christ's Passion, and not as a theological exposition of its meaning.

(v) 13. 46–7.

And Paul and Barnabas spoke out boldly, saying, 'It was necessary that the word of God should be spoken first to you. Since you thrust it from you, and judge yourselves unworthy of eternal life, behold, we turn to the Gentiles. For so the Lord has commanded us, saying,

"I have set you to be a light for the Gentiles, that you may bring salvation to the uttermost parts of the earth".'

26. 16–18.

'I have appeared to you for this purpose, to appoint you to serve and bear witness to the things in which you have seen me and to those in which I will appear to you, delivering you from the people and from the Gentiles —to whom I send you to open their eyes, that they may turn from darkness to light and from the power of Satan to God.'

In the first of these passages we find a verse from the second Servant Song being applied by Paul and Barnabas, not to Jesus, but to their own mission. The context is the failure of the Jews to accept the truth of the gospel; since their countrymen have refused to listen to their preaching, Paul and Barnabas will speak instead to the Gentiles, as was prophesied of them. With this passage we may contrast the use made of this same verse of Deutero-Isaiah in Acts 26. 23 which was noted above:² there, in another speech attributed to Paul, the verse is applied to the work of Christ which he accomplishes through his resurrection.

The way in which this same verse from a Servant passage is applied, first to the apostles, and then to Christ, suggests that in Acts 26. 23

there is no intention of identifying Jesus with the Servant. The method of quoting scriptures which the author employs again recalls the use which is made of 'proof-texts' in the gospels. Further support for this interpretation is found in Acts 26. 18: for here the words used of the mission of Paul, 'to open their eyes, that they may turn from darkness to light', echo Isa. 42. 7. Moreover, they seem to have been suggested by the reference to the Gentiles in *v.* 17, for in Deutero-Isaiah the words 'to open the eyes of the blind' follow immediately after the phrase 'a light of the Gentiles' in Isa. 42. 6. Here, therefore, it seems that words which speak of the Servant's mission have been applied to St Paul, only a few verses before a very similar passage is referred to the resurrection of Christ, and all within the framework of a speech attributed to St Paul.

A possible explanation of this double application of the Servant passages is offered in the suggestion of Lucien Cerfaux[1] that St Paul recognized himself as fulfilling, in a special sense, the vocation of the Servant. Cerfaux offers this, not as an alternative to the usual theory that Jesus was thought of as the Servant, but as a supplement to that view: Jesus had suffered, and thus fulfilled the words of the fourth Servant Song, but Paul was called by Christ to be the 'light to the Gentiles', and thus to continue the work of the Servant which had been begun by Jesus. Thus Cerfaux regards it as significant that words from the Servant Songs are quoted or echoed in these two passages in Acts in connection with the mission of St Paul; he finds further evidence in Acts in the echo of Isa. 41. 10 in the vision of Acts 18. 9f., and in the fact that the account of St Paul's call in chapter 9 speaks of the suffering which he is to endure for the name of Christ. Cerfaux supports his view by reference to the Pauline epistles: he notes the close alliance in language between Gal. 1. 15 and the account of the Servant's call in Isa. 49. 1, the quotation of Isa. 49. 8 in 2 Cor. 6. 2, the quotation of Isa. 52. 15 and 53. 1 with reference to his preaching in Rom. 15. 20f. and 10. 16, and various verbal reminiscences of the Servant Songs.

Cerfaux does not suggest that St Paul thought of himself as a new 'Servant', but that, in continuing, as an apostle, the work of Christ, he felt himself to be entrusted with that part of the Servant's vocation which related to the Gentiles: Jesus, as 'Servant', had delegated this part of his own mission to Paul.[2] Cerfaux's position is thus dependent upon the assumption that the early Church, and Paul in particular, identified Jesus with the Servant. If his interpretation is correct, therefore, it must be considered as evidence of an underlying primitive Servant-Christology. While it is clear, however, from the various passages which Cerfaux examines that Paul was well acquainted with Deutero-Isaiah, the evidence is too slight to show that he was consciously identifying himself with the mission of the Servant. The fact that Acts 9. 15 f. speaks of suffering is no indication that the Servant is in mind: anyone called to be an apostle was inevitably called to suffer for the sake of the name, and Paul, who had been a prime persecutor of the Church, would be doubly conscious of this fact. The promise of Isa. 41. 10, which may lie behind Acts 18. 9f., although it is addressed to Israel as Servant, does not speak of a mission to the Gentiles, and cannot, therefore, be accepted as evidence that Paul thought of himself as fulfilling that part of the Servant's vocation. It was natural that Paul should find the justification of his call to preach to the Gentiles in the Old Testament, but that does not mean that when, in Acts 13 and 26, he spoke of his own mission in terms drawn from Deutero-Isaiah, he was associating himself with the Servant to whom the words were originally spoken: it is more probable that he was using his quotations merely for their own content, and without relation to their original context, as he does elsewhere, and as Cerfaux himself admits to be the case in Rom. 10. 16.

4. THE EPISTLES OF ST PAUL

(i) Rom. 10. 15 f., quotation of Isa. 52. 7 and 53. 1.
(ii) Rom. 15. 21, quotation of Isa. 52. 15.
(iii) 1 Cor. 15. 3. Christ died 'in accordance with the scriptures'.
(iv) Phil. 2. 5–11. Christ took 'the form of a servant'.
(v) Various passages which use words found in Isa. 52–3.

(i) Rom. 10. 15 f.

And how can men preach unless they are sent? As it is written, 'How beautiful are the feet of those who preach good news!' But they have not all heeded the gospel; for Isaiah says, 'Lord, who has believed what he has heard from us?'

A free rendering of Isa. 52. 7 and the LXX reading of Isa. 53. 1 are here used by St Paul to describe the nature and reception of his preaching. The quotation from Isa. 53 does not mean that the rest of this chapter was in St Paul's mind: the point he is emphasizing is the failure of the Jews to believe the gospel, and we may compare the use which is made of the same verse in John 12. 38.

(ii) Rom. 15. 21.
As it is written,
'They shall see who have never been told of him,
and they shall understand who have never heard of him'.

Once again, St Paul applies the LXX rendering of a verse from the fourth Servant Song to justify his preaching. Here, too, there is no indication that he has in mind anything but this one verse.

(iii) 1 Cor. 15. 3.
For I delivered to you as of first importance what I also received, that Christ died for our sins in accordance with the scriptures.

Many scholars have claimed this verse as evidence for a pre-Pauline tradition that Jesus was identified with the Servant of Deutero-Isaiah.[1] The form of the passage, and the words 'what I also received', certainly suggest that Paul is here quoting some very primitive formula of faith.

The reference to Isa. 52-3 has been found in the words 'in accordance with the scriptures'. This phrase, in itself, is again of a quite general nature; it is the equivalent of the similar expressions distributed throughout the gospels and Acts, which have already been considered. It has been claimed, however, that the significant words ὑπὲρ τῶν ἁμαρτιῶν ἡμῶν can refer only to Isa. 53.[2]

While it is justifiable to regard these few verses as representing, to a large extent, pre-Pauline tradition, the possibility of Pauline embellishment must not be overlooked. It would be very dangerous to interpret the pre-Pauline *kerygma* in terms of this passage, if it is found to differ in any substantial way from what we know of that *kerygma* from other sources. It will, therefore, be necessary to make a brief comparison with the various summaries of early Christian faith which are found in Acts.

Examining first this passage in Corinthians, we find that the following statements are made: (1) Christ died for our sins, in accordance with the scriptures. (2) He was buried. (3) He was raised on the third day, in accordance with the scriptures. (4) He appeared to Cephas, the twelve, etc.

It is valuable to compare this summary with the fullest description which Luke gives in Acts of the preaching of Paul. In Acts 13. 26–41, Paul is reported to have made the following exposition of the meaning of Christ's death: (1) The Jews fulfilled the prophets by condemning and killing Jesus. (2) He was then buried. (3) God raised him from the dead...this fulfilled the scriptures. (4) He appeared to those who had come with him to Jerusalem from Galilee, and they are witnesses of his resurrection. (5) Through him forgiveness of sins is proclaimed.

Thus in Luke's report of Paul's preaching we find exactly the same elements as are present in Paul's own summary in 1 Cor. 15. There is no great change in substance, but only in order and emphasis; in Luke's account the forgiveness of sins is not directly connected with Christ's death, but is proclaimed at the end of the narrative. With these two summaries of St Paul's preaching we may now compare two speeches attributed to St Peter, which appear in the early chapters of Acts. First, Acts 2. 22–39: (1) Jesus was delivered up according to the plan and foreknowledge of God. (2) He was killed by lawless men. (3) God raised him, as David prophesied. (4) Peter and his company are witnesses of this resurrection. (5) Christ is now exalted to the right hand of God, and has given the gift of the Holy Spirit. When his hearers ask Peter what they shall do, he replies: (6) Repent, and be baptized in the name of Jesus, for the forgiveness of sins.

The other passage is in Acts 3. 12–21: (1) God has glorified Jesus. (2) The Jews delivered up Jesus and killed him.... His sufferings fulfilled the prophecies. (3) He was raised by God; Peter and his company are witnesses of this resurrection. (4) Repent, that your sins may be forgiven, and that Jesus may return.

According to these two accounts, the preaching of Peter was almost identical with that of Paul: this agrees with Paul's statements in 1 Cor. 15. 3, 11, that he has preached the same gospel as the other apostles. We find in the speeches of Peter the same emphasis on the fact that Christ's death fulfilled the Old Testament scriptures, and on the witness of the disciples to his resurrection; the only differences are the stressing of Christ's exaltation, the omission from Acts 3 of any reference to the burial of his body, and the agreement of these two passages with Acts 13, as against 1 Cor. 15, that the forgiveness of sins was not particularly associated with Christ's death.[1]

In view of the significant fact that ὑπὲρ τῶν ἁμαρτιῶν ἡμῶν is the one phrase in the Corinthian summary which is not supported by these three passages in Acts, it is impossible to take these words as evidence that the tradition which Paul received included the statement that this purpose, or result, of Christ's death was foretold in scripture. Indeed, it seems more probable that the association made between the death and the forgiveness of sins was due to the particular significance which Paul himself attached to the events of the Passion. For this connection is a feature of Paul's theology, and sums up the meaning of his religious experience and preaching. It has been argued that the phraseology is not Pauline, since the word ἁμαρτία is rarely used by St Paul in the sense of particular sins.[2] While this is by no means certain—since there are exceptions to be found elsewhere in the Pauline epistles[3]—it does not affect the validity of our argument, the point of which is not that the phrase is in itself a Pauline addition, but that the association which is made here between Christ's death and the forgiveness of sins is not found in the accounts of the *kerygma* in Acts. While St Paul may well be quoting in rough outline the words of an early 'creed', it is extremely improbable that the form of such a statement could have become so stereotyped by such an early date that no alteration in phrasing or order was possible. Indeed, Paul has clearly added his own name to the original list of witnesses to the resurrection. There is thus no justification for believing that the words κατὰ τὰς γραφάς have special reference to ὑπὲρ τῶν ἁμαρτιῶν ἡμῶν, and do not refer simply to the fact of Christ's death.

Significance has also been found in the fact that the phrase κατὰ τὰς γραφάς is used in connection with both Christ's death and his resurrection, but not with regard to his burial. This, it is claimed, was the result of the recognition by the early Church that while Christ's death and resurrection fulfilled Isa. 53, his burial was not in accordance with that prophecy, since he was buried, not with the wicked, but in an honourable grave.[4] Such an argument reflects the quibblings of biblical scholars, and not the practical purposes of the early disciples. The use which the Church made elsewhere of any text which was relevant or could be adapted to her needs does not suggest such niceties in the use of passages; nor was there much time in the short period before St Paul's conversion for the examination of such subtleties in meaning. The phrase 'in accordance with the scriptures', which, as has been repeatedly emphasized, is a general term, and is not meant to denote any particular passage, is surely used here of Christ's death and resurrection because these were the most significant events, and moreover fulfilled the theme of Old Testament prophecy. We may note that in Acts 2 and 13 similar phrases are applied to both the death and the resurrection, but not to the burial, while in Acts 3 the burial is not mentioned at all. These facts suggest that the burial was included in the *kerygma*, not because it had any particular significance in itself, or fulfilled the scriptures, but because it was the necessary stage between death and resurrection, and moreover confirmed the reality of both.

(iv) Phil. 2. 5–11.

Have this mind among yourselves, which you have in Christ Jesus, who, though he was in the form of God, did not count equality with God a thing to be grasped, but emptied himself, taking the form of a servant, being born in the likeness of men. And being found in human form he humbled himself and became obedient unto death, even death on a cross. Therefore God has highly exalted him and bestowed on him the name which is above every name, that at the name of Jesus every knee should bow, in heaven and on earth and under the earth, and every tongue confess that Jesus Christ is Lord, to the glory of God the Father.

This passage, which speaks of the voluntary humiliation and subsequent exaltation of Christ, has been interpreted by some commentators[1] as based upon the fourth Servant Song. In addition to the general theme of the chapter, references have been seen in the words 'the form of a servant', and in 'he emptied himself...unto death'.

We have already noted[2] that the LXX translates עֶבֶד in the Servant Songs as παῖς, never as δοῦλος, which is the word used here. Furthermore, in the Songs עֶבֶד = παῖς was a title of honour, and denoted the special relationship between God and his Servant. There is thus no connection whatever between that concept and this picture of humiliation. Δοῦλος is used here, not as a title, but indirectly, for Paul is careful not to say that Jesus actually became a slave; furthermore, it denotes, not any honourable position in the sight of God, but the dishonour and limitations of a human body.[3]

There is no linguistic evidence for regarding the words ἑαυτὸν ἐκένωσε...μέχρι θανάτου as a reference to Isa. 53. 11. While κενόω is a possible translation of עָרָה, it is not used in this sense in the LXX, nor is its primary meaning in this passage the actual death of Christ. The words μέχρι θανάτου belong to a completely different construction, and cannot be used as evidence that κενόω refers to the Isaian concept. Lucien Cerfaux[1] links the words to the phrase κενῶς ἐκοπίασα in Isa. 49. 4; this, however, would represent a complete reinterpretation by Paul of their meaning in that passage, where they are used, not of any 'self-emptying', but of the frustrated labour of the Servant.

The general theme of the passage—humiliation and then exaltation —sums up the idea of Isa. 52–3. This, however, does not mean that the concept derived from those chapters; for it is both a succinct summary of the life, death and resurrection of Christ, and also of the early preaching of the Church as portrayed in the first chapters of Acts. The suggestion has been made that this passage is not originally Pauline, but incorporates an early Christian hymn:[2] this would link it closely with the early community. Whoever composed the passage, however, it is possible to understand it, not as an interpretation based upon Isa. 53, but as a summary of what actually happened; for the need of the early Church was to show how this Jesus, who had undoubtedly suffered deep humiliation in his life and death, was now highly exalted and proclaimed as Christ by God himself. Thus this theme of humiliation and exaltation arose primarily out of the actual events, as understood by the disciples, and out of the kerygmatic need of the Church. It is therefore not surprising that the humiliation is described here in terms of incarnation and death, and not in terms of suffering, the main theme of Isa. 53.

Finally, we may note that this chapter says nothing about the forgiveness of sins: the theme of Christ's humiliation and exaltation is introduced to Paul's readers as an example of behaviour.[3]

(v) *Various words echoing the vocabulary of the fourth Song.*

Those who believe that the concept of the Servant was important in the early Church have found reminiscences of the Songs in St Paul's vocabulary. While Paul himself may not have used the Servant concept, it is argued that the language of the Songs has become part of the

Church's vocabulary, so that certain words which are used by Paul reflect an earlier identification of Jesus with the Servant. Thus παραδίδωμι in Rom. 4. 25; 8. 32; Gal. 2. 20; Eph. 5. 2, 25 is traced to Isa. 53, together with οἱ πολλοί in Rom. 5. 19, and the root δικαιόω in Rom. 4. 25; 5. 1, 9; 2 Cor. 5. 21.[1]

The biblical background of παραδίδωμι has already been considered.[2] In Paul, as in Mark 9. 31 and 10. 33, it appears to be the natural word to use, and it is impossible to link it with any particular Old Testament passage; not only is it found repeatedly in the LXX, where it generally translates the common verb נתן, but it is also used frequently in the New Testament and in contemporary writings.[3] As in the Synoptic passages, however, a deeper significance seems to underlie the word, reflecting its Old Testament background, and the finality which is implied by the particle παρά. The Old Testament concept of the divine 'handing over' is used and stressed by Paul in Rom. 1. 24, 26 and 28, and is echoed in 1 Cor. 5. 5 and 15. 24. Where the verb is used of Christ, therefore, we may presume that Paul has in mind the willing activity and purposes of God.

The use of the word πολλοί in Rom. 5. 19 depends upon the rhetorical contrast between the one man and the result for the many. The passage thus has a certain similarity to Isa. 53, where the same contrast is made, but this is no justification for claiming that Paul's argument derives from that chapter. Indeed, in the whole of the section Rom. 5. 12–21 he does not mention the sufferings or the death of Christ.

The root δικαιόω is used frequently in the LXX, mostly in the forms δίκαιος and δικαιοσύνη, and in nearly every case to translate the root צדק. In the New Testament the form δικαίωσις is used only twice, both times in Romans,[4] while δικαιοσύνη and δικαιόω are found, in the majority of cases, in Pauline letters.[5] There is thus no evidence to support the claim, either that it derives from Isa. 53, or that it is a 'primitive' Christian word, reflecting the Servant concept and taken over by St Paul.

Even the combination of these various terms can carry little weight, since it is Paul, not his predecessors, who seems to emphasize the connection between Christ being 'delivered up' and the forgiveness of sins. Although the use of παραδίδωμι and δικαίωσις in Rom. 4. 25 has been stressed by some commentators, the form of the verse suggests that their juxtaposition reflects the parallelism of Hebrew poetry rather than conveys any deep theological significance.[1] In 8. 32f., the fact that παραδίδωμι is followed by words reminiscent of Isa. 50. 8f., in the third Servant Song, can prove nothing, since the ideas which in the original applied to the Servant are here transferred, not to Christ, but to the believer.

5. THE EPISTLE TO THE HEBREWS

9. 28.

So Christ, having been offered once to bear the sins of many, will appear a second time, not to deal with sin but to save those who are eagerly waiting for him.

The words εἰς τὸ πολλῶν ἀνενεγκεῖν ἁμαρτίας in this verse seem to echo the phrase αὐτὸς ἁμαρτίας πολλῶν ἀνήνεγκεν found in Isa. 53. 12 (LXX). They occur in a passage in which the author of the epistle is depicting the work of Christ as our great High Priest, in terms drawn from the ritual of the Day of Atonement. Jesus, as High Priest, has entered the innermost sanctuary, bearing a sacrifice for the sins of the people, and so 'carrying their sins'. He, however, unlike his earthly counterpart, does not enter once a year (ἅπαξ τοῦ ἐνιαυτοῦ, v. 7), but once for all (ἅπαξ), so that we are still waiting for his reappearance, which will take place only at the Second Coming. The fact that Christ 'bears the sins of many', therefore, depends, not upon Isa. 53, but upon his work as High Priest.

To the author of this epistle, however, Jesus is not only the High Priest: he is also the Victim. The Jewish high priest, at the yearly ritual, enters the Holy of Holies with 'blood not his own' (v. 25), 'which he offers for himself and for the errors of the people' (v. 7). Jesus, however, is himself offered[2] as the sacrifice: it is his own blood with which the new covenant is sealed.

How was it that the writer to the Hebrews came to this remarkable understanding of Jesus as both Victim and Priest? What was the link in his mind between the concept of the living High Priest who offers sacrifice for the sins of others, and the idea that the death of Christ was itself that sacrifice? A possible clue to the solution of this problem may lie in the phrase 'to bear the sins of many'. We have already seen that the idea which underlies these words is derived from the high-priestly ritual. When the author goes on to consider in what way this 'bearing of sins' was accomplished, however, his answer is that Christ was himself the Victim who was offered for sin. He may well have derived this concept from a consideration of Isa. 53, which also speaks of one who 'bore the sin of many', not as a priest, but in his own death. While, therefore, there is no identification of Jesus with the 'Suffering Servant', the concept of Isa. 53 very probably lies behind this New Testament passage.

6. I PETER

(i) 1. 10f. Prediction of Christ's suffering and glory in the prophets.
(ii) 1. 18f. The lamb without blemish or spot.
(iii) 2. 21–5. The example of Christ's sufferings.

(i) 1. 10f.[1]

The prophets sought and searched diligently...what time or what manner of time the Spirit of Christ which was in them did point unto, when it testified beforehand the sufferings of Christ and the glories that should follow them.

Here once more the reference to the Old Testament is of a general nature, and 'the prophets' implies the whole prophetic tradition[2] rather than any one particular passage. In view of the passage in chapter 2, however, there is no doubt that Isa. 53 was to the author an outstanding example of the prefiguring of Christ's suffering and glory.

(ii) 1. 18f.

You know that you were ransomed from the futile ways inherited from your fathers, not with perishable things such as silver or gold, but with the precious blood of Christ, like that of a lamb without blemish or spot.

The use of the word ἀμνός here has again been traced to Isa. 53.7.[3] Once more the main theme of the passage, however, is quite different from that of the Old Testament verse and its context: it does not speak of humiliation, or even of sin-bearing, but of redemption, expressed in the verb λυτρόω.[4] E. G. Selwyn writes of this passage: 'The reference is to the Paschal lamb, which was connected *par excellence* with Israel's redemption; and it belongs to a series of "redemption formulae" based on the traditional Jewish exegesis of Exod. 12–14 and interwoven with the "consecration formulae" derived ultimately from Lev. 17–26.'[5] The word ἄμωμος, 'without blemish', is found frequently in the LXX in connection with animal sacrifice.[6]

We have already noted that it is not the ἀμνός which is killed in Isa. 53. 7, but the πρόβατον.¹ It would, therefore, be very dangerous, on the basis of this one word alone, to claim that the author had that passage in mind. The use which is made of the fourth Servant Song in the following chapter, however, together with the possible echo of Isa. 52. 3 (LXX οὐ μετὰ ἀργυρίου λυτρωθήσεσθε) in 1. 18 (οὐ φθαρτοῖς, ἀργυρίῳ ἢ χρυσίῳ ἐλυτρώθητε), suggests that there may well be a very subsidiary reference to Isa. 53. 7.

(iii) 2. 21–5.

εἰς τοῦτο γὰρ ἐκλήθητε, ὅτι καὶ Χριστὸς ἔπαθεν ὑπὲρ ὑμῶν, ὑμῖν ὑπολιμπάνων ὑπογραμμόν, ἵνα ἐπακολουθήσητε τοῖς ἴχνεσιν αὐτοῦ· ὃς ἁμαρτίαν οὐκ ἐποίησεν, οὐδὲ εὑρέθη δόλος ἐν τῷ στόματι αὐτοῦ· ὃς λοιδορούμενος οὐκ ἀντελοιδόρει, πάσχων οὐκ ἠπείλει, παρεδίδου δὲ τῷ κρίνοντι δικαίως· ὃς τὰς ἁμαρτίας ἡμῶν αὐτὸς ἀνήνεγκεν ἐν τῷ σώματι αὐτοῦ ἐπὶ τὸ ξύλον, ἵνα ταῖς ἁμαρτίαις ἀπογενόμενοι τῇ δικαιοσύνῃ ζήσωμεν οὗ τῷ μώλωπι ἰάθητε. ἦτε γὰρ ὡς πρόβατα πλανώμενοι, ἀλλ' ἐπεστράφητε νῦν ἐπὶ τὸν ποιμένα καὶ ἐπίσκοπον τῶν ψυχῶν ὑμῶν.

There can be no doubt at all that this passage is based, in part, upon Isa. 53. The phrases which have been underlined resemble strongly the following passages in the LXX version of that chapter:

v. 9. ὅτι ἀνομίαν οὐκ ἐποίησεν, οὐδὲ δόλον ἐν τῷ στόματι αὐτοῦ.
v. 12. παρεδόθη...ἁμαρτίας πολλῶν ἀνήνεγκεν.
v. 5. τῷ μώλωπι αὐτοῦ ἡμεῖς ἰάθημεν.
v. 6. πάντες ὡς πρόβατα ἐπλανήθημεν.

In these few verses of 1 Peter we find a blending of phrases from Deutero-Isaiah with the historical events of Christ's Passion: these events are not distorted to agree with Isa. 53,² but are interpreted in the light of that chapter. In this passage we find the fourth Servant Song used, not only to emphasize the fact of Jesus' willing submission to humiliation, but also to connect the sufferings of Christ with the sins of others. It is interesting to note how this second theme seems to be called up by the first, which we have already met used alone. Thus the author first recalls the humiliation of Christ as the great example of the behaviour which slaves should adopt in the face of unjust punishment; but this picture of Christ's suffering, expressed in terms of Isa. 53, leads into an exposition of the further value of those sufferings in defeating sin.[3]

7. REVELATION

The Apocalypse of St John seems far removed from the Servant concept. Nevertheless, it has been maintained that the title ἀρνίον, used repeatedly of the exalted Christ in this book, but never elsewhere, is derived from Isa. 53.

As with ἀμνός in John 1. 29, 36, this word has been referred to both Isa. 53. 7 and the double meaning of the Aramaic טַלְיָא. Regarding Isa. 53. 7, V. Taylor[1] even goes so far as to say that the phrase ὡς ἐσφαγμένον in Rev. 5. 6 'clearly shows' that the concept is derived from this passage. It is difficult to see what justification he has for making this statement: the fact that the root σφάζω, used quite commonly in the LXX, appears in both passages is of no significance, and the word for 'sheep' used in all the the Greek versions of Isa. 53. 7 is not ἀρνίον but πρόβατον.

J. Jeremias[2] regards the title ἀρνίον used in this book as the equivalent of ἀμνός in John 1. 29, 36, and traces them both to the παῖς of Isa. 52. 13 –53. 12, although he also recognizes a reference to the Passover lamb. The complete absence of the title from other early Christian literature, however, shows that this is not a name which the author has taken over from tradition. If it in any way referred to Isa. 53, therefore, we should expect to find other evidence of the influence of the passage in his work; such evidence is completely lacking.

If we are to relate the use of this word to the rest of the book, then we must look for a clue to its meaning in the symbolism of Jewish apocalyptic. It is significant that an exact parallel to John's description is to be found there in the use of the image of a lamb to symbolize a Messianic figure.[3] There can be little doubt that this is the primary origin of the term in the book of Revelation. The fact that the Christian Messiah was slain before his triumph connects the figure with the Old Testament concept of sacrifice, but there is no reason to associate it in particular with the metaphor of Isa. 53. 7.

8. CONCLUSION

This examination of the remaining relevant New Testament passages completes our investigation of the canonical material. It will be helpful to summarize the facts which emerge from our study.

In general, the evidence of the Acts of Apostles follows the same pattern as that in the Synoptics. In the gospels, Jesus was found to refer to the prophets when speaking of the necessity for his violent death: the same theme is found in the speeches of the Apostles, who declare that the Passion of Jesus fulfilled the things which were written of him. It is possible that the title 'παῖς' in the early chapters of Acts is derived from a primitive Christian identification of Jesus with the Servant, but the evidence for this is doubtful. A definite link with the Servant passages is found only in the actual quotations: here, however, we find that, as in the gospels, the theme of suffering is missing; indeed, in 13. 47 and in 26. 18 they are applied, not to Jesus, but to Paul. The one great exception to this common pattern is found in Acts 8, where the fourth Servant Song is definitely associated with the sufferings of Christ. Here we have clear proof that at a quite early date the relevance of this chapter to the Passion of Jesus was seen. We observed, however, that the connection was only noted, and was in no way expounded: no mention is made of the vicarious nature of the Servant's sufferings, and the account does not suggest that Philip used the passage as a basis to preach that Jesus' sufferings and the forgiveness of sins were associated. Here, as elsewhere in the New Testament, no connection is made between these two elements in the *kerygma*.[1]

In the writings of the theologians of the early Church, we found little evidence that the identification of Jesus with the Servant played any great part in the thinking of St Paul, St John, or the author of the Epistle to the Hebrews, and no *proof* that it was known to them at all. If the Church did apply the Servant passages to Jesus in this specialized way, then these writers did not consider it to be of central importance, for it appears, at the most, in the background of their work. In the first epistle of St Peter, however, we find proof that the concept was important to at least one writer. For here not only do we find, as in Acts 8, a definite application of the fourth Song to Jesus, but the significance of this application is expounded: the passage is not used merely as a 'proof-text' of the necessity for Christ's death, but is shown to be relevant to the experience of divine forgiveness through the sufferings of Christ. The second chapter of 1 Peter is the earliest definite proof for the full identification of Jesus with the Servant in all its Christological significance.

Our study has thus revealed that there is little evidence that the Servant-Christology held any important place in Christian thought of the New Testament period. There is, therefore, no sound basis, either in the gospels, or in other literature of the early Church, to support the view of Vincent Taylor,[1] who, speaking of 'the popularity of the Servant-conception in primitive Christianity', maintains that 'it is a mark of the fidelity of the evangelists to historic tradition that it emerges so rarely in the gospels, and with manifest restraint in the sayings of Jesus'. The evidence which we have found for this 'popularity' is so scanty, and so dubious, that it is not surprising that the concept has failed to leave any impression upon the gospel narratives through the medium of the Church's influence.

The Synoptic gospels failed to offer any conclusive proof that Jesus thought of himself as the 'Servant': further study has not revealed that the idea held any great significance for the early Church. Those who maintain the traditional view that Jesus interpreted his death in terms of the vicarious sufferings of the Servant must therefore explain, not only the absence of evidence for this view in the Synoptics, but also why the Church apparently overlooked for so many years the significance of the passages which Jesus saw as the key to his Passion, and why it was only gradually that she came to make the connection between his sufferings and the Servant's vicarious atonement. Since our investigation has exposed the weakness of the evidence for the traditional view, it is proposed to turn in the following chapter to a wider consideration of the themes which are involved, in order to see whether there is any explanation for this absence of evidence.

APPENDIX

It is to be expected that Christian literature of the first period after the era of the New Testament will continue the general tendencies of the New Testament use of the Servant concept. If this is so, it will provide corroborative evidence for our judgement of the New Testament material. We shall therefore consider very briefly the evidence for the use of the Servant concept in the writings of the Sub-Apostolic Age.

THE SERVANT IN THE EARLY CHURCH

I. THE APOCRYPHAL NEW TESTAMENT

(i) The Preaching of Peter: the sufferings of Christ foretold in the prophets. (ii) The Acts of Peter: quotation of Isa. 53. 8, 2.

(i) *The Preaching of Peter.*

But we having opened the books of the prophets which we had, found, sometimes expressed by parables, sometimes by riddles, and sometimes directly and in so many words naming Jesus Christ, both his coming and his death and the cross and all the other torments which the Jews inflicted on him, and his resurrection and assumption into the heavens before Jerusalem was founded, even all these things as they had been written, what he must suffer and what shall be after him. When, therefore, we took knowledge of these things, we believed in God through that which had been written of him.

This passage from the lost book *The Preaching of Peter* is quoted by Clement of Alexandria in *Stromateis* VI. 15. 128. It demonstrates the continued importance in the early Church of finding scriptural foundation for the necessity of Christ's sufferings.

(ii) *The Acts of Peter.*

Presumest thou to speak thus, whereas the prophet saith of him: Who shall declare his generation? And another prophet saith: And we saw him and he had no beauty nor comeliness.

(Latin MS. of *The Acts of Peter*, 24.)

These two phrases from Isa. 53 introduce a long list of quotations which are brought forward by Peter to refute the argument of Simon at the end of 23: 'Ye men of Rome, is God born? Is he crucified? He that hath a master is no god.' It seems certain, therefore, that the author regards the first phrase as answering the question 'Is God born?', and the second as answering the question 'Is he crucified?' It is strange that although both quotations come from Isa. 53, the writer refers to the second as being from 'another prophet'. This suggests, first, that he may have been quoting, not from the original, but from proof-texts well known in the early Church, and secondly that passages used in this way were not necessarily applied *in toto*.

2. THE APOSTOLIC FATHERS

References to the Servant are found in the following passages, and in nearly every case take the form of direct quotations:

(i) 1 Clement 16. 1–17. Quotation of Isa. 53. 1–12.
(ii) Epistle of Polycarp 8. 1–2. Quotation of 1 Pet. 2. 22–4.
(iii) Epistle of Barnabas 5. 1 f.; 13 f.; 6. 1 f. Quotation of Isa. 53. 5, 7 and 50. 6–9.
(iv) Epistle of Barnabas 14. 6–9. Quotation of Isa. 42. 6 f.
(v) *Shepherd* of Hermas. The Fifth Similitude. Parable of the slave in the vineyard.
(vi) Epistle to Diognetus 9. 5. Language faintly reminiscent of Isa. 53.

(i) 1 Clement 16. 1–17.

For it is to the humble-minded that Christ belongs, not to those who exalt themselves above His flock. The Sceptre of the Divine Majesty, the Lord Jesus Christ, did not, for all His power, come clothed in boastful pomp and overweening pride, but in a humble frame of mind, as the Holy Spirit has told concerning Him; for He says:

'Lord, who has believed our teaching?...'

You see, beloved, what the example is that has been given us; for, if the Lord was so humble-minded, what ought we to do who have come under the influence of His grace through Him?

The entire fifty-third chapter of Isaiah, together with Ps. 21. 7–9, is here quoted by Clement, in a form very close to that of the LXX. The purpose of introducing the passage is made clear in both the opening and the concluding words: Christ belongs to the humble-minded, for he himself came to men ταπεινοφρονῶν: since this is the example given to Christians by their Lord, then they also should be humble-minded.

(ii) Epistle of Polycarp 8. 1–2.

Unceasingly, then, let us cling to our Hope and the Pledge of our justification, that is, Christ Jesus, who in His own Body took the weight of our sins up to the Cross; who did no wrong; nor was treachery found on His lips. On the contrary, for our sakes—that we might live in Him—He endured everything. Therefore let us become imitators of (His) patient endurance and glorify Him whenever we suffer for the sake of His name. This is the example He has set us in His own Person, and this is what we have learnt to believe.

In this passage the author quotes two phrases from 1 Pet. 2. 24, 22, which, as we have already seen, are based on Isa. 53. 12, 9. Not only does he quote from this epistle, he also follows its exposition, for although he adopts the words about Christ bearing our sins, and speaks of Christians living in him through his suffering, the purpose of the quotation is once again to direct his readers to imitate the example of Christ's patient endurance in the face of suffering; he develops this theme in the next chapter by calling on the example of those early Christians who have shared in Christ's sufferings.

(iii) *Epistle of Barnabas* 5. 1 f., 13 f., 6. 1 f.

It is indeed with this purpose in view that the Lord endured to surrender His body to destruction: we are to be sanctified by the remission of sins, that is, through the sprinkling of His blood. For this is what the Scripture says in speaking of Him partly to Israel, and partly to us. It says as follows:

> He was wounded because of our iniquities, and languishes because of our sins; by His bruises we were healed; as a sheep He was led to the shambles, and as a lamb that is dumb before its shearer.

But this suffering was due to His own choice. It was ordained that He should suffer on a tree, since the inspired writer attributes to Him the following words:

> Save me from the sword,

and

> Pierce my flesh with nails, because bands of evil-doers have risen against me.

And again He says:

> Behold, I present my back for scourgings, and my cheeks for blows; my face I set as a solid rock.

And when He has obeyed the command, what does He say?

> Who wants to quarrel with me? Let him confront me! Who wants to bring me to justice? Let him come near the Servant of the Lord! Ruin awaits you! You will all grow old like a garment, and the moth will devour you!

The heart of Isa. 53 is here applied directly to a clear declaration that the purpose of Christ's death was to sanctify men by the remission of sins. His suffering was due to the voluntary submission of Christ himself, foretold in Isa. 50. 6–9. It should be noted that these quotations are only two among many which the author applies to Christ's death.

(iv) Epistle of Barnabas 14. 6–9.

For the Scripture tells how the Father enjoins Him to ransom us from darkness and prepare for Himself a holy people. This then the prophet says:....

These words introduce three quotations: Isa. 42. 6f.; 49. 6f., and 61. 1f.

In this fourteenth chapter of the epistle the author shows how the Jews proved themselves unworthy to receive the covenant at Sinai, and how Christians have been enabled to receive it instead, through the sufferings of Christ: Moses a servant (θεράπων) and bearer of the covenant between God and the people is contrasted with Christ the Heir, who appeared in person in the flesh. These three passages illustrate how Christ was to ransom men from darkness, establishing a covenant among them and preparing a holy people: through his sufferings the early Christians have become 'the people of inheritance' (Epistle of Barnabas 14. 4).

(v) The *Shepherd* of Hermas, Sim. 5. (The parable of the slave in the Vineyard.)

The real purpose of this fifth parable seems to be to show the value of supererogatory works; its exposition, however, is Christological, and the slave of the story, who performs more than his duties require, and is exalted to the status of Sonship, is identified with the Son of God. In chapter 6 of the Similitude, however, the Shepherd denies that the Son of God is in the form of a slave.

It is possible that some concept of a Servant-Christology may lie behind this parable. The whole passage is so confused, however, that it is impossible to consider it as evidence.[1]

(vi) Epistle to Diognetus 9. 5.

O sweetest exchange! O unfathomable accomplishment! O unexpected blessings—the sinfulness of many is buried in One who is holy, the holiness of One sanctifies many who are sinners!

The language of the fourth Servant Song is faintly echoed in this one verse of the epistle, but it is unlikely that it is a direct reference to that passage, in view of the author's dislike of Judaism, and his lack of Old Testament quotations. The words which are used are all part of the common vocabulary of the Church,[1] and there is nothing to show that they were derived ultimately from Deutero-Isaiah.[2]

Conclusion

In these early extra-canonical documents there is nothing to suggest that the identification of Jesus with the Servant was widely known or used in the primitive Church. Only in one passage in the Epistle of Barnabas is the fifty-third chapter of Isaiah applied to Jesus, through whose sufferings Christians receive the forgiveness of their sins. Elsewhere the passage is taken, either merely as a prophecy of the fact of his sufferings, or as the description of the one whose example of humility Christians are exhorted to follow.

We have now examined the literature of the early Church up to the middle of the second century A.D., a period sufficiently long to show whether or not the failure of the New Testament writers to make much use of Isa. 53 was accidental; the paucity of positive evidence in the extra-canonical material supports the conclusion to which the evidence of the New Testament has already led us, that the early Church did not attach any great significance to the Servant passages, or regard them as the key to their understanding of the Atonement.

CHAPTER 6

THE CONCEPT OF SUFFERING

1. INTRODUCTION

In the last two chapters we have been concerned with the examination of individual passages in the New Testament and with their possible relationship, in language and thought, to Isa. 53. Before we attempt to investigate this evidence further, it will be appropriate in the present chapter to consider the theme of suffering in general, in order that this may form the background of our discussion in the final chapter. This vast subject, which merits further study, cannot be treated in detail here: it requires a separate investigation. Even in the light of material which is already to a great extent familiar, however, it should be possible to discover whether any alternative solution to the question of the influence of the Servant passages in the New Testament is suggested by the biblical and apocalyptic attitude to the problem of suffering. We shall, therefore, briefly examine this theme, first in the New Testament, and secondly in Jewish thought, without at the moment referring to the problem of the influence of the Servant concept. Since Jesus speaks repeatedly of the sufferings of the Son of Man, we must also consider the relationship of that figure to suffering in apocalyptic literature.

2. SUFFERING IN THE NEW TESTAMENT: THE SYNOPTIC GOSPELS

(a) The Sufferings of Jesus

The four principal predictions of his Passion which are attributed to Jesus in the Synoptic gospels have already been discussed in chapter 4.[1] We may note here a few of their outstanding characteristics.

(i) The predictions all contain a note of necessity: Jesus is announcing, not simply what he thinks will happen, but what he knows must happen. This is expressed in two forms: first, the vocabulary and grammatical structure of the sentence imply that Christ's death forms a part of the plan of God; second, this fact has been made known in the scriptures.

(ii) The passages all speak of the sufferings of the Son of Man.

(iii) None of the passages—except Matthew's addition 'for the forgiveness of sins' in 26. 28—connect Christ's sufferings with the forgiveness of sin.

Besides the actual predictions, there are many passages where Jesus speaks of his approaching death. While these sayings are not detailed expositions, they nevertheless suggest the attitude of Jesus to his sufferings. Here again we may note certain characteristics.

(i) These sayings, also, imply the necessity for Christ's death. Thus in the Gethsemane prayer (Mark 14. 34–6; Matt. 26. 38f.; Luke 22. 41f.) Jesus speaks of God's will being done. The metaphor which he uses there, of the 'cup' of suffering, is found again in Mark 10. 38f. (Matt. 20. 22f.), and is a common Old Testament metaphor for the destiny, good or bad, which God has ordained for the righteous or for the wicked.[1] His death is also a 'baptism' which he must go through (Mark 10. 38f.; Luke 12. 50). The tone of the sayings about the bridegroom who is taken away (Mark 2. 19f.; Matt. 9. 15; Luke 5. 34f.), the Son of Man who has come to serve and to give his life (Mark 10. 45; Matt. 20. 28), and the ointment which is used in preparation for his burial (Mark 14. 8; Matt. 26. 12), all imply that his death is inevitable: for Jesus, this must mean that it is the will of God.[2]

(ii) These passages do not refer to the Son of Man, except in Mark 10. 45 (Matt. 20. 28), and in Mark 14. 21 (Matt. 26. 24; Luke 22. 22), where the appeal by Mark and Matthew to what is 'written' reminds us of the four Passion predictions.[3]

(iii) None of these passages, except Mark 10. 45, offers any explanation as to the meaning of Christ's death.

(b) The Sufferings of Those Living before the Time of Christ

In some passages we find that Jesus refers to the sufferings of those who have preceded him. A notable example is his reference in Mark 9. 13 (Matt. 17. 12) to the sufferings of Elijah, which, like those of the Son of Man, were 'written' of him. The parable of the Wicked Husbandmen in Mark 12. 1–12 (Matt. 21. 33–46; Luke 20. 9–19) is clearly based, in its present form, upon the treatment which was accorded by Israel to the messengers whom God had sent to her. In Matt. 23. 29–36 (Luke 11. 47–51) we find a passage which speaks of the prophets and 'the righteous blood shed on earth, from the blood of Abel to the blood of Zechariah the son of Barachiah'. Matt. 23. 37–9 (Luke 13. 34f.) also speaks of the killing of the prophets.

It is noteworthy that these sufferings of the prophets are associated with those of Jesus himself. Thus the fulfilment of the sufferings foretold of Elijah confirms the forthcoming fulfilment of those foretold of the Son of Man. The parable of the Wicked Husbandmen suggests that Jesus saw his own sufferings as the climax to a whole series of persecutions. Even if this interpretation is due to the allegorization of the early Church, the parable itself shows that Jesus knew that God's final revelation was to be rejected, as all his previous appeals had been; he must have realized, therefore, that he, as the bearer of that revelation, must expect the same treatment as his predecessors.[1] Matthew's words in 23. 32, 'Fill up, then, the measure of your fathers', reflect the same belief, as do those in Luke 13. 33: 'it cannot be that a prophet should perish away from Jerusalem'.[2]

(c) *The Sufferings of the Disciples*

The gospel narrative makes it quite clear that Jesus expected that those who became his disciples would also have to undergo suffering. It is possible that he expected them to be killed with him. Whether or not this was so, however, he told his followers quite plainly that they must be prepared to meet with the same treatment and death as their Master; this warning is well summed up by the words in John 15. 20: 'If they persecuted me, they will persecute you.'

Thus we find the stern saying of Jesus, which is recorded twice by Matthew and Luke, that his disciples must be prepared, quite literally, to take up their cross (Mark 8. 34; Matt. 16. 24; Luke 9. 23; Matt. 10. 38; Luke 14. 27). They are warned that they will be subjected to persecution (Mark 13. 9–13; Matt. 24. 9–14; Luke 21. 12–19; Matt. 5. 10–12;[3] 10. 17–23); John and James are to share the same fate as Jesus (Mark 10. 39; Matt. 20. 23).

Once again we may note that the sufferings of others are associated with those of Jesus himself. In shouldering their cross, the disciples are following the example of Jesus; when they are persecuted, it is for his sake; they are to drink from the same cup and to undergo the same baptism. They will, however, also share in his glory, for when the Son of Man returns, then those who have been persecuted unjustly for the sake of Jesus will receive their reward. There can, indeed, be no entry into that glory except by the path of suffering (Mark 10. 37f.; Matt. 20. 21).

3. SUFFERING IN THE NEW TESTAMENT: BOOKS OTHER THAN THE SYNOPTIC GOSPELS

In the rest of the New Testament the Cross is at the centre of the Church's *kerygma*.[1] Here also we find that the sufferings of the prophets and of the followers of Christ are mentioned.

(a) The Sufferings of Jesus

(i) As in the Synoptic gospels, emphasis is laid upon the fact that the sufferings and death of Jesus were part of God's foreordained plan. In arguments with the Jews, it is natural that the apostles appealed to the scriptures for proof that the crucified Jesus could be the Messiah. The idea of the necessity for the Cross is found in Acts in the speeches of Peter (2. 23; 3. 18), the prayer of the Church (4. 28) and the arguments of Paul (17. 3; 26. 22f.). We may compare the teaching which Luke attributes to the Risen Christ himself in his gospel (Luke 24. 25-7; cf. *vv.* 45-7).

We have already noted that Paul speaks of Christ's death and resurrection as being 'in accordance with the scriptures',[2] and we have seen that his use of the verb παραδίδωμι probably implies the active purposes of God.[3] The same concept seems to underlie Rom. 5. 8; 8. 32 and Gal. 1. 4. The author of the Epistle to the Hebrews agrees with this fundamental idea, when he writes in 2. 10 that it was fitting that God should make Christ 'perfect through suffering' for the work of salvation.

The belief that Christ's death was part of the purpose of God is reflected in the fourth gospel by the statement of Jesus in 3. 14, that the Son of Man must be lifted up. In the prayer of Jesus in John 12. 27f., he rejects the thought that he might pray to be delivered from the hour of death. We see here the strengthening of the tradition that Jesus saw his death as part of the will of God; in the Gethsemane prayer in the Synoptics there is still a possibility that, after all, his death may not be necessary; but for John this suggestion is impossible, since the death of Jesus is seen as the purpose for which his whole life has been a preparation.

(ii) The death of Christ is almost always connected with his resurrection and exaltation. We should expect, indeed, that the apostles would be concerned to proclaim the fact of Christ's resurrection, and proof of this is found in Acts 2. 23 f., 36; 3. 14 f. In Acts 7. 55 f., Stephen, having spoken of the death of Jesus, immediately sees a vision of the exalted Son of Man at the right hand of God. This double motif of humiliation and exaltation appears repeatedly in the epistles of Paul[1] and underlies the emphasis on exaltation in Hebrews.[2] John, as we have already noted,[3] has developed this theme into an identification of the actual suffering with the resurrection and ascension.

(iii) The primitive *kerygma*, as represented in Acts, makes no connection between the sufferings of Christ and the forgiveness of sins, although it speaks of both.[4] This connection is found, however, in the New Testament epistles, whose writers clearly associated their experience of deliverance from sin with the Passion of their Lord: this fact is expressed in such passages as Rom. 4. 25; 1 Cor. 15. 3; Heb. 9. 26; 1 Pet. 2. 24 and 1 John 1. 7.

(b) *The Sufferings of Those living before the Time of Christ*

As in the Synoptic gospels, reference is sometimes made to those who suffered before the time of Christ. The most outstanding exposition of this theme is found in Heb. 11, where the author, in speaking of the meaning of faith, describes the example which was set in time past by various heroes of Israel from the time of Abel down to the Maccabaean martyrs. Many of these figures met with opposition, death and suffering, but remained obedient to God. Through this impressive list the author builds up to the supreme example of faith, Jesus himself: once again, therefore, the connection is made between the sufferings of Jesus and those of his predecessors; the association is clearly expressed in *v.* 26, where the sufferings of Moses are described as the reproach of Christ.

The same theme is found in Acts 7 where, in the speech of Stephen, the treatment which was accorded to Joseph, Moses and the prophets by Israel prefigures the rejection of Christ. In *vv.* 51–2 Stephen accuses his hearers of killing Jesus, just as their fathers had killed the prophets who foretold his coming.

St Paul, too, uses this concept in Gal. 4. 21–30, when he sees, in the persecution of Christians by Jews and Judaizers, a continuation of the old persecution of Israel by the Gentiles.

(c) The Sufferings of the early Christians

References to the sufferings of Christians are numerous in the New Testament, as we might expect. The Acts of the Apostles tells of one persecution after another; Paul speaks frequently of the suffering which he himself has undergone in the course of his ministry; the epistles are often concerned with the sufferings which the Church is called upon to endure.

It is noteworthy that once again these sufferings of his followers are linked with those of Jesus himself. In Acts 5. 41, after they had been beaten for preaching in the name of Jesus, we find Peter and John 'rejoicing that they were counted worthy to suffer dishonour for the name'. In Acts 9. 16 it is said that Paul is to suffer many things for the sake of the Lord's name, and we find that this prophecy has been fulfilled in 2 Cor. 6. 4-10 and 11. 23-9. When Paul speaks of suffering or persecution, it is 'for the sake of Christ' (Phil. 1. 29), or 'for the cross of Christ' (Gal. 6. 12). There is, indeed, an even deeper association than this between the sufferings of Christ and those of his followers: each shares in the experience of the other. All three accounts of Paul's conversion contain the words 'Why do you persecute me?...I am Jesus, whom you are persecuting' (Acts 9. 4f.; 22. 7f.; 26. 14f.). Paul himself, in his epistles, speaks of suffering with Christ (Rom. 8. 17), and of sharing his sufferings (Phil. 3. 10); the sufferings of the apostles are the manifestation of the death of Jesus (2 Cor. 4. 10), and persecution is itself the 'stumbling-block of the cross' (Gal. 5. 11).[1]

Those who share in the sufferings of Christ, however, will also share in his glory. This belief is well summed up by Paul in Rom. 8. 16-18: 'We are children of God, and if children, then heirs, heirs of God and fellow heirs with Christ, provided we suffer with him in order that we may also be glorified with him. I consider that the sufferings of this present time are not worth comparing with the glory that is to be revealed to us.' It is reflected also in passages such as 2 Cor. 4. 17; 1 Pet. 5. 1, 10 and 2 Tim. 2. 11 f.

4. THE CONCEPT OF SUFFERING IN JEWISH THOUGHT

The perplexity of the problem of suffering for the Hebrew is apparent in the many attempts in the Old Testament and in subsequent writings to find a solution. The orthodox attitude to the question was the doctrine of retribution, which has its roots in the story of the Fall in Gen. 3: if man sins, punishment will follow, because God is morally good. The natural, though illogical, conclusion was drawn that if a man suffered, then he must have sinned.

This orthodox teaching is set out in Ps. 32, where the speaker claims that his sufferings ceased when he confessed the sin which he had committed.[1] The pattern of life was not always so conveniently arranged, however, as the author of Ps. 73 discovered; while this psalm also supports the official view, and claims that ultimately the righteous will be rewarded and the wicked destroyed, the author confesses that the present prosperity of the wicked and the suffering of the righteous, in which he himself is personally involved, had at one time led him to doubt the truth of the doctrine.

The realization that life often failed to support this explanation of suffering resulted in the search for more adequate solutions. The most notable attempts in the Old Testament to solve the problem are found in the books of Habakkuk and of Job, in Isa. 52-3, and in Ps. 73. None of their authors, however, was able to find a logical answer to the problem: Habakkuk, like the author of Ps. 73, finds satisfaction in trust in God; Deutero-Isaiah discovers the concept of redemptive suffering; Job's problem loses its significance in the final vision of Yahweh. We may note that in all these cases the righteous receive, or are promised, ultimate vindication and restoration: indeed, the final glory in Job and in Isa. 52 is as overwhelming in scale as the suffering.

The problem of suffering, far from diminishing as time passed, became still more acute. The bitterness of the problem lay, for many, in the fact that while they themselves were suffering, the godless and wicked were flourishing, and indeed profiting at the expense of the righteous. Thus we find in the Psalms frequent references to the sufferings of the righteous man, who is persecuted by his enemies.[2] In the post-Exilic period Israel also became subject to increasing persecution through external domination; the situation at this time is well pictured in the four books of Maccabees. In this period, not only were the righteous subject to persecution, but it was actually on account of their righteousness, and obedience to the Law, that they suffered.

The author of the book of Wisdom was clearly concerned with the problem of suffering in this situation.[1] In chapters 1–5 he declares that the present triumph of the wicked over the righteous is short-lived, and he describes the final reward of the righteous and the punishment of their tormentors. In 3. 5 f. he suggests that the suffering has fallen on the righteous as a trial of their worth; ultimately it is they who will, under Yahweh, become the judges and rulers of the nations. In Wisdom, hope of any reasonable restoration or reward in this life is abandoned; under foreign influence, the solution has been sought in a future life where rewards and punishments are at last in accordance with men's deeds.

It was this problem of suffering and persecution which gave rise to the apocalyptic movement. We have already noted the attempts which were made by the authors of the books of 1 and 2 Baruch and 2 Esdras to deal with the dilemma:[2] their solution, the hope of a glorious age to come, is the apocalyptic version of the general belief in an ultimate vindication and compensation for the righteous. If at present Israel were persecuted by her neighbours, and the Jews who remained faithful to the Torah were persecuted by their own countrymen, then, if the moral justice of God were to be upheld, the answer must be found in some future restoration of the righteous, when they would receive the reward of their obedience and the consolation for their sufferings, when their enemies would receive eternal punishment, and they themselves would be exalted to a position of honour and glory.[3]

Suffering and poverty, therefore, could no longer be explained as the punishment of the wicked; instead, in unofficial circles at least, it came to be regarded as the frequent lot of the righteous man who is perfectly obedient to the will of God. It is noteworthy that it was at this time that the legends about the deaths of the prophets grew up; this is the background of those New Testament references to their sufferings which receive no explanation from the Old Testament. Vivid examples of these descriptions of the sufferings of the prophets are to be found in the apocryphal 'Lives of the Prophets'.[4]

5. THE SON OF MAN

The phrase 'Son of Man', while it is as strange in Greek as it is in English, is a perfectly normal idiom in Hebrew or Aramaic. In the Old Testament is is found in two senses: normally the phrase conveys the meaning 'man', and is used as a synonym for the word אִישׁ; although not common elsewhere, it occurs frequently in Ezekiel. On the one occasion where the phrase is used in Aramaic, however, in Dan. 7. 13, it has a symbolic meaning, and stands for the saints of the Most High. It was from Daniel that the phrase passed into the apocalyptic vocabulary, and this symbolic use is the one that is normally employed in the book of Enoch, where the phrase first becomes prominent.

In Daniel, the phrase is found in the author's first dream, in which he sees four beasts which are, respectively, like a lion, like a bear, like a leopard, and the beast with horns: Daniel next has a vision of God, who is sitting in judgement; following this judgement, the last beast is destroyed and the others are stripped of their power, while one who is like a man is presented to the 'Ancient of Days' and is given 'dominion and glory and kingdom' for ever. The dream is followed by the interpretation: 'These four great beasts are four kings who shall arise out of the earth. But the saints of the Most High shall receive the kingdom, and possess the kingdom for ever, for ever and ever.'[1]

In view of this clear explanation of the meaning of the vision, any attempt to interpret the 'one like a Son of Man' as the Messiah is quite unjustified: as the four beasts represent the four kings, so the final figure represents the 'saints of the most high'. The fact that the beasts represent individuals, not nations, does not mean that there is any inconsistency: the king, as we have already seen,[2] was the symbol of his people, and the interchangeability of the terms 'king' and 'kingdom' is seen in *v.* 22 of the following chapter in Daniel. Moreover, one text of the Aramaic, together with the LXX, Theodotion, and the Vulgate, reads 'kingdoms' in 7. 17.[3] Here, therefore, we have another example of the oscillation in Hebrew thought between the corporate and the individual, and the representation of the many by the one. Furthermore, this phenomenon explains how, although the 'one like a son of man' in Daniel clearly represents the saints of Israel, it was possible at an early stage for the figure to be transformed into an individual.[4]

Like the rest of the book, this vision of Daniel is concerned also with the question of persecution and suffering: the second beast is told 'Arise, devour much flesh', and it is said of the fourth that 'it devoured and broke in pieces, and stamped the residue with its feet'. The word 'residue' translates the Aramaic שְׁאָרָה, which is an emphatic form of שְׁאָר; this latter word appears also in Hebrew, and is derived from the verb שָׁאַר, to remain; both the noun and the participle of the verb were used in the technical sense of 'Remnant'.[1] Now it is generally agreed that the fourth beast represents Greece, so that the residue which it is described as trampling down will be those who suffered under the rule of that nation: in fact, the sufferings of this period fell on those who remained faithful to the Law and refused to compromise with Hellenism —in other words, on the very people who saw themselves as the faithful Remnant of Israel. After the triumph of the beasts, however, Daniel sees the Ancient of Days presiding over a court of judgement, and as a result the four beasts are overthrown and the kingdom is given to the saints of God. Thus dominion and power are taken away from the other nations and given to the Remnant—those who hitherto have been trampled underfoot, but now are vindicated as the saints of the Most High.

The Son of Man in 1 Enoch is a far more complex problem, and many interpretations, both individual and collective, have been offered. One thing, however, is certain: whatever other influences may have played their part in shaping its character, and however far it may have developed, the figure comes ultimately from Dan. 7; the connection between that chapter and Enoch 46, where the title 'Son of Man' is first used in this book, is indisputable. This fact alone suggests that there is at the basis of the concept some relationship between the Son of Man in Enoch and the saints of God whom he represents in Daniel. This relationship is confirmed by an examination of the theme of the Similitudes, and the occurrences of the title there.

The second book of 1 Enoch consists of three Similitudes, and the main theme of them all is the same: the wicked are to be judged and condemned to destruction, but the righteous, whom they have oppressed, are to receive blessing and honour. This is, in fact, an elaborate enlargement of the theme treated in Dan. 7. 9–18: the present triumph of the Gentiles and the subjugation of Israel, which were described in Dan. 7. 1–8, have dropped out of the picture, and the coming

Judgement, with the consequent reward and punishment, has become all-important. Into this pattern comes the figure of the Son of Man, now far more important than in Daniel; to him the titles of 'The Elect One', 'The Righteous One' and 'The Anointed One' are also given.

The passages where these titles occur are as follows:

(a) The Righteous One. 38. 1–2.
(b) The Righteous and Elect One. 53. 6–7.
(c) The Elect One. 39. 6–7; 40. 5; 45. 3–5; 49. 2–3; 51. 2–5; 52. 6, 9; 55. 4; 61. 5–8, 10; 62. 1–2.
(d) The Son of Man. 46. 1–4; 48. 2–7; 62. 5–9, 13–15; 69. 26–9; 70. 1; 71. 14–17.[1]
(e) The Anointed. 48. 10; 52. 4.

Although the title 'The Righteous One' is used so rarely, it should be noted that righteousness is one of the characteristics of the Son of Man, and is frequently mentioned, as, for example, in 46. 3: 'This is the Son of Man who hath righteousness and with whom dwelleth righteousness.'[2]

An examination of these passages shows that the predominant feature of this figure, by whatever title he is designated, is that he is to be Judge: for on the one hand he is to condemn the wicked, and to destroy the kings and mighty of the earth, and on the other he is to ensure that the righteous and the elect receive their reward. As a prelude to this judgement the Son of Man is to cast down the kings from their thrones; as a sequel he is to dwell on a renewed earth with the elect ones. This activity will be a decisive event: the phrase 'on that day' often occurs, and there is even a reference to 'the day of the Elect One';[3] this would appear to be a continuation of the idea of the prophetic 'Day of Yahweh'. The fact that it is now the Son of Man who is to be Judge, and no longer the Ancient of Days, as in Daniel, together with the constant reiteration of the idea of his enthronement, shows that he has become important as the representative of Yahweh.[4]

The activity of the Son of Man, therefore, is inextricably bound up with the theme of the whole of this second book of 1 Enoch. He is most intimately concerned with both the reward of the righteous ones and the destruction of those who have persecuted them. His work of judgement, however, is not performed by an outsider, but by one who has the closest affinity with those whom he helps, for he, like them, is

THE CONCEPT OF SUFFERING

'righteous' and 'elect'. Moreover, almost every time that the Son of Man is mentioned, it is in connection with these righteous and elect ones; thus when they appear he appears, and where they live he is to live:[1] their life and salvation, in fact, seem to depend in some way upon him, so that in chapter 48. 4, 7, we are not surprised to find that

> He shall be a staff to the righteous whereon to stay themselves and not fall....
> For he hath preserved the lot of the righteous....
> For in his name they are saved, and according to his good pleasure hath it been in regard to their life.

Whatever decision we make concerning the Son of Man in Enoch—and it is impossible to consider here the many other aspects of the problem—we must at least recognize, not only that the figure derives ultimately from Dan. 7, but also that it retains certain of the corporate associations of that passage. It may be that here again we have an example of the typical Hebrew oscillation between the ideas of individual and community, for the features of representation and close association are certainly present.[2] The society, as in Daniel, is again the community of the righteous, or the Remnant of Israel; but whereas in Daniel's vision the societary element was undoubtedly dominant, in Enoch it is the individual element which has prevailed.[3]

While many scholars have attempted to show that 'Son of Man' was a Messianic title at the time of Jesus, there is little evidence for such an assumption.[4] The earliest witness to a Messianic interpretation of Daniel is not found until the third century A.D. As for Enoch, the most that can be said is that the Son of Man shares many of the characteristics of the Messiah; this, however, as we have already noted in considering the relationship between the Son of Man and the Servant, is not proof of identification. W. Manson[5] has drawn attention to certain characteristics which are shared by the Servant, the Messiah and the Son of Man; but none of these features belongs exclusively to these three figures. Thus the word 'anointed', which is used twice of the Son of Man in Enoch, is not necessarily a reference to the 'Messiah'; originally, the verb meant no more than the anointing of some individual—prophet, priest or king—to a particular office.[6] Although in the Old Testament the title is used most commonly of the king,[7] it could be applied also to an individual with some especial task,[1] and even to the nation.[2] Righteousness is no more than we expect to find in these three figures: it is a quality which was always demanded of any ruler in Israel, and one of the features of Yahweh's own reign.[3] The choice of the Son of Man, like that of the Servant, has its background in the persistent Old Testament theme of election.[4] Even those phrases in 1 Enoch which seem to have been taken directly from the Old Testament pictures of Messiah and Servant do not convey the essential features of those figures:[5] it is, in fact, these essential elements which are missing from the portrait of the Son of Man. Thus there is no reference to the Son of Man being subjected to any kind of suffering, such as was endured by the Servant; he is not himself in need of vindication, but is the vindicator of others; he is the Saviour, not of the wicked, whom on the contrary he condemns, but of the righteous. Similarly, the essential features of the Messiah are missing from the Enochian figure: nowhere is he said to be of the Davidic line; his function is that of Judge, rather than that of Ruler: the Son of Man, in fact, takes over the role of Yahweh, rather than that of the Messiah, and his importance and centrality are in striking contrast to the position of the Messiah, whose rule was always kept subordinate to, and quite distinct from, that of Yahweh. In view of these fundamental differences, it is more reasonable to suppose that the features which these three figures share are drawn from a common source,[6] or were borrowed from each other without any intention of identification, rather than that the author of the Parables in 1 Enoch has consciously tried to combine the figures of Messiah and Servant, and in so doing has made use only of what they share in common, thus neglecting their distinctive attributes.

Finally, any direct equation of Son of Man and Messiah makes nonsense of the evidence of the gospels, which shows clearly that neither the disciples of Jesus, nor the Jews in general, understood the title 'Son of Man' as a Messianic term.

CHAPTER 7

THE SERVANT CONCEPT IN THE THOUGHT OF JESUS AND THE EARLY CHURCH

1. THE RESULTS OF OUR INVESTIGATION

The evidence which is relevant to our study has now been investigated, and it is necessary to consider what conclusions may be drawn from a comparison of the results.

(a) *The Old Testament*

An examination of the Old Testament evidence, although not having a direct bearing upon the problem of the use of the Servant concept in New Testament times, suggested that the original meaning of the Servant 'Songs' was inextricably bound up with the whole message of Deutero-Isaiah. The originality of the prophet's thought owed much to the time in which he lived, since he was able to interpret the disasters of the past and the sorrows of the present in the light of the glory which he foresaw for the immediate future. Like his near-contemporaries, Jeremiah and Ezekiel, Deutero-Isaiah speaks of the Restoration of his people: for him, however, this Restoration is imminent, and the signs of the New Age are about to be fulfilled.

Since for Deutero-Isaiah the Return is all-important, there seemed to be every justification for interpreting the Servant Songs in terms of the same theme. In spite of the highly individualized characteristics of the Servant, we saw no reason to isolate him as a figure in separation from the other oracles: since the rest of Deutero-Isaiah's prophecies were about Israel, we expected the Songs to be about Israel. If, indeed, the Servant Songs may be distinguished at all from the other oracles, it is because they describe the nature of the active mission of Israel, whether this to is be fulfilled by Israel herself or by some representative of the nation. Neither form nor theme nor context of the Songs suggested that it was necessary to interpret the Servant in terms of any other figure. The sufferings of the Servant, therefore, are the sufferings of Israel, or of the righteous within Israel, who has now at last learnt to be submissive to the will of Yahweh: having learnt obedience through suffering, Israel is to discover that the very instrument of discipline is to be transformed, through the coming exaltation, into the means of accomplishing her mission to the nations.

(b) Judaism

Jewish literature did not provide any evidence that a Messianic interpretation of the sufferings described in Isa. 50 and 53 was ever made in the pre-Christian era. While it is possible that the descriptions of the Servant's triumphs may have been applied to the Messiah during this period, the doctrine of a suffering Messiah still seems to have been foreign to Jewish thought. There is no evidence to show that the Servant Songs had as yet assumed any important role in Judaism; on the contrary, there is no mention of 'the Servant' as such. While the suffering of Israel and of her righteous members continued to be a pressing problem, the solution of Deutero-Isaiah seems to have been largely ignored.

(c) The Synoptic Gospels

Our examination of the Synoptic gospels revealed a considerable number of possible references to the oracles of Deutero-Isaiah. Many of these are associated with the person and work of Jesus. Thus Mark sums up the activity of Jesus in the word εὐαγγέλιον, a term which we traced back to בשׂר, the Hebrew root used by Deutero-Isaiah for the proclamation of Yahweh's salvation. Mark introduces his gospel with a description of John the Baptist, the forerunner of Jesus, applying to him the words which Deutero-Isaiah used to announce the coming redemption by Yahweh. In all the gospels, many of the features of Christ's ministry are found to fulfil the details which are foretold as forming part of that salvation, and the parallels with Deutero-Isaiah's promises are echoed in words and phrases taken from his oracles. The healing of the diseased (Luke 4. 18f.; 7. 22), the casting out of demons (Mark 3. 27), the gift of the Spirit (Mark 1. 8, 10), the gathering of the Elect (Mark 13. 27), are all part of the New Era which is, we are to infer, inaugurated in the person of Jesus.

There is, however, no certain reference to the Songs themselves, which in any way suggests that Jesus was identified with a Messianic interpretation of the 'Servant', or which is concerned with the significance of his suffering and death. While Matthew quotes from both the first and the fourth Songs, it is with reference to Jesus' command of silence to those whom he heals, and—a surprising use of Isa. 53—to the healing miracles themselves. Matthew's partiality for Old Testament prophecies suggests that the significance of these quotations lies in his desire to find passages which foreshadow particular events, and not in any intention to identify Jesus with the Servant of the Songs. A similar motive would seem to lie behind Luke's use of a phrase from Isa. 53 in 22. 37: no doctrinal significance is attached to the passage, which has apparently been used to stress the necessity for the things which were being done. The use which is made of these quotations from Deutero-Isaiah does not support the suggestion that they imply an identification of Jesus with the 'Servant'. It is truer to say that these passages, together with other allusions to Deutero-Isaiah in the gospels, refer to the redemptive activity of God himself. The signs of the New Era which Jeremiah and Ezekiel foretold, and which Deutero-Isaiah believed to be imminent, are now at last being fulfilled in the person of Jesus. These references must therefore be understood against the larger background of the significance which Deutero-Isaiah's whole message of redemption held for the mind of Jesus.

If, however, the definite quotations from Deutero-Isaiah do not suggest that Jesus thought of himself as 'Servant', we must be very wary of regarding possible linguistic references as 'proof' that he did so. There is, indeed, no justification for assuming that individual words, even though they may be thought to derive from the Servant Songs, point to such an identification. Equally, there is no basis for assuming that a possible reference to one 'Song' implies *ipso facto* the use of the concepts found in all four.[1] For if there is no evidence that the Servant figure, as such, played an important role in the thought of Jesus, there is no guarantee that there was any link in his mind between one 'Song' and another.

Our examination showed clearly that no sure reference to any of the Servant Songs exists in those passages where Jesus speaks of the *meaning* of his death: there is no evidence that either he or the evangelists had the suffering of the Servant in mind. Even in the passages where he announces the *fact* of his approaching death, there is no indication that the third and fourth Songs held for him any particular significance: the reference is in every case a general one to the necessity which is laid upon him by the divine will, and which is expressed in scripture as a whole.

Finally, we may note that the Synoptic writers are all agreed in their evidence. While it is true that the quotations from the Songs are found only in Matthew and Luke, they are not used in a way that suggests any deviation from Mark's understanding of Jesus. In spite of this increased use of the Servant Songs in Matthew and Luke, as compared with Mark, there is no indication that they have in any way distorted the primitive tradition, or have done more than draw in clearer detail, as they do continually, the parallel between the events of Jesus' life and passages from the Old Testament.

(*d*) *The early Church*

The account of the beliefs of the early Christians which is given in the Acts of the Apostles does not suggest that the primitive community ever thought of Jesus as 'the Servant' of Deutero-Isaiah. Nor is there any evidence that the author of the book himself made such an identification. We found no reason for linking either the title 'παῖς' or the term 'δίκαιος' with Deutero-Isaiah in particular, nor for understanding the references to the prophets as pointing only to Isa. 50 and 53. The use which is made of Isa. 49. 6 and of 42. 6f. in Acts 13 and 26 shows clearly that no identification of Jesus with any 'Servant figure' is intended; the concepts have been found to be relevant to both Jesus and Paul.

These facts are the more significant, since in Acts 8 we find a quotation from Isa. 53 actually applied to the sufferings and death of Christ. While it is evident from the context, however, that Philip interpreted the passage as a description of the Passion of his Lord, this by no means implies that he must have in mind an equation of the nature: Jesus = the Servant. For it must be stressed once again that the words which are quoted speak only of the *fact* of the sufferings and death of the Servant, and do not mention their *significance*. These facts, however, are precisely those features which were *already present in the primitive* of the Church. Once this comparison has been made, however, it is easy to imagine hints at the Servant concept in the New Testament where none is intended. Our understanding of New Testament thought will not be seriously affected, so long as these linguistic similarities are regarded merely as references to Old Testament passages, which were seen to be relevant to the facts of Christ's life and death; centuries of Christian thought about the Atonement, however, have led critics to understand them as implying a whole Christological doctrine based on the identification of Jesus with the Servant. Much of the so-called 'evidence' for a New Testament Servant-Christology is therefore based upon a fundamental error: for in the absence of any passage in the primitive tradition which clearly applies Isa. 53 to the *meaning* of Christ's death, and not merely the *fact* of that event, it is impossible to accept linguistic similarity as evidence that any connection was intended *doctrinally* with the Servant concept; if quotations from Deutero-Isaiah are used only as 'proof-texts', we have no right to assume that mere words and phrases were intended to bear any other significance.

How was it, then, that apparently neither Jesus nor his disciples made use of an idea which to us seems so obvious? Why did both Jesus, who spoke of the necessity of his death, and the early Church, which grappled with the perplexing problem of his Passion, and actually quoted the fourth Servant Song in their apologetic, fail to identify him with the Servant?

The solution to this problem would seem to lie in the fact that modern scholarship, in over-estimating the importance of the Servant concept for Jesus and the early Church, has also inevitably exaggerated the part played by the same concept in contemporary Judaism. Consequently, too much emphasis has been placed, first upon the figure of the Servant himself, and secondly upon his experience of suffering.

(*a*) *The Servant 'Figure'*

It will be remembered that in discussing the interpretation of the Servant Songs in Jewish literature, it was found that the Servant theme played a very small part indeed in the thought of the centuries B.C.: not only was there no evidence for a Messianic interpretation of the Servant figure, but there were no references to 'the Servant', and very little use was made of the idea of vicarious suffering. It was suggested that the failure to use the ideas of the fourth Servant Song was due, in part, to the inability of Deutero-Isaiah's successors to combine the hope of future exaltation and triumph for Israel with the wider vision which included the other nations of the world.

There is, however, yet another reason for the absence of the Servant image from Jewish writings. This lies in the fact that the 'neglect' of the Servant in Judaism is apparent only, in so far as the concept of the figure which it presupposes rests upon a false evaluation of the original text. Ever since Duhm first isolated the Servant Songs, modern criticism has been so obsessed by the problem of the identity of the Servant that it has overlooked the possibility that the question it has set itself to answer may be a false one: for to ask 'Who is the Servant?' is to assume the existence of some particular figure—or possibly several particular figures—entitled 'Servant of Yahweh'. The constant posing of this question has thus conjured up some mysterious image, an unknown x who has to be identified. We have to ask, however, whether this picture is true to the original thought-world of the author: was there, in fact, ever a 'Servant' in the sense which is now attached to this concept?

Whatever our interpretation of the Servant passages, it is clear that the nation, group or person which is described as 'Servant of Yahweh', must have existed in the mind of the author before the designation 'Servant': he, at any rate, did not start with the enigmatic title 'Servant', and then seek some figure to fit it. This fact is so obvious that its implications are often overlooked; for if it is the figure, and not the title, which is primary, this surely suggests that the words 'my Servant' may be meant, not as an independent designation, but as a description of one part of the character of the person or nation so described, or as an indication of their relationship to Yahweh. This shift in emphasis may seem slight, but it points us, not to a 'Servant figure' as he is normally understood, but to the concept of someone who, because of the quality of his life, may, like Moses and David, be described as a true Servant of God.

Our examination of the Servant passages themselves has already led us to believe that they are firmly embedded in their context, and that isolation of them from Deutero-Isaiah's other oracles must lead to a misinterpretation of his meaning. If we believe that the 'Servant' of the Songs is Israel, however, this strongly strengthens our contention that the words 'my Servant' are intended to express, not an independent title, but a quality of the person who is so described. While Israel is addressed as 'Servant' in the oracles outside the Songs, she is also spoken of in terms far less complimentary! Clearly the title 'Servant', as it applies to Israel, cannot cover her whole character. We have suggested that the Servant Songs were the expression of Deutero-Isaiah's vision of the nature of Israel's vocation: it is therefore not surprising to find that here, where she fulfils the mission which God has given her, and becomes finally obedient to his will, she is addressed by the term of honour 'my Servant'. Thus the words represent, not a concrete figure, for whom an identification must be sought, but the qualities of an already existing figure, the people who serve their God in obedience to his strange plan: the primary concept is not 'The Servant' of modern terminology, but Israel *as* a servant of Yahweh.

Pre-Christian Judaism was, therefore, true after all to the intention of Deutero-Isaiah. The absence of the title 'Servant' in any reference to his oracles shows that the Jews did not interpret the words as a proper name: there are no references to 'the Servant' because for them there *was* no 'Servant'. They were surely right in assuming that Deutero-Isaiah never intended to use the term independently, but only in the sense in which it is employed elsewhere in the Old Testament. Here, therefore, we find an answer to the problem why Jesus was not identified with the Servant. It was for the simple reason that there was not, and never had been, a 'Servant figure' with whom to identify him. Moses, David, Israel—all were 'servants of Yahweh', and in Deutero-Isaiah, as in the rest of the Old Testament, the term was but an additional title of honour given to one who already had a name. Thus it was not a particular figure which became lost in these centuries B.C., but the concept of Israel's vocation to be the Servant of Yahweh: the theme of the Servant Songs is missing from Judaism because Israel did not fulfil her mission, and forgot that she was called to be 'a light to the Gentiles'.

The evidence of Jewish literature thus offers an explanation of the absence of the title 'Servant' in the gospels. The gospels themselves, like all writings prior to the third century A.D., continue the normal

Jewish view of the term, which is true to that of Deutero-Isaiah himself. The words 'Thy Servant' are indeed used of Jesus in Acts. It will be remembered, however, that we saw no reason to suppose that they were, in the first instance, intended to apply to the passages in Deutero-Isaiah, but concluded that unless we found evidence to show that the 'Servant' was a living concept in Judaism at this time, the words must be regarded as a continuation of the general Old Testament usage. Since we now believe the 'Servant' to be non-existent as an independent figure, we may presume that in Acts, as indeed in the Servant Songs themselves, the title is a general one.

We must conclude, therefore, that the traditional belief that Jesus saw himself as the 'Suffering Servant' not only lacks any sufficient evidence in the New Testament, but is based upon an incorrect interpretation of the Jewish concept. The present position of deadlock which has been reached in discussion of the New Testament use of the Servant theme is scarcely surprising, since the approach which presupposes the existence of a 'Servant' is fundamentally false. The solution to the problem can thus no longer be sought in terms of a straightforward answer to the question whether Jesus was identified with the Servant.

(b) The Suffering of the Servant

The second fact which has led modern scholars to exaggerate the importance of the Servant Songs is the failure to consider them in the context of other passages which deal with a similar situation. While it is true that Deutero-Isaiah's solution to the problem of suffering is far more profound than those of his successors, the Servant's experience of persecution is by no means unusual: it is the interpretation of that experience that is unique. The fact that the Christian normally turns to the Old Testament for his knowledge of Jewish thought may cause us to forget the great influence which the apocryphal literature played in the time of Christ. This literature was undoubtedly popular during this period, and it was here, in particular, that the problem of persecution was debated, and the apocalyptic answer given. The argument which is so often advanced, that only in Isa. 53 could Jesus have found the reason for his death, ignores not only the important references to suffering in the Psalms, but also the existence of non-biblical Jewish literature which, although subordinate to the books which came to be regarded as 'canonical', nevertheless had a considerable popular appeal in the first century A.D.

The Servant passages have been seized upon by Christian thinkers because, although we have found no evidence to suppose that the sufferings of the Servant were ever interpreted of the Messiah in pre-Christian Judaism, they are nevertheless clearly open to a Messianic interpretation once the figure of the Servant has been isolated. The element in the Servant Songs which has appealed to Christian exegetes is, of course, the vicarious character of the Servant's sufferings. Since, however, we have found no evidence that this distinguishing feature of *vicarious* suffering was significant for either Jesus or the primitive community, there is no reason to suppose that these passages held any particular importance for them merely because they spoke of suffering as such, a feature which, after all, they share with many other passages.

3. THE PATTERN OF SUFFERING AND EXALTATION

If, then, the evidence is overwhelmingly against the view that Jesus thought of himself as 'the Servant', and if there are good reasons to explain this fact, are we to conclude that Jesus made no use at all of the Servant concept, or was he in fact influenced by the Servant passages, while not actually thinking of himself as their fulfilment? To answer this problem we must consider briefly the relationship between the theme of suffering and the words of Jesus about his own person and work.

The gospels are agreed that Jesus spoke of the Son of Man, a figure who was in some way closely associated with Jesus himself. It has frequently been commented upon that the overwhelming majority of cases where this title is used occur after Peter's confession at Caesarea Philippi, and that almost all are connected with either suffering or future exaltation.[1] The relationship of this title to the events at Caesarea Philippi is of particular significance, since it was immediately after Peter's declaration that Jesus was the Messiah, that Jesus himself first spoke of the sufferings of the Son of Man. The conclusion is inevitable that Jesus was deliberately rejecting the popular conception of Messiahship: while he did not deny that he was the Messiah, he clearly found that the title was a misleading one, since the common idea of Messiahship, which led to Peter's rebuke of Jesus, was quite different from Jesus' own understanding of his work.

Traditional Christianity has been reluctant to believe that Jesus' thought about himself could have been seriously influenced by apocalyptic literature. It was, however, the apocalyptic movement which was popular in the everyday life of first-century Palestine, since it was supremely relevant to the conditions of that period. The situation was the same as that which had given rise to the book of Daniel and its successors, and this literature accordingly had a strong appeal. We may believe, therefore, that as a child Jesus would have become very familiar with these stirring stories. We have already discussed the pre-Christian use of the phrase 'Son of Man', an apocalyptic term which is developed by the author of the Similitudes in 1 Enoch from the phrase in Dan. 7. In Daniel, the most popular of the apocalyptic books, the climax is reached in the revelation of the Son of Man in 7. 12: it is this verse which Jesus quotes when he finally makes a public acknowledgement of his Messiahship.[1]

This apocalyptic background provides a ready explanation of the many passages in the gospels which speak of the future glory and exaltation of the Son of Man. There are, however, a similarly large number of passages which speak of his sufferings, and it is these which have led scholars to speak of the Son of Man being 'reinterpreted' in terms of the Suffering Servant. Is there, however, nothing in Daniel itself which associates the Son of Man with suffering, and could thus explain these words of Jesus? We have already seen that the whole book of Daniel is concerned with the problem of suffering: it is one of the first apocalyptic answers to the trials of Israel. While it is true that the Son of Man himself does not suffer, he is the symbol of the righteous Remnant, the restored people of God, who are at present enduring afflictions: the Son of Man thus represents those who have passed through persecution; the righteous community which is suffering today will tomorrow be the glorified Son of Man.

Whether or not we believe that Jesus used the term as a corporate designation, this Jewish background suggests that the phrase has some kind of corporate significance; this is strongly supported by the close association which we have seen to exist between the sufferings and glory of Jesus and of his disciples—the very themes which are spoken of in connection with the Son of Man. We may expect the Son of Man in the gospels, therefore, to be concerned with the same community as he represents in Judaism. In Daniel, the Son of Man is the symbol of God's righteous people; in Enoch he is their head. In the gospels, we find that Jesus is gathering round him a small group who are the nucleus of the true Israel.

We have already noted that Jesus himself is addressed by the heavenly voice in words which were used, in the Old Testament, to describe Israel.[1] During the course of his ministry, Jesus calls twelve disciples, the symbol of the twelve tribes of Israel, to be his close companions. It is round this small group that Jesus gathers the true members of Israel, those who are to be the elect with the Son of Man. This is the kernel of the community which is to inherit the benefits of the New Age, when the sufferings of the Son of Man accomplish the redemption which brings about the Second Exodus;[2] this is the Israel with whom the new covenant in Jesus' blood is made.

Those who are called to be members of this new community are not, however, as we might expect, the 'righteous' in the present society. The beginning of the gospel of Jesus Christ, says Mark, was the preaching of John the Baptist. John, the eschatological prophet, calls people to repentance; now that Judgement is near, the privilege of birth is no longer enough to make one a true 'son of Abraham'. Jesus, too, has come to call sinners to repentance; while few of those who already thought themselves 'righteous' followed him, the outcasts of society were willing to do so. The Pharisees held that the sign of the Remnant of Israel, the righteous members of the community, was the keeping of the Law, and in particular the Sabbath; but Jesus, gathering the true Remnant around him, declared that he had come to fulfil the Law, and that the Son of Man was Lord of the Sabbath.

Jesus' attitude to the political situation of his time was reflected, as in Daniel, in the figure of the Son of Man. While he recognized himself as the chosen Messiah, the Son of David, he does not use these titles as self-designations, because he realizes that the deliverance of Israel will come, not with the movement of armies and the overthrow of Rome by any human agency, but by the direct activity of God. Thus in rejecting the political role of the Messiah, and instead attributing to God the activity which will lead to the destruction of his enemies, Jesus must choose the alternative which was offered by Jewish apocalyptic: the way which leads to the revelation of the Son of Man. Ultimately, the Son of Man is a greater figure than the Messiah, for he is both Judge of all men, and Saviour of his people. But the path which leads to this revelation is the path of suffering for the righteous community: before the final consummation the measure of suffering must be fulfilled, and the righteous pass through the fire of persecution. With the coming of Jesus the New Age foretold by Jeremiah, Ezekiel, Deutero-Isaiah and the Apocalyptists is dawning; he is gathering the righteous community round him. But Jesus realized that the Son of Man himself must suffer with his people, since he alone was the perfectly righteous man; in Jesus we find the consummation of the sufferings of the martyrs, one who was perfectly obedient to God, and was thus in the truest sense his servant:[1] his dying words were fittingly taken from the prayer of the Old Testament psalmist, who also had remained faithful throughout unmerited suffering, and was ultimately saved and vindicated:[2] 'My God, my God, why hast thou forsaken me?'

Jesus, therefore, the true representative of Israel, may well have seen in Deutero-Isaiah's oracles the description of Israel's sufferings, of which his own were a part. The portrait of Isa. 52-3, however, is only one element in the whole pattern of suffering and exaltation which marks all Deutero-Isaiah's thought, and which runs through Jewish literature, from ritual psalms to apocalyptic visions. This is a theme which illumines all Jewish history, from the time of the First Exodus itself, so that when Jesus interpreted the scriptures to his disciples, he began with Moses, and appealed to *all* the prophets: this was the pattern which made it necessary 'that the Christ should suffer these things and enter into his glory'.[3] The two concepts of suffering and glory are thus indissolubly joined: the prefiguring of Christ's future glory at the Transfiguration is immediately followed by a prediction of the Passion, and Luke says that it was on this subject that Jesus was actually conversing with Moses and Elijah[4]—two prophets who had themselves borne 'the reproach of Christ'.[5]

The volume of literature which has been written on this subject shows how vital this question is for the Christian understanding of the work and person of Jesus. Has the Church been wrong, then, in thinking of Jesus in terms of Isa. 53? While the gospel evidence suggests that Jesus inherited Deutero-Isaiah's universalism, and believed that his own vocation, and that of the new community, was to gather the nations of the world to worship, we have found no indication that he directly associated his sufferings—in which his followers also were to share—through which this vocation was to be largely achieved, with that prophet's concept of vicarious suffering. Christian experience, however, has shown the rightness of the Church's interpretation: as the onlookers in Deutero-Isaiah's vision can speak, after the event, of the saving efficacy of Israel's sufferings, so Christians too can look back and know, through the realization of their own sin and salvation and the injustice of Christ's sufferings, the vicarious and atoning power of the Cross. While Jesus himself, therefore, was not profoundly influenced by the Servant passages in particular, he, and his followers with him, finally fulfilled Israel's vocation to the world: the fourth evangelist was right when he said[1] that it was through his death that Jesus would draw all men to himself.

NOTES

PAGE 1

1 E. Hoskyns and N. Davey, *The Riddle of the New Testament* (1931; 3rd ed. 1947), p. 55.
2 F. C. Burkitt, *Christian Beginnings* (1924), pp. 35–6.
3 *A New Commentary on Holy Scripture*, ed. C. Gore, H. L. Goudge, A. Guillaume (1928), New Testament vol. pp. 205–7.

PAGE 2

1 J. E. Carpenter, *The First Three Gospels* (1906), p. 92. Cf. B. H. Streeter, 'The Historic Christ', essay in *Foundations*, ed. Streeter (1912), pp. 121–7.
2 Part I, vol. I (1920), pp. 381–92.
3 Ibid. p. 383.

PAGE 3

1 Cf. J. M. Creed, *The Gospel According to St Luke* (1930), p. 271, on Luke 22. 37: 'The only clear reference in the Gospels to Isa. 53.' See also F. C. Burkitt, op. cit. p. 37.
2 Op. cit. p. 391. Cf. J. M. Creed, op. cit. p. 271; F. C. Burkitt, op. cit. p. 37.
3 Op. cit. pp. 38–9.
4 Ibid. p. 41.

PAGE 4

1 In *Beginnings*, vol. V (1933), pp. 364–70.
2 Ibid. p. 366. Cf. J. M. Creed, op. cit. p. 267.
3 W. Bousset, *Kyrios Christos* (Göttingen, 1926), pp. 69–72.
4 Ibid. p. 71. Cf. also M. Dibelius, *From Tradition to Gospel* (Eng. trans. 1934), pp. 184–8.

PAGE 5

1 R. Bultmann, *Jesus and the Word* (Eng. trans. 1935), pp. 213–14.
2 R. Bultmann, *Theology of the New Testament*, vol. I (Eng. trans. 1952), p. 31.
3 In particular Pss. 22 and 69. See *Die Geschichte der synoptischen Tradition* (Göttingen, 1931), pp. 303 ff.
4 *Theology of the New Testament*, loc. cit.
5 See also C. G. Montefiore, *The Synoptic Gospels*, vol. I (2nd. ed. 1927), pp. 210, 273–5.

PAGE 6

1 I. Engnell, 'The 'Ebed Yahweh Songs and the Suffering Messiah in "Deutero-Isaiah"', in *B.J.R.L.* vol. 31 (1948), p. 54. Engnell's assumption is, of course, based upon his belief that this combination of Messiah and Servant in the mind of Jesus was the revival of an ancient cult-pattern lying behind both the Servant Songs and the Psalms of suffering. On this question of a pre-Christian identification of the Servant with the Messiah see below, pp. 56f.

2 E. O. James, 'Sources of Christian Ritual', in *The Labyrinth*, ed. S. H. Hooke (1935), p. 253. Cf. also G. H. Box, 'The Value and Significance of the Old Testament in Relation to the New', in *The People and the Book*, ed. A. S. Peake (1925), pp. 454, 466.

3 E. Hoskyns and N. Davey, *The Riddle of the New Testament* (1931; 3rd ed. 1947), pp. 73–4.

PAGE 7

1 Ibid. pp. 80–1.

2 Ibid. p. 93.

3 Ibid. pp. 114–15.

PAGE 8

1 *Jesus and His Sacrifice* (1937; 2nd ed. 1948), p. 97.

2 Ibid. pp. 101 ff., 127.

3 Ibid. p. 113.

4 Ibid. pp. 193–4.

5 Ibid. p. 281. See, further, V. Taylor, *The Names of Jesus* (1953), pp. 36–7; *The Atonement in New Testament Teaching* (2nd ed. 1945), pp. 13–36, 57–67, 135–9.

6 'The Origin of the Markan Passion-Sayings', in *N.T.S*, vol. 1 (1955), pp. 159–67.

7 Ibid. p. 163.

PAGE 9

1 R. Otto, *The Kingdom of God and the Son of Man* (Eng. trans. 1938), pp. 249–55.

2 C. J. Cadoux, *The Historic Mission of Jesus* (1941), pp. 37 ff.

3 Ibid. pp. 186–7, 253.

4 H. W. Wolff, *Jesaja 53 im Urchristentum* (Berlin, 1942; 2nd ed. 1950). See especially pp. 55–70.

PAGE 10

1 W. Manson, *Jesus the Messiah* (1943), pp. 110–13.

PAGE 11

1 J. W. Bowman, *The Intention of Jesus* (1945), p. 108.
2 Ibid. p. 76.

PAGE 12

1 Ibid. p. 84.
2 Ibid. p. 103.
3 Ibid. p. 108.
4 Ibid. p. 128.

PAGE 13

1 Ibid. p. 131.
2 Pp. 23–7. North, however, appears to misunderstand the point made by Jackson and Lake. He writes that Bultmann agrees with them in admitting the influence of the Old Testament—including Isa. 53—on the gospel narrative (p. 24). Such an influence, however, with regard to the predictions of suffering, is precisely what Jackson and Lake are concerned to deny. Moreover Bultmann, in the work cited by North (*Die Geschichte der synoptischen Tradition*, pp. 303 ff.), is dealing with the narrative of the Passion itself, not with the Son of Man prophecies. Since North wrote, Bultmann, as we have already noted (see above, pp. 12–13), has emphatically denied the influence of Isa. 53 in these sayings.
3 Mark 10. 38 f.; 14. 36; Luke 12. 50.
4 *The Cross of the Servant* (1926), pp. 68–9. Wheeler Robinson finds further evidence for the traditional view in the words of Mark 1. 9–11 and the story of the Temptation, and argues that influence by the Servant concept is the most reasonable explanation of Jesus' acceptance of his death as the will of God. See pp. 66–71.

PAGE 14

1 *The Atonement in New Testament Teaching* (2nd ed. 1945), p. 65.
2 Vol. v (1954); see especially pp. 709 ff. The article by Jeremias was published in 1952.
3 Jeremias cites Mark 9. 12, 31; 10. 45; 14. 8, 24; Luke 23. 34; John 10. 11, 15, 17 as examples.
4 Mark 9. 12 b; Luke 9. 44; 12. 50; 13. 32 ff.; 17. 25.
5 Mark 8. 31; 14. 8; Luke 22. 37; Mark 9. 12 b.

PAGE 15

1 T. W. Manson, *The Servant Messiah* (1953), p. 54.
2 Ibid. p. 64.
3 Ibid. p. 73.
4 H. E. W. Turner, *Jesus, Master and Lord* (1953). See especially pp. 149, 207–11.
5 Ibid. p. 208.

PAGE 16

1 Ibid. p. 209.
2 *The Mission and Achievement of Jesus* (1954). See especially pp. 52–95, 102–8.
3 Ibid. pp. 58–9.
4 Ibid. pp. 108, 88.
5 Ibid. pp. 107, 103.

PAGE 17

1 *Peter: Disciple, Apostle, Martyr* (Eng. trans. 1953), pp. 66–9.
2 Acts 3. 13, 26; 4. 27, 30.
3 *Primitive Christian Application of the Doctrine of the Servant* (Durham, U.S.A., 1929), p. v.
4 Ibid. pp. 161–7.
5 Ibid. p. 62.

PAGE 18

1 *The Apostolic Message* (New York, 1925), pp. 186–7, 203–4, 213–15, 259, 272; *The Story of Jesus* (New York, 1927), pp. 311–19. Although Bacon denies that the use of the Servant concept goes back to Jesus, in *The Apostolic Message* he takes a stand quite opposite to that of Jackson and Lake over the question of its use in the Synoptics, for he maintains that the Servant doctrine was on the wane by the time they were written, and that the vicarious aspect of it has completely disappeared from Luke.
2 *The Intention of Jesus* (1945), p. 73.

PAGE 19

1 Ibid. p. 105.
2 See below, pp. 25–7.

PAGE 20

1 See, e.g. the arguments of J. Moffatt in *The Theology of the Gospels* (1912), pp. 139–49.
2 C. H. Dodd, *According to the Scriptures* (1953), pp. 88–96.

PAGE 21

1 Cf. T. W. Manson, 'The Life of Jesus', in *B.J.R.L.* vol. 27 (1943), pp. 333–4.
2 Loc. cit.

PAGE 22

1 In *Beginnings*, vol. v, pp. 369–70.
2 Cf. C. H. Dodd, *The Old Testament in the New* (1952), p. 9. See also the views of H. W. Wolff, above, pp. 9f.

PAGE 23

1 *The Idea of Atonement in Christian Theology* (1920), pp. 23–56, 63–83.
2 Cf. R. Bultmann, *Jesus and the Word* (Eng. trans. 1935), pp. 170, 212–15.
3 Cf. J. Weiss, *The History of Primitive Christianity*, vol. I (1937), pp. 113–18.

PAGE 24

1 Cf. W. O. E. Oesterley, *Sacrifices in Ancient Israel* (1937), p. 286. Of the passages reflecting Isa. 53 (Matt. 8. 17; Mark 9. 12; Matt. 26. 24; Luke 22. 37 and Mark 15. 28 in his judgement) he writes: 'not one of them makes any reference to what, from the point of view of the Atonement, are the crucial passages of Isa. 53.'

PAGE 25

1 The material is dealt with fully by C. R. North, *The Suffering Servant*.

PAGE 26

1 See, e.g., C. R. North, op. cit. pp. 156–91; O. Eissfeldt, 'The 'Ebed-Jahwe in Isaiah xl–lv', in *E.T.* vol. 44 (1933), pp. 261–8. The great diversity of opinion as to the actual extent of the Songs is good evidence for their essential oneness with the rest of Deutero-Isaiah. Cf. N. H. Snaith, 'The So-called Servant Songs', in *E.T.* vol. 56 (1945), pp. 79–81, and 'The Servant of the Lord in Deutero-Isaiah', in *Studies in Old Testament prophecy presented to Prof. T. H. Robinson*, ed. H. H. Rowley (1950), pp. 187f.; E. J. Kissane, *The Book of Isaiah*, vol. II (1943), p. lxv.
2 Cf. I. Engnell, 'The 'Ebed Yahweh Songs and the Suffering Messiah in "Deutero-Isaiah"', in *B.J.R.L.* vol. 31 (1948), pp. 54ff. He writes (p. 64): 'Thus it must be denoted as fundamentally erroneous to treat these songs

without regard to the rest of the text, or, still more, to treat one of them not considering the others.' See also E. J. Kissane, op. cit. p. lxv, who relates the Songs to their immediate context: 'The context is the guide to the interpretation, and disregard of the context leads to chaos'; N. H. Snaith, 'The So-called Servant Songs': 'It is a false antithesis to put the songs so definitely on one side, and the remainder of Isa. 40–55 *en bloc* on the other'; J. Lindblom, *The Servant Songs in Deutero-Isaiah* (Lund, 1951), p. 9, while feeling that Kissane's regular scheme is too extreme, nevertheless maintains that there is 'a certain order, if not in the book as a whole, at any rate in the arrangement of the individual oracles in relation to each other'. As representative of the ultra-critical approach, cf. S. Mowinckel, *He That Cometh* (Eng. trans. 1956), p. 188: 'I take it for granted that these four poems form a special group, that they treat of the same figure, the Servant, uniformly conceived, and that they must be interpreted in their own light and in relation to each other, without any preconceived theory of their relation to other sayings in the Deutero-Isaianic collection.' He writes also: 'Kissane's method represents a neglect of the understanding which has been gained in recent years of the detached character of the individual prophetic words, and of the composition of the prophetic books, and is a return to out-of-date literary theories', p. 189 n. See also W. F. Lofthouse, 'Some Reflections on the "Servant Songs"', in *J.T.S.* vol. 48 (1947), pp. 169–76.

PAGE 29

1 42. 1. Cf. 41. 8f.; 43. 10, 21; 44. 1.
2 49. 3. Cf. 44. 23; 43. 21.
3 49. 5.
4 49. 6; 42. 1–4. Cf. 45. 21f.
5 50. 4–6. Cf. 48. 9f.
6 50. 7–9. Cf. 40. 1f.; 49. 24–6; 51. 22.
7 53. 3; 50. 6f. Cf. 49. 7; 51. 23.
8 52. 13–15; 53. 10–12. Cf. 49. 7, 23; 54. 7f.
9 53. 10–12. Cf. 49. 19–21; 54. 1–3.

PAGE 30

1 41. 8, 9; 44. 1, 2, 21; 45. 4.
2 For further details of comparison, see H. H. Rowley, *The Servant of the Lord and other Essays on the Old Testament* (1952), pp. 49f., *Israel's Mission to the World* (1939), pp. 14–20.
3 See, e.g., Amos 5. 18–20; 7. 7–9; Hos. 2. 9–13; 9. 1–9; Micah. 1. 2–9; 3. 9–12; Isa. 5. 1–7; 6. 10–13.

4 Many of these prophecies are probably scattered through the books attributed to the pre-Exilic prophets, especially Isaiah; see, e.g., Amos 9. 11–15. Cf. also Haggai and Zechariah.

5 See Isa. 42. 19–25; 43. 22–8; 50. 1–3.

PAGE 31

1 Cf. S. Mowinckel, *He That Cometh* (Eng. trans. 1956), pp. 153 f.: 'Deutero-Isaiah himself does not yet present a true eschatology. We miss the conception of a definite end to the present order, and of a new world of an essentially different character from this one. The historical empires of Cyrus and of others have their place in Deutero-Isaiah's picture of the future.' See also S. Smith, *Isaiah Chapters XL–LV* (1944), pp. 18 f.; J. Lindblom, *The Servant Songs in Deutero-Isaiah* (Lund, 1951), pp. 94–102.

2 Cf. e.g. Isa. 2. 2–4 with Isa. 11. 11–14.

3 See, e.g., Hos. 11.

4 On this point see the discussion in A. Bentzen, *Introduction to the Old Testament*, vol. II (Copenhagen, 1949), pp. 108 f.

PAGE 32

1 The similarity extends to the actual phrases:

ואתה אל־תירא עבדי יעקב...ואל תחת ישראל...
כי אתך אני נאם יהוה להושיעך: (Jer. 30. 10 f.)
ואתה ישראל עבדי יעקב אשר בחרתיך...
אל־תירא כי עמך־אני: (Isa. 41. 8, 10.)

PAGE 35

1 Jer. 32. 35.

2 Note also Isa. 48. 11.

PAGE 36

1 The term בְּרִית is found in Hos. 2. 20 (Eng. 2. 18), but the primary sense is not, here, of a covenant made between Yahweh and his people, but of an agreement between Israel and the animals which was imposed by Yahweh upon the latter.

2 Cf. W. O. E. Oesterley and T. H. Robinson, *Hebrew Religion: Its Origin and Development* (2nd ed. 1937), pp. 264 f.

3 G. A. Cooke, in his *Commentary on Ezekiel* (1936), p. 400, maintains that the covenant of Ezek. 37. 26 is not a covenant which Yahweh makes *with* Israel, but one made by him on her behalf: 'a gracious dispensation ensuring peace and security'. This interpretation is not, however, necessitated by the construction וְכָרַתִּי לָהֶם בְּרִית since the preposition לְ does not have here its

strict meaning of 'to' or 'for': it is true that לְ does carry the force of 'for' in Hos. 2. 20, but this is clear from the context. In Jer. 32. 40 we find the same construction, וְכָרַתִּי לָהֶם בְּרִית, with apparently no change in meaning from Jer. 31. 31, which reads בְּרִית... אֶת־בֵּית יִשְׂרָאֵל: Isa. 55. 3 also uses the preposition לְ. The fact that לְ is used more frequently than either אֶת or עִם in speaking of covenants between men shows that it could have the full sense of 'with' (see, e.g., Exod. 23. 32; 34. 12, 15); the use of the same construction in 2 Chron. 29. 10 to describe Hezekiah's intention to make a covenant לַיהוָה is conclusive evidence on this point. Nor does the context of the phrase in Ezek. 37. 26 support Cooke's interpretation that בְּרִית here means a dispensation on Israel's behalf, and not a personal relationship between God and his people. This relationship is implicit in the promise that God is to dwell in the midst of Israel, and that they are to be God and people (v. 27): it is difficult to understand why Cooke should regard this in a different light from the very similar promises in Jer. 31–2. Moreover, Cooke himself describes the בְּרִית of Ezek. 16. 60 as expressing the same idea of a new relationship as does Jeremiah's covenant (p. 180), and speaks of the promise in Ezekiel 34. 25 as identical with that of Lev. 26. 6 (p. 378): in both cases, however, the banishment of wild beasts is not the actual בְּרִית itself, but the result of the covenant effected between God and his people.

PAGE 37

1 See, e.g., Jer. 30. 22; 32. 38. Ezek. 36. 28; 37. 23.

PAGE 38

1 Cf. H. Frankfort, *Kingship and the Gods* (Chicago, 1948), p. 341: 'The relation between the Hebrew monarch and his people was as nearly secular as is possible in a society wherein religion is a living force. The unparalleled feature of this situation is the independence, the almost complete separation of the bonds which existed between Yahweh and the Hebrew people, on the one hand, and between Yahweh and the House of David, on the other. Yahweh's covenant with the people antedated kingship. His covenant with David concerned the king and his descendants, but not the people... (2 Sam. 7. 12–16).... Only in later times, when this promise was made the foundation of Messianic expectations, did the people claim a share in it.'

2 Jer. 33. 16; 31. 1, 33; Isa. 40. 9; 43. 15.

PAGE 39

1 See, e.g., C. R. North, *The Suffering Servant*, pp. 129f.

PAGE 40

1 This remains true even if we follow those scholars who regard these chapters as later than Deutero-Isaiah.

PAGE 41

1 Cf. H. S. Nyberg, 'Smärtornas man' (1942), in *Svensk Exegetisk Årsbok* 7 (quoted in C. R. North, op. cit. p. 220): 'The usual disjunctive, collective *or* individual, is false.' See also C. H. Dodd, *According to the Scriptures* (1952), pp. 95 f.: 'What is clear is that in the text of Isaiah as it has come down to us there is an alternation between the corporate connotation, where the Servant is equated with "Israel" or "Jacob", and the individual, where he is a quasi-prophetic figure with a mission to Israel...it is not impossible that the alternation of meaning is integral to the conception.' H. H. Rowley, in *The Servant of the Lord and Other Essays on the Old Testament* (1952), writes (p. 49): 'No simple, clear-cut solution is likely to do justice to all the evidence ...the views that emphasize the many strands that went into the thought and the fluidity that marks it in the Servant songs are likely to be in the right direction.'

2 E.g. S. Smith, *Isaiah Chapters XL–LV* (1944), pp. 49–75; C. R. North, op. cit. pp. 207–19; E. J. Kissane, *The Book of Isaiah*, vol. II (1943), pp. lxiv–lxviii.

PAGE 42

1 Cf. H. H. Rowley, *Israel's Mission to the World* (1939), p. 12: 'I believe the writer himself would have found difficulty in defining with precision what was in his own mind....There was a fluidity in the writer's thought that makes all our efforts to pin him down to a single identification doomed to failure.'

2 See 'The Hebrew Conception of Corporate Personality', pp. 49–62 in *Werden und Wesen des Alten Testaments*, *B.Z.A.W.* 66 (Berlin, 1936); *The Cross of the Servant* (1926), pp. 22–39; 'Hebrew Psychology', pp. 353–82 in *The People and the Book*, ed. A. S. Peake (1925), especially pp. 375–80. For similar views, see O. Eissfeldt, 'The 'Ebed-Jahwe in Isaiah xl–lv', in *E.T.* vol. 44 (1933), pp. 261–8; A. R. Johnson, *The One and The Many in the Israelite Conception of God* (1942); J. Pedersen, *Israel: Its Life and Culture*, vol. I–II (1946), pp. 275–9; W. L. Wardle, 'Currents of Old Testament Study', in *London Quarterly and Holborn Review*, vol. 160 (1935), pp. 436 f.

3 The most common example of this in the Old Testament is the way in which the prophets speak of the Exodus as though the present generation had taken part in it.

PAGE 43

1 See A. R. Johnson, 'The Role of the King in the Jerusalem Cultus', pp. 71–111, in *The Labyrinth*, ed. S. H. Hooke (1935), especially pp. 73–7; S. H. Hooke, 'The Myth and Ritual Pattern of the Ancient East', pp. 7f., and W. O. E. Oesterley, 'Early Hebrew Festival Rituals', pp. 142–5, both in *Myth and Ritual*, ed. S. H. Hooke (1933); A. S. Tritton, art. 'King', in *E.R.E.* vol. 7, pp. 726b–727, on the king as representative in the Babylonian penitential psalms.

2 A. Lods, *Israel from Its Beginnings to the Middle of The Eighth Century* (Eng. trans. 1932), p. 413: 'Finally, it is in the conception of the monarchy that we can trace some of the sources of the Messianic hope: on the one hand the yearning for the vanished glories of the early kings clearly helped to awaken the expectation of the glorious ruler of the future; on the other hand, the titles and honours of the king were extended to Jahweh himself. Thus arose the hope of a day when "the kingdom of God" would be finally set up over the whole earth.' On p. 473 Lods quotes the following from S. Mowinckel, *Psalmenstudien* (Oslo, 1921–4), vol. II, pp. 506f.: 'Israel's messianic hope...is the projection into the more remote future of the glorious accession of Jahweh, the renewal of which, from the earliest times of the monarchy, was eagerly awaited at the beginning of each new year....' Cf. also S. Mowinckel, *He That Cometh* (Eng. trans. 1956), p. 156: 'It is, therefore, a fundamental principle for understanding the content of the Messianic conceptions, that whatever applies to the Israelite ideal of kingship also applies to the Messiah, but in a still greater measure. *The Messiah is the future, eschatological realization of the ideal of kingship.*' See J. Pedersen, op. cit. vol. III–IV, p. 465, S. H. Hooke, *The Origins of Early Semitic Ritual* (1938), Schweich Lectures for 1935, p. 56.

3 Cf. the parallel examples in the Tell-el-Amarna letters given by A. R. Johnson in *The One and the Many in the Israelite Conception of God* (1942), pp. 14f., where there is vacillation between 'servant' and 'servants', both used of the social unit.

4 See Ps. 44 for an example of this oscillation.

PAGE 44

1 Cf. H. H. Rowley, *The Servant of the Lord and Other Essays on the Old Testament* (1952), pp. 22, 54; *The Unity of the Bible* (1953), p. 60; C. Ryder Smith, *The Bible Doctrine of Salvation* (1941), p. 72.

2 Cf. the words of Solomon Astruc in the fourteenth century A.D., in his exposition of the fourth Servant Song: 'When he speaks of the king Messiah, the people is comprehended with him'; see S. R. Driver and A. Neubauer,

The Fifty-Third Chapter of Isaiah according to the Jewish Interpreters, vol. II (1877), p. 129.

3 Cf. C. Ryder Smith, loc. cit.

4 'Messianic' is used here in the broadest sense of the word, not with any eschatological content. See the discussion in A. Bentzen, *King and Messiah* (Eng. trans. 1955), pp. 35–8. Cf. also S. B. Frost, *Old Testament Apocalyptic* (1952), pp. 57–61.

5 Cf. S. Mowinckel, op. cit. p. 173: 'In the earlier Jewish future hope, then, the Messiah does not actually establish the future kingdom, but is the Davidic ruler in the restored Israel, in so far as it is thought of as political and this-worldly. Only rarely is he regarded as Yahweh's instrument in crushing the enemy and establishing the state of bliss... the emphasis was not laid on this aspect of the royal figure. In the restoration Yahweh Himself dominated the scene and all attention was directed to Him.... Generally speaking it is only after the restoration that the future king comes into action.'

PAGE 45

1 Contrast the Servant Songs and oracles which speak of Yahweh's care for Israel with the description of Cyrus in ch. 45; Cyrus is Yahweh's anointed only 'for the sake of Jacob my servant, and Israel my chosen'.

2 An ingenious solution to the Servant problem has recently been offered by J. Lindblom, in *The Servant Songs in Deutero-Isaiah* (Lund, 1951). He suggests that the 'Songs' should be understood as allegories, in which Deutero-Isaiah depicts the fate and mission of Israel in terms of an unknown vassal-king, his own prophetic calling, his experiences of suffering, and finally in a vision; each allegory is followed—or in the case of the fourth Song, preceded—by an interpretative passage, which must be considered as forming a unity with the Song. Lindblom thus ranks himself with the 'individualists' (p. 105), while maintaining that the figure of the Servant is meant to *represent* Israel. While this theory offers an explanation for the individual traits in the Songs, however, there is little evidence to support it. Although it is true, as Lindblom claims, that there are other cases of allegories in the Old Testament, the examples which he quotes are mostly not parallel to the passages which we are considering, while those which can be compared with them are metaphorical, rather than allegorical. It is essential to the nature of an allegory that its characters should be sufficiently different from the real subjects to be distinguishable from them: this, however, is clearly not the case in Deutero-Isaiah; there is little difference in subject or language between the Songs and their so-called 'interpretations'. These 'interpretations', moreover, continue the theme of the Songs, rather than explain them. If these passages were intended to be 'allegorical oracles' we would surely find,

if not an actual statement to that effect, at least a clear indication of the parallel which was intended. An allegory which does not clarify the issue, but only confuses it, as the Songs on this interpretation have done, is hardly worthy of the name. On this subject we must be very careful to distinguish between allegory and metaphor, which is a quite different matter, and is used extensively in the Songs.

3 Isa. 61. 3. An expression of Deutero-Isaiah's faith, even if not his actual words.

PAGE 46

1 Cf. *Cambridge Ancient History*, vol. III (1925), where S. A. Cook, in his article 'The Prophets of Israel', writes (p. 492): 'if Israel had received double for her sins (Isa. 40. 2), might not the surplus have a saving efficacy for others?'

2 This interpretation of the Hebrew text is supported by reference to the LXX and other Greek versions, and to the Targum. The Targum transfers the sufferings to others, who suffer deservedly; the LXX, in its use of the passive, emphasizes that the Servant is a recipient, rather than an actor. The phrase 'he poured out his soul unto death' in 53. 12 is usually interpreted as a positive offering on the part of the Servant. Once again, however, this reflects the preconceived theory of voluntary suffering. It is significant that the LXX translates the phrase by παρεδόθη εἰς θάνατον ἡ ψυχὴ αὐτοῦ, which suggests that it may have understood the Niph'al, עֵרָה. As the phrase stands in the Hebrew, there is no reason to suppose that it implies a self-offering, any more than does the English phrase 'to give up the ghost'. It may well be a more emphatic form of the Hebrew expression נָפַח נֶפֶשׁ found in Jer. 15. 9 and Job 11. 20; 31. 39. Cf. also the other occasion where ערה is used with the idea of death, in Ps. 141. 8. Similarly, in Isa. 50. 6f., submission should not be taken to mean voluntary offering: the words 'I gave my back to the smiters...' no more imply willingness than those used of Israel in 51. 23: 'you have made your back like the ground and like the street for them to pass over'. We may compare also the submissive attitude of Job at the beginning of his sufferings: the acceptance of suffering expressed in Job 1. 21 and 2. 10 certainly does not imply an active self-offering.

PAGE 47

1 Cf. also the taunt song over Babylon in Isa. 47.

2 The 'resurrection' is described in terms of offspring, prosperity and spoil; cf. 49. 19–26.

3 The comparison with Ezek. 37 is noted by H. W. Robinson in *The Cross of the Servant* (1926), pp. 62f.

4 Cf. H. H. Rowley, *The Servant of the Lord and Other Essays on the Old Testament* (1952), pp. 52f. This criticism applies also to the view that the prophet's disciples wrote the fourth Song about his death.

5 Cf. H. H. Rowley, loc. cit.

6 For this view see C. R. North, *The Suffering Servant*, pp. 207–19.

PAGE 48

1 Principally, H. S. Nyberg, 'Smärtornas man' (1942), in *Svensk Exegetisk Årsbok* 7; I. Engnell, 'The 'Ebed Yahweh Songs and the Suffering Messiah in "Deutero-Isaiah"', in *B.J.R.L.* vol. 31 (1948), pp. 54ff.; see also S. H. Hooke, *Prophets and Priests* (1938), pp. 40ff.; H. Riesenfeld, *Jésus Transfiguré* (1947), pp. 82f. For details of the ritual on the fifth day of the New Year Festival, which included the humiliation of the king, see J. B. Pritchard (ed.), *Ancient Near Eastern Texts Relating to the Old Testament* (Princeton, U.S.A., 1950), pp. 332–4; S. H. Hooke, *Babylonian and Assyrian Religion* (1953), pp. 59f., 109f.; H. Frankfort, *Kingship and the Gods* (Chicago, 1948), p. 320; S. Langdon, *The Babylonian Epic of Creation* (1923), pp. 25f.

2 Cf. H. H. Rowley, op. cit. p. 251: 'The prophet's language might be reminiscent of the language of the Tammuz cult....But if so, he was applying the language of that cult to the Servant, and not conforming the Servant to the ideas of the Tammuz cult, for which he could have had nothing but contempt...in so far as the prophet's language had any cultic background it is more likely to have been in the Yahwistic ritual of his own people.' For a description of this ritual, see A. R. Johnson, 'The Role of the King in the Jerusalem Cultus', in *The Labyrinth*, ed. S. H. Hooke (1935), pp. 98–111.

3 See, e.g., Pss. 22, 30 and 88, and cf. the discussion of these psalms in A. Bentzen, *King and Messiah* (Eng. trans. 1955), pp. 27ff., although he distinguishes between the concept here and in Isa. 53.

4 *The Suffering Servant*, pp. 205–6. See also pp. 178–84.

5 Ibid. pp. 178–80.

PAGE 49

1 Cf. 43. 10 and 49. 6. In both cases the primary thought is of witnessing. The R.V. translation of the second passage is misleading: Yahweh's salvation is not identified with the Servant, but becomes effective through his witness.

PAGE 50

1 Cf. E. J. Kissane, *The Book of Isaiah*, vol. II (1943), pp. lxvi–lxvii.

2 Isa. 43. 10.

PAGE 51

1 It should be noted that this interpretation of the Servant is fully in agreement with the historical background, a point which is stressed by S. Smith in *Isaiah Chapters XL–LV* (1944). The chapters must be read against the contemporary background, but this does not necessitate adopting the particular identification of the Servant which Smith makes, as he himself recognizes in his preface, pp. vii–viii.

2 C. R. North, *The Suffering Servant*, p. 205.

PAGE 53

1 Cf. Isa. 53. 11–13. See H. L. Ginsberg, 'The Oldest Interpretation of the Suffering Servant', in *V.T.* vol. 3 (1953), pp. 400–4; W. H. Brownlee, 'The Servant of the Lord in the Qumran Scrolls I', in *B.A.S.O.R.* no. 132 (1953), pp. 12–15. Brownlee argues that the reference to the Servant is confirmed by the fact that the wise are said to suffer persecution in Dan. 11. 33, 35; in Dan. 12. 10 and 8. 24f., the many are themselves the sufferers. It should be noted, however, that it is nowhere said in Daniel that it is through their sufferings that the mission of the wise is accomplished. A similar criticism may be made of Brownlee's conclusion concerning Dan. 9. 24–7: 'It is difficult to resist the impression that, whether the anointed one which is cut off be Onias III or some other, we have here the doctrine of a suffering Messiah based on an interpretation of Second Isaiah.' This sweeping statement is based upon the flimsiest of evidence: there is no mention whatever of any sufferings on the part of the 'anointed one', only of his sudden death, nor is he associated with the atonement spoken of in *v.* 24. Furthermore, there is no justification for Brownlee's statement that 'the "prophet" and the anointing of "the most holy", whatever they may refer to, introduce one into the realm of messianic ideas'; nor is there any necessary connection between the use of the term 'anointed' here, and in the Qumran text of Isaiah.

PAGE 54

1 See C. C. Torrey, *The Apocryphal Literature* (New Haven, U.S.A., 1945), pp. 98–103.

2 Ibid. pp. 93–7.

3 Ibid. pp. 103–6.

4 Ibid. pp. 110–14.

5 E.g. W. Manson, *Jesus the Messiah* (1943), pp. 171–4; S.–B., *Kommentar*, vol. I, p. 481; W. D. Davies, *Paul and Rabbinic Judaism* (1948), pp. 279f.

6 Thus those scholars who see in the Son of Man a pre-Christian combination of the Servant with the Messiah are basing their theory on a fact which is really strong evidence against it.

PAGE 55

1 1 Cor. 1. 23.

2 *Jesaja 53 in Hexapla, Targum und Peschitta* (Gütersloh, 1954). See also the review of this book by M. Black in *N.T.S.* vol. 1 (1955), pp. 313f.

3 Cf. J. F. Stenning, *The Targum of Isaiah* (1949), pp. ix–x.

4 Isa. 52. 13.

PAGE 56

1 A possible exception has been noted in the phrase 'he delivered up his soul to death' in 53. 12. On this phrase, however, see C. R. North, *The Suffering Servant*, pp. 11f.

2 C. R. North, op. cit. p. 13, notes that this phenomenon appears repeatedly in later Jewish interpretation of the Servant, even after the idea of a suffering Messiah was established: 'there is not a single full-length exposition on Messianic lines in which the principle embodied in the Targum is not in some degree adhered to.... While the Jews allowed that the Messiah, Son of David, would suffer, it was no part of their expectation that his sufferings would end in a violent death.'

3 Cf. G. R. Driver, 'The Hebrew Scrolls from the Neighbourhood of Jericho and the Dead Sea', *Friends of Dr Williams's Library*, Lecture 4 (1951). Cf. also passages from the 'Manual of Discipline' in A. Dupont-Sommer, *The Jewish Sect of Qumran and the Essenes* (1954), pp. 134, 143.

4 For reminiscences of Deutero-Isaiah in the Zadokite Fragments, cf. C. Rabin, *The Zadokite Fragments* (1954), pp. 78f. W. H. Brownlee, 'The Servant of the Lord in the Qumran Scrolls II', in *B.A.S.O.R.* no. 135 (1954), pp. 33–8, argues that certain passages in the 'Manual of Discipline' contain allusions to the Servant. His evidence, however, is unconvincing; even if we accept the linguistic parallels, there is no reference here to the essential feature of Isa. 53, that of suffering bringing salvation to others.

5 See H. E. Ryle, *Philo and Holy Scripture* (1895), p. 297. Josephus' impassioned offer of his own life at the close of *Bel. Jud.* 5. 9 has no connection with the concept of vicarious atonement for sin.

6 See examples in S.-B., *Kommentar*, vol. II, pp. 279–82; C. G. Montefiore, *Rabbinic Literature and Gospel Teaching* (1930), pp. 300–5; G. F. Moore, *Judaism*, vol. I, pp. 546–53.

7 A Büchler, *Studies in Sin and Atonement* (1928).

8 Cf. also C. G. Montefiore, *The Old Testament and After* (1923), pp. 400–17.

9 E. Stauffer, *New Testament Theology* (Eng. trans. 1955), p. 334, maintains that the theme of the sufferings of the martyrs in Jewish thought includes the concept of expiatory suffering. While it is true that the sufferings of the

martyr are regarded as atoning for his own sins, Stauffer's evidence for the idea that 'the blood of the martyr atones for the sin of his people' (par. 44) is unconvincing. Of the passages which he quotes, few are really concerned with this concept: Deut. 32. 43 speaks of Yahweh's vengeance on Israel's enemies; 2 Mac. 7. 37f. is a prayer for God's mercy on his people, which is not dependent upon the martyrs' death; in 4 Mac., vicarious atonement is not mentioned in either 1. 11, where the example of the martyrs brings about the downfall of the tyrant, or in 12. 7f. Only in 4 Mac. 6. 28f. and 17. 21f. is the concept really found. The evidence gathered in S.-B., *Kommentar*, vol. II, pp. 274ff., 281f., and that of the Midrash, is of a later date.

PAGE 57

1 The figure of honour here, of course, is not the Messiah but the Son of Man.

2 Although older commentators referred these words to the Messiah, such an interpretation is extremely unlikely. See S. B. Frost, *Old Testament Apocalyptic* (1952), pp. 136f.; H. G. Mitchell, in *Commentary on Haggai, Zechariah, Malachi and Jonah* (1912), pp. 330f.; R. H. Kennett in *A Commentary on the Bible*, ed. A. S. Peake (1924), p. 582b; J. C. H. How in *A New Commentary on Holy Scripture*, ed. C. Gore, H. L. Goudge, A. Guillaume (1929), pp. 623–624a.

3 Dan. 12. 3 and Ecclus. 48. 10 contain no idea of either suffering or Messianism.

4 It is impossible to consider in detail here the arguments which have been brought forward in support of a pre-Christian suffering Messiah. On this question the discussion by H. H. Rowley in his essay 'The Suffering Servant and the Davidic Messiah' (published in *The Servant of the Lord and Other Essays on the Old Testament* (1952)) appears to be conclusive. Others who maintain this view are G. F. Moore, *Judaism*, vol. I, pp. 551f., vol. III, p. 166 n. 255; S.-B., *Kommentar*, vol. II, p. 274; H. W. Robinson, *Redemption and Revelation* (1942), p. 201; H. W. Wolff, *Jesaja 53 im Urchristentum*, Berlin, 2nd ed. (1950), pp. 42f.; J. Klausner, *Jesus of Nazareth* (1925), p. 201; V. H. Stanton, art. 'Messiah', in *H.D.B.* vol. III, pp. 354b–355a; C. W. Emmet, 'Messiah', in *E.R.E.* vol. VIII, pp. 579b–580a; E. Schürer, *A History of the Jewish People in the times of Jesus Christ* (Eng. trans. 1895), vol. II, ii, pp. 184–7. For the opposing view, see W. D. Davies, *Paul and Rabbinic Judaism* (1948), pp. 274–84; J. Jeremias, 'παῖς Θεοῦ', in *T.W.N.T.* vol. V, pp. 685–98; 'Zum Problem der Deutung von Jes. 53 im palästinischen Spätjudentum', in *Aux Sources de la Tradition Chrétienne*, Mélanges offerts à M. Maurice Goguel (Neuchâtel, 1950), pp. 113–19; C. C. Torrey, 'The Influence of Second Isaiah in the Gospels and Acts', in *J.B.L.* vol. 48

(1929), p. 25; H. Riesenfeld, *Jésus Transfiguré* (Copenhagen, 1947), pp. 81–96, 314–17; W. Manson, *Jesus the Messiah* (1943), pp. 171–4; I. Engnell, 'The 'Ebed Yahweh Songs and the Suffering Messiah in "Deutero-Isaiah"', in *B.J.R.L.* vol. 31 (1948), pp. 54–60.

5 See I. Engnell, op. cit.; A. Bentzen, *King and Messiah* (Eng. trans. 1955).

PAGE 58

1 A. Bentzen, op. cit. p. 79.

2 R. A. Aytoun, 'The Servant of the Lord in the Targum', in *J.T.S.* vol. 23 (1922), pp. 172–80, argues that the interpretation of the Targum was the normal one at the time of Jesus.

3 C. H. H. Wright, 'The Pre-Christian Jewish Interpretation of Isaiah LII, LIII', in *The Expositor*, 3rd series, vol. 7 (1888), pp. 364–77, 401–20, held that the Jewish interpretation was of the righteous. Evidence for the collective interpretation at a later period is found in Origen, *Contra Celsum* I, ch. 55 (pp. 50f. in Chadwick's translation).

4 C. C. Torrey, *The Apocryphal Literature* (New Haven, U.S.A., 1945), pp. 59ff., 116ff., 123ff.; R. Pfeiffer, *History of New Testament Times with an Introduction to the Apocrypha* (New York, 1949), pp. 409ff.

5 A similar passage is found in Ps. Sol. 11; this also is clearly based on the thought and language of Deutero-Isaiah, and may be dependent on 1 Baruch, or *vice versa*. See C. C. Torrey, op. cit. p. 62.

PAGE 59

1 C. C. Torrey, op. cit. pp. 123ff.; R. H. Charles, *The Apocrypha and Pseudepigrapha of the Old Testament*, vol. II (1913), pp. 470ff.

PAGE 60

1 Cf. S. B. Frost, *Old Testament Apocalyptic* (1952), pp. 8–11.

2 E.g. in 49. 22–6. J. Lindblom, *The Servant Songs in Deutero-Isaiah* (Lund, 1951), pp. 64–74, finds in this fact one of the main reasons for his division of Deutero-Isaiah's oracles into two groups, which he believes come from two distinct periods in the prophet's life: 'I cannot imagine that the prophet whom we call Deutero-Isaiah proclaimed at the same time the conversion or salvation of the Gentiles *and* their subjugation or annihilation' (p. 67). Lindblom surely underestimates, here, however, not only the considerable element of exaggeration in Hebrew prophecy, but also the different feelings which the author of these oracles must have had for Babylon, the cruel tyrant, on the one hand, and for the rest of the nations, subject like Israel, on the other.

3 See G. F. Moore, *Judaism*, vol. I, pp. 219–34; W. O. E. Oesterley, *The Jews and Judaism during the Greek period* (1941), pp. 111–18. Cf. C. Guignebert, *The Jewish World in the Time of Jesus* (1939), p. 157: 'in Palestine universalism was nothing more than an extension of particularism, implying the absorption of the Gentile world by the chosen people.'

PAGE 63

1 See, e.g., H. Wheeler Robinson, *The Cross of the Servant* (1926), p. 68.

PAGE 66

1 The verb occurs also in Joel 2. 32, where the LXX has understood the root בשׂר in the Hebrew text.

2 See B.D.B. p. 142; G.T. pp. 256f.; E. Hoskyns and N. Davey, *The Riddle of the New Testament* (1931), pp. 85 ff.; L.S. pp. 704f.; G. Friedrich, art. 'εὐαγγελίζομαι', in *T.W.N.T.* vol. II, pp. 705–7, 722f.

3 Cf. R. H. Fuller, *The Mission and Achievement of Jesus* (1954), pp. 36f.

PAGE 67

1 See 2 Sam. 4. 10; 18. 27; 1 Kings 1. 42; Jer. 20. 15; Isa. 52. 7. Cf. W. K. L. Clarke, *Divine Humanity* (1936), p. 88.

2 Matthew and Luke have quoted only the words from Isaiah at this point, but they use the rest of Mark's quotation in the words of Jesus about John the Baptist in Matt. 11. 10 and Luke 7. 27. T. W. Manson, *The Sayings of Jesus* (1949), pp. 68–70, has drawn attention to the fact that, although this quotation is usually presumed to be from Mal. 3. 1, the first part of it is, in fact, an exact quotation from Exod. 23. 20, while the second part agrees with neither passage; Manson attributes the use of the text in both Luke and Mark to influence by Matthew's book of 'testimonies'. In John 1. 23 a slightly different version of part of Isa. 40. 3 is used, and the words from Malachi—or Exodus—are not found at all.

PAGE 68

1 Cf. Isa. 6. 5–7.

2 For the use of these symbols in Jewish writings, see S.–B., *Kommentar*, vol. I, pp. 123–5; *The Jewish Encyclopaedia*, ed. I. Singer, vol. IV, pp. 644f. Cf. also C. K. Barrett, *The Holy Spirit and the Gospel Tradition* (1947), pp. 35–9; A. Plummer, *The Gospel according to St Luke*, 5th ed. (1922), p. 99; G. W. H. Lampe, *The Seal of the Spirit* (1951), pp. 35f.; W. F. Flemington, *The New Testament Doctrine of Baptism* (1948), pp. 27f.

PAGE 69

1 H. Wheeler Robinson, *The Cross of the Servant* (1926), pp. 66f., describes Mark 1. 11 as a combination of Isa. 42. 1 with Ps. 2. 7. See also C. H. Dodd, *According to the Scriptures* (1952), p. 89; C. R. North, *The Suffering Servant*, p. 25; L. L. Carpenter, *Primitive Christian Application of the Doctrine of the Servant* (Durham, U.S.A., 1929), pp. 43–7; J. Denney, *The Death of Christ*, ed. R. V. G. Tasker (1951), p. 17; H. E. W. Turner, *Jesus, Master and Lord* (1953), pp. 97f., 216; J. Moffatt, *The Theology of the Gospels* (1912), pp. 132, 149; A. E. J. Rawlinson, *The Gospel According to St Mark*, 7th ed. (1953), pp. 10f.; C. J. Cadoux, *The Historic Mission of Jesus* (1941), pp. 37f.; R. H. Fuller, *The Mission and Achievement of Jesus* (1954), p. 53; J. W. Bowman, *The Intention of Jesus* (1945), p. 76; W. Manson, *Jesus The Messiah* (1943), pp. 110–12; A. Loisy, *L'Evangile selon Marc* (Paris, 1912), p. 62; G. W. H. Lampe, *The Seal of the Spirit* (1951), pp. 36ff.; H. B. Swete, *The Gospel According to St Mark* (1898), p. 9; V. Taylor, *The Gospel According to St Mark* (1952), p. 162; C. G. Montefiore, *The Synoptic Gospels*, vol. I (2nd ed. 1927), p. 11; O. Cullmann, *Baptism in the New Testament* (Eng. trans. 1950), pp. 16–18.

2 Cf. J. Jeremias, *The Parables of Jesus* (Eng. trans. 1954), p. 57.

3 Cf. C. C. Torrey, *The Apocryphal Literature* (New Haven, U.S.A.), pp. 116–23. There are references to 'my son' in 4 Ezra 7. 28f.; 13. 32, 37, 52; 14. 9; the first two of these appear to be insertions. In Ps. Sol. 17. 23–51, a passage based upon Ps. 2, there is no reference to the Messiah; it is, in fact, the people of God who are there called 'sons of God' (*v.* 30). We may note also that the Targum paraphrases Ps. 89. 27 as 'King Messiah', and changes Ps. 2. 7 to a comparative phrase; this passage is also interpreted comparatively in Midrash Tehillah. Cf. W. Sanday, art. 'Son of God', in *H.D.B.* vol. IV, p. 571; E. G. Hirsch, art. 'Son of God', in *The Jewish Encyclopaedia*, ed. I. Singer, vol. XI, pp. 460f.; E. Huntress, '"Son of God" in Jewish Writings Prior to the Christian Era', in *J.B.L.* vol. 54, pp. 117–23.

4 Cf. J. Y. Campbell, art. 'Christ', in *T.W.B.* p. 45b: 'It is often said that he knew himself to be the Messiah, but not the Messiah whom the Jews expected. But why should he have used the term at all, if he had to give it a new and different meaning? To do this, without explanation, would only have misled his hearers'; H. E. W. Turner, *Jesus, Master and Lord* (1953), p. 92: 'It would plainly be unwise to claim Messiahship either directly or prematurely for fear that many people would interpret the mission of Jesus in terms of the pattern of Messiahship existing in their own minds.' It is generally agreed that for Jesus the concept of Sonship, not of Messiahship, was primary. Cf. J. Moffatt, *The Theology of the Gospels* (1912), p. 132; H. Wheeler Robinson, *The Cross of the Servant* (1926), p. 65; C. J. Cadoux,

The Historic Mission of Jesus (1941), pp. 34, 52; H. E. W. Turner, op. cit. p. 214; G. H. Box, art. 'The Value and Significance of the Old Testament in Relation to the New', in *The People and the Book*, ed. A. S. Peake (1925), p. 455.

PAGE 70

1 J. Jeremias, art. 'παῖς Θεοῦ', in *T.W.N.T.* vol. v, p. 699; O. Cullmann, *Baptism in the New Testament* (Eng. trans. 1950), pp. 17f.

2 C. J. Cadoux, *The Historic Mission of Jesus* (1941), pp. 37f.; L. L. Carpenter, *Primitive Christian Application of the Doctrine of the Servant* (Durham, U.S.A., 1929), pp. 53f.

3 It appears also in Ps. 67. 12 and Isa. 26. 17, where the Hebrew understood by the LXX differs from the Massoretic text.

PAGE 71

1 See C. H. Turner, art. 'ὁ υἱός μου ὁ ἀγαπητός', in *J.T.S.* vol. 27, pp. 113–29. He is followed by H. E. W. Turner, *Jesus, Master and Lord* (1953), pp. 216–18, and by C. H. Dodd, *Parables of the Kingdom* (1935), p. 130. Cf. V. Taylor, *The Gospel According to St Mark* (1952), p. 161.

2 This is the reading which is quoted by J. H. Moulton and W. F. Howard, *A Grammar of New Testament Greek*, part II (1929), p. 458, as that of the LXX. It is, however, found only in Theodotion's version, as given in the margin of Codex Marchalianus. See *The Old Testament in Greek according to the LXX*, ed. H. B. Swete, 4th ed. (1909–12), vol. III, p. 177.

PAGE 72

1 B.D.B., p. 953a, classifies this as a use of רָצָה with the accusative. Gesenius, *Hebrew and Chaldee Lexicon to the Old Testament Scriptures*, trans. S. P. Tregelles (1859), p. 779a, regards the בוֹ as carried over from the first part of the verse.

2 See, e.g., Hos. 11. 1; Exod. 4. 22f.; Deut. 1. 31. Cf. K. Grayston, art. 'Family', *T.W.B.* pp. 77b–78a; W. R. Smith, *Lectures on the Religion of the Semites*, 3rd ed., ed. S. A. Cook (1927), p. 41.

3 The term is used in comparison in Mal. 3. 17 and Ecclus. 4. 10, and directly in Ps. Sol. 17. 30; Wisd. 2. 16, 18; 5. 5.

PAGE 73

1 Cf. especially Joel 2. 28–32; Isa. 63. 11 and 64. 1. The parallel between the preaching of John and Mal. 3–4, a passage which calls for repentance, condemns social unrighteousness and proclaims judgement for the unrepentant, but deliverance for those who fear the Lord, is most clearly seen in Luke 3.

2 Cf. C. H. Dodd, *According to the Scriptures* (1952), p. 92.

PAGE 74

1 W. Grundmann, art. 'ἰσχύω' in *T.W.N.T.* vol. III, pp. 402 ff., links the Lucan version of this passage to Isa. 53. 12 as well as to 49. 24f., and then to the death of Jesus. Luke 11. 22, however, is, like Mark 3. 27, sufficiently explained by the parallel in Isa. 49. Further, the passage is concerned only with Jesus' expulsion of demons; there is no reference to his death. He has power over the demons because he has *already* overcome Satan and entered his house.

2 See C. H. Dodd, op. cit. p. 93; J. Moffatt, *The Theology of the Gospels* (1912), pp. 144 ff.; V. Taylor, *Jesus and His Sacrifice* (1937), pp. 99–105; A. E. J. Rawlinson, *The Gospel According to St Mark*, 7th ed. (1953), pp. 240 ff.; R. Otto, *The Kingdom of God and the Son of Man* (Eng. trans. 1938), pp. 251–61; W. F. Howard, art. 'Great Texts Reconsidered: Mark 10. 45', in *E.T.* vol. 50, pp. 107 ff.; C. J. Cadoux, *The Historic Mission of Jesus* (1941), p. 38; G. Dalman, *Jesus-Jeshua* (Eng. trans. 1929), pp. 170–2; J. Denney, *The Death of Christ*, ed. R. V. G. Tasker (1951), pp. 33 f.; R. H. Fuller, *The Mission and Achievement of Jesus* (1954), pp. 55–9; W. Manson, *Jesus the Messiah* (1943), p. 132; H. Rashdall, *The Idea of Atonement in Christian Theology* (1920), pp. 29 ff.

3 G.T. p. 137; L.S. p. 348.

4 Δοῦλος is used for עֶבֶד as follows: 42. 19 (pl.); 48. 20; 49. 3, 5, 7 (pl.; the servants of rulers, not of Yahweh). Δουλεύω is used for עֶבֶד at 53. 11. παῖς is used in 41. 8, 9; 42. 1, 19 (pl.); 43. 10; 44. 1, 2, 21, 26; 45. 4; 49. 6; 50. 10; 52. 13. In Trito-Isaiah δοῦλος is used at 56. 6; 63. 17 and 65. 9, each time in the plural. Παῖς is not used.

5 W. F. Howard links this account with the saying in Luke 22. 37, which is parallel to Mark 10. 44. See *The Fourth Gospel in Recent Criticism and Interpretation* (1921), p. 148. Cf. also J. H. Bernard, *The Gospel According to St John* (1928), vol. II, p. 459.

6 In Isa. 49. 7, the Hebrew speaks of Israel as a servant of rulers. The LXX, however, translates by τὸν βδελυσσόμενον ὑπὸ τῶν ἐθνῶν τῶν δούλων τῶν ἀρχόντων, thus making the nations, not Israel, the servants of rulers.

PAGE 75

1 Exod. 14. 31; Deut. 34. 5; Josh. 1. 1; 1 Chron. 6. 49; 2 Chron. 24. 9; Neh. 10. 29; Dan. 9. 11.

2 Gen. 26. 24; Deut. 9. 27; Ps. 105. 42; Ezek. 28. 25; 37. 25; Josh. 24. 29; Judg. 2. 8; Job 1. 8; 2. 3; 42. 8; 2 Sam. 3. 18; Pss. 18 and 36 (titles); Dan. 6. 20; Isa. 20. 3; Jer. 25. 9; 27. 6; 43. 10.

3 Cf. what appears to be a variant of the saying of Mark 10. 43 f. in Matt. 23. 11; Mark 9. 35; Luke 9. 48.

4 G.T. pp. 329, 332, 339.

5 The Hebrew word behind πρῶτος is רֹאשׁ (רֵישָׁא in Aramaic).

6 It is the *attitude* of the Servant to suffering which is remarkable; the suffering itself was apparently heaped upon him, not sought voluntarily. Cf. J. K. Mozley, *The Doctrine of the Atonement* (1915), p. 29 n.'

7 E.g. H. Rashdall, *The Idea of Atonement in Christian Theology* (1920), pp. 29, 49–56; R. Bultmann, *Jesus and The Word* (Eng. trans. 1935), p. 214; F. Büchsel, art. 'λύτρον', in *T.W.N.T.* vol. IV, p. 343; V. Taylor, *The Gospel According to St Mark* (1952), pp. 445 f., argues for its genuineness.

PAGE 76

1 Λύτρον is used in the LXX in Exod. 21. 30; 30. 12; Lev. 19. 20; 25. 24–6, 51 f.; 27. 31; Num. 3. 12, 46–51; 18. 15; 35. 31 f.; Prov. 6. 35; 13. 8; Isa. 45. 13. Cf. A. E. J. Rawlinson, *The Gospel According to St Mark*, 7th ed. (1953), p. 147.

2 Exod. 6. 6; 15. 13, 16; Deut. 7. 8; 9. 26; 13. 5; 15. 15; 21. 8; 24. 18. Λύτρον is used of the ransom of a slave or captive in Lev. 25. 51 f. and Isa. 45. 13.

3 The uses of λυτρόω are as follows: Hos. 13. 14; Micah 4. 10; Zeph. 3. 1; Isa. 35. 9; 41. 14; 43. 1, 14; 44. 22–4; 52. 3; 62. 12; 63. 9; Jer. 27 (50). 34— translating גָּאַל; Hos. 7. 13; Micah 6. 4; Zech. 10. 8; Isa. 51. 11; Jer. 15. 21; 38 (31). 11—translating פָּדָה.

4 See Isa. 35. 9; 41. 14; 43. 1, 14; 52. 3; 51. 11. For the idea of the Return as a Second Exodus, cf. E. J. Kissane, *The Book of Isaiah*, vol. II (Dublin, 1943), pp. 39–70.

5 Cf. F. J. Taylor, art. 'Redeem', in *T.W.B.* pp. 185 f.; H. Wheeler Robinson, *Redemption and Revelation* (1942), pp. 220–8.

PAGE 77

1 The references are given and discussed by N. H. Snaith in *The Distinctive Ideas of the Old Testament* (1944), pp. 85 f.

2 See Hos. 13. 14; Jer. 38 (31). 11; Isa. 35. 9 f.; 51. 10 f.

3 E.g. J. Denney, *The Death of Christ*, ed. R. V. G. Tasker (1951), p. 34; W. Manson, *Jesus the Messiah* (1943), p. 132; R. H. Fuller, *The Mission and Achievement of Jesus* (1954), pp. 56 ff. Cf. on the other hand, F. Büchsel, art. 'λύτρον', in *T.W.N.T.* vol. IV, p. 344. In n. 22 on that page Büchsel writes: 'Dass das Lösegeldwort Ähnlichkeit mit Js. 53 aufweist, ist nicht zu leugnen. Es ist auch zuzugeben, dass Js. 53 für seine Entstehung Bedeutung haben kann. Aber jedenfalls nimmt es nicht ausdrücklich, auch nicht deutlich Bezug

auf Js. 53; deshalb ist es methodisch auf jeden Fall unrichtig, zwar Erklärung des Lösegeldwortes von Js. auszugehen.' See also Jackson and Lake, *Beginnings*, vol. I, pp. 386f.; F. C. Burkitt, *Christian Beginnings* (1924), p. 37.
4 Cf. F. Büchsel, art. 'ἀντί', in *T.W.N.T.* vol. I, p. 373.

PAGE 78

1 Luke 24. 21.
2 See below, pp. 142–6.
3 See above, p. 56.

PAGE 79

1 As is implied by J. Jeremias, *The Eucharistic Words of Jesus* (Eng. trans. 1955), pp. 123ff., 148ff.
2 *According to the Scriptures* (1952), p. 91.
3 See, e.g., Isa. 27. 12; Jer. 23. 3; 29. 14; 31. 8, 10; 32. 37; Ezek. 11. 17; 20. 34, 41; 34. 13; 39. 27; Micah 2. 12; Zech. 10. 10.

PAGE 80

1 Jackson and Lake, *Beginnings*, vol. I, p. 386.
2 A. E. Abbott, *Paradosis* (1904), pp. 1–10.
3 Ibid. p. 115.
4 Loc. cit.
5 Op. cit. p. 3. For the view that παραδίδωμι is derived from Isa. 53. 12 see also L. S. Thornton, *The Common Life in the Body of Christ*, p. 229; and 'The Body of Christ in the New Testament', in *The Apostolic Ministry*, ed. K. E. Kirk (1946), pp. 61, 71ff., 92–6.

PAGE 81

1 See, e.g., R. Otto, *The Kingdom of God and the Son of Man* (Eng. trans. 1938), pp. 289–95; C. H. Dodd, *According to the Scriptures* (1952), p. 93; L. L. Carpenter, *Primitive Christian Application of the Doctrine of the Servant* (Durham, U.S.A., 1929), pp. 56f.; R. H. Fuller, *The Mission and Achievement of Jesus* (1954), pp. 70–5; C. J. Cadoux, *The Historic Mission of Jesus* (1941), p. 38; V. Taylor, *Jesus and His Sacrifice* (1937), pp. 125–39.
2 See, e.g., Judg. 2. 1; Jer. 31. 31–3; Josh. 8. 33; Isa. 59. 21; Num. 25. 12f.; Gen. 17. 2; 6. 18; Ps. 89. 3; 2 Kings 11. 17; 2 Sam. 5. 3.
3 See, e.g., Josh. 9. 6; Gen. 21. 27. Cf. Gen. 31. 44–54, where God is named as the witness to such a covenant.
4 Exod., 24. 3–8. It is probable that Jesus had in mind also Zech. 9. 11, the only other occasion where the phrase occurs.
5 *The Eucharistic Words of Jesus* (Eng. trans. 1955), pp. 133–5.

NOTES TO PP. 82–86

PAGE 82

1 Jeremias also objects to the phrase on the grounds that in late Judaism דַּם בְּרִית is a recognized term for 'the blood of circumcision'. There is no evidence that this meaning was current in the first century A.D., however, and Dalman, *Jesus-Jeshua* (Eng. trans. 1929), pp. 167f., does not consider it to be a reason for doubting the authenticity of the words.

2 G.T. p. 210.

3 B.D.B. p. 1049.

4 H. Rashdall, *The Idea of Atonement in Christian Theology* (1920), p. 38; V. Taylor, *Jesus and His Sacrifice* (1937), p. 127; R. Otto, *The Kingdom of God and the Son of Man* (Eng. trans. 1938), p. 322.

PAGE 84

1 Cf. Isa. 9. 2; Mal. 1. 11.

PAGE 85

1 See, e.g., J. W. Bowman, *The Intention of Jesus* (1945), p. 130; C. J. Cadoux, *The Historic Mission of Jesus* (1941), pp. 37f.; L. L. Carpenter, *Primitive Christian Application of the Doctrine of the Servant* (Durham, U.S.A., 1929), pp. 47f.

2 J. Jeremias, *The Parables of Jesus* (1954), p. 151 n., points out that the quotation of Isa. 61. 1f. in Luke 4. 18f. breaks off immediately before the words 'and the day of vengeance of our God'. If this is deliberate, as it surely must be, then we have here an example of a quotation which extends precisely to the limits of the reference which is intended. This suggests that the same may be true elsewhere, and that Dodd is wrong in supposing that references to a single Old Testament verse imply that a whole passage is in mind (see above, pp. 21–3).

PAGE 86

1 Among those who associate this passage with the Suffering Servant are J. W. Bowman, op. cit. pp. 103, 113; C. J. Cadoux, loc. cit.

2 Cf. C. G. Montefiore, *The Synoptic Gospels*, 2nd ed. (1927), vol. II, pp. 601–5; J. M. Creed, *The Gospel According to St Luke* (1930), p. 271.

3 *Beginnings*, vol. I, p. 390.

4 H. J. Cadbury in *Beginnings*, vol. V, p. 366; *The Making of Luke–Acts* (1927), p. 280 and note.

5 See, e.g., C. J. Cadoux, *The Historic Mission of Jesus* (1941), pp. 37f.; L. L. Carpenter, *Primitive Christian Application of the Doctrine of the Servant*

NOTES TO PP. 86–93

(Durham, U.S.A., 1929), pp. 58f.; J. Jeremias, art. 'παῖς Θεοῦ' in *T.W.N.T.* vol. v, p. 712; W. Manson, *Jesus the Messiah* (1943), pp. 111, 132; V. Taylor, *Jesus and His Sacrifice* (1937), pp. 190–4.

6 See, e.g., W. Bousset, *Kyrios Christos*, 3rd ed. (Göttingen, 1926), pp. 69–72; R. Bultmann, *Die Geschichte der synoptischen Tradition* (Göttingen, 1931), pp. 303 ff.; M. Dibelius, *From Tradition to Gospel* (Eng. trans. 1934), pp. 184–8.

PAGE 89

1 Cf. A. H. McNeile, *The Gospel According to St Matthew* (1949), p. 400; W. Bousset, op. cit. p. 72.

2 Cf. A. Plummer, *An Exegetical Commentary on the Gospel According to St Matthew*, 2nd ed. (1910), pp. 377 ff.

PAGE 90

1 See C. H. Dodd, *According to the Scriptures* (1952), p. 93; W. Bousset, loc. cit.; R. Bultmann, op. cit. p. 304.

PAGE 91

1 Thus the evidence of these passages does not support the view of F. Jackson and K. Lake, *Beginnings*, vol. I, pp. 391 f.

PAGE 92

1 Loc. cit.

2 Cf. the judgement of A. H. McNeile, *The Gospel According to St Matthew* (1949), p. 419: 'Reflexion on the words of Isaiah may have led the early Christians to attach importance to the crucifixion of the robbers, but that it led them to invent the account is not suggested by anything in the records.' See also McNeile in *Cambridge Biblical Essays*, ed. H. B. Swete (1909), p. 246.

3 R. Bultmann, *Die Geschichte der synoptischen Tradition* (Göttingen, 1931), p. 17; C. H. Dodd, *Parables of the Kingdom* (1935), p. 116; M. Dibelius, *From Tradition to Gospel* (Eng. trans. 1934), p. 65; B. H. Branscombe, *The Gospel of Mark* (1937), pp. 53 f.

4 Cf. A. E. J. Rawlinson, *The Gospel According to St Mark*, 7th ed. (1953), p. 31.

PAGE 93

1 Cf. F. C. Grant in *The Interpreter's Bible*, vol. VII, ed. N. B. Harmon (New York, 1951), pp. 767f. See also the discussion in V. Taylor, *The Atonement in New Testament Teaching*, 2nd ed. (1945), pp. 85–97; L. L. Carpenter, *Primitive Christian Application of the Doctrine of the Servant* (Durham, U.S.A., 1929), pp. 51–4; R. Bultmann, *Theology of the New Testament*, vol. I (Eng. trans. 1952), pp. 29f.

PAGE 110

1 See below, pp. 111f. Cf. *Recueil Lucien Cerfaux*, vol. II (Gembloux, 1954), pp. 139–43.

2 We may note that in the other passages there is no connection with the Isaian Servant theme. The word 'raised' in 3. 26 is not taken from Deutero-Isaiah, and in any case probably does not here refer to the resurrection or exaltation of Jesus. The use of the words 'holy' and 'anoint' in chapter 4 is in keeping with the general Old Testament concept of Yahweh's servant.

3 J. Jeremias, in *T.W.N.T.* vol. V, p. 702, argues that it is a Messianic title which could be derived only from Deutero-Isaiah. This argument is valid, however, only if παῖς Θεοῦ were ever understood as a title. See above, ch. 3.

PAGE 111

1 Some texts read in v. 24: ’Αθῷός εἰμι ἀπὸ τοῦ αἵματος τοῦ δικαίου τούτου.

2 L. L. Carpenter, *Primitive Christian Application of the Doctrine of the Servant* (Durham, U.S.A., 1929), p. 68; C. C. Torrey, *J.B.L.* vol. 48 (1929), p. 29, in art. 'The Influence of Second Isaiah in the Gospels and Acts'; *Recueil Lucien Cerfaux*, vol. II (Gembloux, 1954), pp. 141f. For the opposite view, see *Beginnings*, vol. V, pp. 363f.

3 See below, pp. 143–5.

PAGE 112

1 Cf. also 17. 11.

2 See above, ch. 4, p. 99, notes 1 and 3. In Acts we find the singular ἡ γραφή used in 1. 16; 8. 32, 35, each time of a particular reference, and the plural used in 17. 2, 11; 18. 24, 28, each time in a general sense.

3 See below, pp. 114–16.

PAGE 113

1 The incident is generally attributed to Caesarean tradition, and therefore probably derives from Philip himself. Cf. K. and S. Lake, *An Introduction to the New Testament*, revised ed. (1938), p. 69.

PAGE 114

1 Cf. H. J. Cadbury, *The Making of Luke–Acts* (1927), pp. 280f. n.: 'It is noticeable how out of the middle of a passage with a dozen "vicarious" phrases (Isa. 53. 4–12), Acts quotes verses 7bcd, 8abc, which have none.'

2 See p. 112.

PAGE 115

1 *Recueil Lucien Cerfaux*, vol. II (Gembloux, 1954), pp. 439–54, 'Saint Paul et le "Serviteur de Dieu" d'Isaïe'.

2 Cf. e.g. p. 441: 'Paul et Barnabé ne perdent pas de vue cette signification première, et savent que c'est le Christ qui est le Serviteur souffrant, réalisant la grande prophétie de 52–53, comme il est lumière des nations (cf. Lc. 2. 32), pacte du peuple, etc. Mais ils savent également que l'achèvement de l'œuvre du Serviteur parmi les nations leur est confié et que, dans la mesure où ils sont ses représentants et ses serviteurs, le texte les visait également.'

PAGE 117

1 E.g. J. Jeremias, in *T.W.N.T.* vol. v, pp. 703f.; *The Eucharistic Words of Jesus* (Eng. trans. 1955), pp. 67, 139f.; A. M. Hunter, *The Unity of the New Testament*, 2nd ed. (1944), p. 89; L. S. Thornton, 'The Body of Christ in the New Testament', in *The Apostolic Ministry*, ed. K. E. Kirk (1946), p. 71. Cf. V. Taylor, *The Atonement in New Testament Teaching*, 2nd ed. (1945), p. 22; 'The Origin of the Markan Passion-Sayings', in *N.T.S.* vol. 1 (1955), p. 161.

2 J. Jeremias, op. cit. pp. 703f.

PAGE 119

1 Cf. C. H. Dodd, *The Apostolic Preaching and its Developments*, new ed. (1944), p. 25.

2 J. Jeremias, *The Eucharistic Words of Jesus* (Eng. trans. 1955), pp. 129f.

3 Cf. article on ἁμαρτία by G. Stählin, in *T.W.N.T.* vol. I, p. 297.

4 L. S. Thornton, *The Common Life in the Body of Christ* (1942), pp. 257f.; J. Moffatt, *The First Epistle of Paul to the Corinthians* (1938), p. 237. If valid, this objection would apply also to the crucifixion, since Isa. 53. 9 reads 'and with the rich in his death'.

PAGE 120

1 L. S. Thornton, *The Dominion of Christ* (1952), p. 95 and n.; J. H. Michael, *The Epistle of Paul to the Philippians* (1928), pp. 90f.; L. L. Carpenter, *Primitive Christian Application of the Doctrine of the Servant* (Durham, U.S.A., 1929), p. 78; V. Taylor, *The Atonement in New Testament Teaching*, 2nd ed. (1945), p. 65; *The Names of Jesus* (1953), p. 36; *Recueil Lucien Cerfaux*, vol. II (Gembloux, 1954), pp. 425–36.

2 Cf. above, p. 74.

3 Cf. Paul's use of the concept of slavery elsewhere for the state of men, e.g. Rom. 6. 16f.; Gal. 4. 3. L. Cerfaux, op. cit. pp. 426ff., points out that the phrase μορφὴν δούλου has verbal echoes in the translation of Aquila, who translates עֶבֶד by δοῦλος in 52. 13, and תֹּאַר by μορφή (not εἶδος as in LXX) in 52. 14; 53. 2f. This is the translation which we should expect from Aquila, who kept rigidly to the literal meaning of the Hebrew: it would hardly have been acceptable to St Paul, even if it had been written in his time.

PAGE 121

1 Op. cit. p. 428.
2 A. M. Hunter, *Paul and His Predecessors* (1940), pp. 45–51; V. Taylor, 'The Origin of the Markan Passion-Sayings', in *N.T.S.* vol. 1 (1955), p. 162.
3 See below, p. 125.

PAGE 122

1 Cf. L. S. Thornton, *The Common Life in the Body of Christ* (1942), pp. 53–6, 229, 284; 'The Body of Christ in the New Testament', in *The Apostolic Ministry*, ed. K. E. Kirk (1946), pp. 72f.; L. L. Carpenter, op. cit. p. 74; V. Taylor, *The Atonement in New Testament Teaching*, 2nd ed. (1945), p. 65, in *N.T.S.* vol. 1 (1955), p. 161; G. S. Duncan, *The Epistle of Paul to the Galatians* (1934), pp. 73f.; J. Jeremias, in *T.W.N.T.* vol. v, pp. 703f.; A. M. Hunter, op. cit. pp. 33f.; E. Stauffer, *New Testament Theology* (Eng. trans. 1955), p. 132.
2 See above, pp. 70, 94f.
3 Cf. E. Hatch and H. A. Redpath, *Greek Concordance to the LXX*, 2 vols. (1897); J. H. Moulton and G. Milligan, *The Vocabulary of the New Testament* (1930); J. H. Moulton and A. S. Geden, *Concordance to the Greek Testament*, 3rd ed. (1926).
4 Rom. 4. 25; 5. 18.
5 Even in Acts they usually appear in speeches attributed to Paul.

PAGE 123

1 Cf. C. H. Dodd, *The Epistle of Paul to the Romans* (1932), p. 70: 'The concluding verse of the chapter is rhetorical rather than logical in form.'
2 The verb προσφέρω is the same here as in *v.* 7.

PAGE 124

1 The translation given here is that of the Revised Version.
2 Cf. the reference to the prophets in Zech. 1. 4–6.
3 C. Bigg, *The Epistles of St Peter and St Jude*, 2nd ed. (1910), pp. 119f. Cf. C. H. Dodd, *The Interpretation of the Fourth Gospel* (1953), pp. 230f.
4 See above, pp. 76–8.
5 E. G. Selwyn, *The First Epistle of St Peter* (1946), pp. 145f.
6 See especially Num. 28–9.

PAGE 125

1 See above, p. 104, n. 2.

2 Cf. E. G. Selwyn, op. cit. p. 95: 'The core of the matter lies in the observed historical fact of Christ's patience and meekness when suffering unjustly, Himself innocent.'

3 Ibid. p. 92: 'the doctrine of the Atonement grows out of Christ's meekness and patience in suffering.'

PAGE 126

1 *The Atonement in New Testament Teaching*, 2nd ed. (1945), p. 36.

2 J. Jeremias, articles on 'ἀμνός', etc., in *T.W.N.T.* vol. I, pp. 342–5, and on 'παῖς Θεοῦ', vol. v, p. 700.

3 See Enoch 89, where the term is ἀρήν, and Test. Joseph 19, where it is ἀμνός. Cf. C. H. Dodd, *The Interpretation of the Fourth Gospel* (1953), pp. 231 f.

PAGE 127

1 See further below, pp. 150f.

PAGE 128

1 *The Names of Jesus* (1953), pp. 36f.

PAGE 132

1 See the comments on Hermas in S. Cave, *The Doctrine of the Person of Christ* (1925), pp. 71 f.; C. Gore, *The Reconstruction of Belief* (1926), pp. 496, 524f.

PAGE 133

1 This whole passage suggests reflection on Rom. 5 and 6, as well as on 1 Peter.

2 As examples of the use of Isa. 53 later in the second century A.D., we may note the quotations of Isa. 53. 7 in Justin, *Dialogue with Trypho*, 111, and Melito, *Homily on the Passion*, 64.

PAGE 134

1 Mark 8. 31; 9. 31; 10. 33f.; 9. 12 and their parallels. See above, pp. 92–7.

PAGE 135

1 See, e.g., Ps. 11. 6; 23. 5; Isa. 51. 17; Jer. 49. 12.

2 Cf. E. Fascher, 'Theologische Beobachtungen zu δεῖ', in *Neutestamentliche Studien für Rudolf Bultmann* (Berlin, 1954), pp. 228–60.

3 Luke omits the reference to scripture, preferring the word ὡρισμένον.

PAGE 136

1 Cf. the discussions of this parable in C. H. Dodd, *The Parables of the Kingdom* (1935), pp. 124-32; J. Jeremias, *The Parables of Jesus* (Eng. trans. 1954), pp. 55-60.

2 Cf. E. Stauffer, *New Testament Theology* (Eng. trans. 1955), pp. 98f.

3 It is to be noted that the sufferings of the disciples are here linked to the persecution of the prophets.

PAGE 137

1 The available evidence fails to support the arguments of S. G. F. Brandon, *The Fall of Jerusalem and the Christian Church* (1951), pp. 74-87, that the apostles depicted the crucifixion as 'a tragic accident' (p. 75), or that 'beyond the passing reference to its fulfilment of prophecy, the death of Jesus thus assumed no essential place in their exposition of the new faith which they professed' (p. 77). The various summaries of the *kerygma* in Acts (see 2. 14-39; 3. 13-26; 4. 10-12; 5. 30-2; 10. 36-43; 13. 17-41), together with that in 1 Cor. 15. 3 ff., all have the death of Christ as an essential item, and most stress that this death was predetermined. The space which St Mark's gospel devotes to the Passion narrative is surely an indication of the importance of Christ's death for the primitive community.

2 1 Cor. 15. 3f. See above, pp. 117-20.

3 Above, pp. 122f.

PAGE 138

1 See, e.g., Rom. 5. 6-11; 6. 1-11; 7. 4; 1 Cor. 15; 2 Cor. 5. 15; Phil. 2. 1-11.

2 Cf. Heb. 2. 9; 10. 12f.; 12. 2.

3 Above, pp. 105f.

4 See above, pp. 117-19.

PAGE 139

1 Cf. E. Stauffer, *New Testament Theology* (Eng. trans. 1955), pp. 185-8.

PAGE 140

1 This psalm is very probably a set formula of confession, so that it is not strange if it reflects the orthodox teaching; see T. H. Robinson, *Poetry and Poets of the Old Testament* (1947), p. 132. For a dogmatic assertion of the orthodox view, cf. also Ps. 37.

2 E.g. Pss. 22; 54-7; 64; 69-71; 142.

PAGE 141

1 We may note the hint at persecution by fellow-Israelites in 2. 12.

2 Above, pp. 58-60.

3 Cf. S. B. Frost, *Old Testament Apocalyptic* (1952), p. 7: 'Thus the ultimate purpose of [apocalyptic] literature is to deal with a *Sitz im Leben*: to compensate for their present despair by the hope of a Golden Age, and to present a theodicy which may explain the way of Yahweh with His people.'

4 The importance of the martyr-theme in Jewish thought is stressed by E. Stauffer in *New Testament Theology* (Eng. trans. 1955); see his Appendix I, pp. 331–4.

PAGE 142

1 Dan. 7. 17f. On 'Son of Man' here, see J. A. Montgomery, *The Book of Daniel* (1927), pp. 317–24; S. R. Driver, *The Book of Daniel* (1900), pp. 102–10.

2 Above, p. 43.

3 See *Biblia Hebraica*, critical apparatus.

4 Cf. H. H. Rowley, *The Relevance of Apocalyptic*, 2nd ed. (1947), p. 30; T. W. Manson, 'The Son of Man in Daniel, Enoch and the Gospels', in *B.J.R.L.* vol. 32 (1950), pp. 173–5; G. F. Moore, *Judaism*, vol. III, pp. 333–5; V. Taylor, *Jesus and His Sacrifice* (1937), p. 22.

PAGE 143

1 See B.D.B. pp. 114a, 983b–984b; *T.W.B.* pp. 188f.

PAGE 144

1 The phrase is also used in 60. 10, where it has the sense of 'man' common in Ezekiel.

2 Cf. also 39. 6; 66. 1f.

3 61. 5.

4 These themes are well illustrated by 43. 3–6 and 69. 27.

PAGE 145

1 38. 1f.; 45. 3f.

2 Cf. T. W. Manson, op. cit. pp. 188–90.

3 For further discussion of the Son of Man, see R. Otto, *The Kingdom of God and the Son of Man* (Eng. trans. 1938), pp. 176–218; S. B. Frost, *Old Testament Apocalyptic* (1952), pp. 217–29; T. W. Manson, op. cit. pp. 171–90.

4 T. W. Manson, op. cit. pp. 175f.

5 *Jesus the Messiah* (1943), pp. 98–101, 171–4.

6 See, e.g., 1 Kings 19. 16; Exod. 28. 41; 1 Kings 1. 39.

7 See, e.g., 1 Sam. 26. 16.

PAGE 146

1 See Isa. 45. 1. Cf. Isa. 61. 1; 2 Chron. 22. 7.

2 A corporate interpretation seems likely in Ps. 20. 6; 28. 8; 105. 15; Lam. 4. 20; Hab. 3. 13.

3 See, e.g., Deut. 1. 16; Ps. 9. 8.

4 Cf. Neh. 9. 7; Deut. 7. 6f.; 18. 5; 1 Sam. 10. 24.

5 Cf. e.g. Enoch 48. 4 with Isa. 42. 6; Enoch 49. 3 with Isa. 11. 2.

6 Cf. the discussion on the 'First Man' by A. Bentzen, *King and Messiah* (Eng. trans. 1955).

PAGE 149

1 As is assumed, e.g., by O. Cullmann in *Baptism in the New Testament* (Eng. trans. 1950), p. 18: 'For he who is addressed in Isa. 42. 1 has certainly to fulfil the mission which is more closely described in the 53rd chapter of Isaiah.'

PAGE 152

1 See above, pp. 16–18.
2 The Preaching of Peter.
3 The Acts of Peter.
4 1 Cl. 16; Epistle of Polycarp 8.
5 Epistle of Barnabas 5.

PAGE 153

1 48. 7–9; 62.

PAGE 154

1 47. 4.
2 48. 4.
3 See above, pp. 2f.
4 See Origen, *Contra Celsum*, in particular Book 1, 54–5.

PAGE 159

1 Cf. T. W. Manson, *The Teaching of Jesus* (2nd ed. 1935), pp. 211–34.

PAGE 160

1 Mark 14. 62.

PAGE 161

1 See above, pp. 68–73.
2 Mark 10. 45.

PAGE 162

1 E. Schweizer, 'Discipleship and Belief in Jesus as Lord', article in *N.T.S.* vol. II (1956), pp. 87–99, sees the suffering of the righteous in Israel as the pathway along which Jesus, the 'Eschatological' righteous One, is bound to go, together with his disciples. He suggests that this is the real origin of the term παῖς in Acts: Jesus is seen as one who is truly obedient to God.

2 Mark 15. 34; Ps. 22. 1.
3 Luke 24. 26f.
4 Luke 9. 31. Cf. Mark 9. 9–13; Matt. 17. 9–13.
5 Heb. 11. 26.

PAGE 163

1 John 12. 32.

BIBLIOGRAPHY

1. WORKS OF REFERENCE

Abbot-Smith, G., *A Manual Greek Lexicon of the New Testament*, 3rd ed., Edinburgh, 1937.

Brown, F., Driver, S. R. and Briggs, C. A., *A Hebrew and English Lexicon of the Old Testament*, Oxford, 1906.

Cruden, A., *Complete Concordance to the Old and New Testaments*, ed. C. H. Irwin, A. D. Adams and S. A. Waters, London, 1930.

Gore, C., Goudge, H. L. and Guillaume, A., eds., *A New Commentary on Holy Scripture*, London, 1929.

Grimm, C. L. W., *A Greek-English Lexicon of the New Testament*, trans. and revised by J. H. Thayer, 4th ed., Edinburgh, 1901.

Hastings, J., ed., *A Dictionary of the Bible*, 4 vols. and extra vol., 1909.

Hastings, J., ed., *Encyclopaedia of Religion and Ethics*, 12 vols. and index, 1908–21.

Hatch, E. and Redpath, H. A., *A Concordance to the Septuagint and the other Greek Versions of the Old Testament*, 2 vols., 1897.

Huck, A., *Synopsis of the First Three Gospels*, 9th ed. by H. Lietzmann, Eng. ed. by F. L. Cross, Oxford, 1951.

Kittel, G. and Friedrich, G., eds., *Theologisches Wörterbuch zum Neuen Testament*, Stuttgart, 1933– .

Liddell, H. G. and Scott, R., *A Greek-English Lexicon*, new ed. by H. Stuart Jones, Oxford, 1925.

Moule, C. F. D., *An Idiom Book of New Testament Greek*, Cambridge, 1953.

Moulton, J. H., *A Grammar of New Testament Greek*, part I, 3rd ed., 1908; part II, completed W. F. Howard, Edinburgh, 1929.

Moulton, J. H. and Milligan, G., *The Vocabulary of the Greek Testament*, London, 1930.

Moulton, W. F. and Geden, A. S., *A Concordance to the Greek Testament*, 3rd ed., Edinburgh, 1926.

Peake, A. S., ed., *A Commentary on the Bible*, London, 1924.

Richardson, A., ed., *A Theological Word Book of the Bible*, London, 1950.

Singer, I., ed., *The Jewish Encyclopaedia*, 12 vols., New York and London, 1901–6.

Tregelles, S. P., trans., Gesenius' *Hebrew and Chaldee Lexicon to the Old Testament Scriptures*, London, 1859.

2. TEXTS

Biblia Hebraica, ed. R. Kittel, 6th ed., Stuttgart, 1950.
The Old Testament in Greek according to the Septuagint, ed. H. B. Swete, 4th ed., 3 vols., 1909–12.
The Dead Sea Scrolls of St Mark's Monastery, vol. I, ed. M. Burrows, New Haven, U.S.A., 1950.
The Apocrypha and Pseudepigrapha of the Old Testament in English, 2 vols., ed. R. H. Charles, Oxford, 1913.
Novum Testamentum Graece, ed. A. Souter, 2nd ed., Oxford, 1947.
Revised Standard Version of the Bible, 1952.
The Apocryphal New Testament, trans. M. R. James, Oxford, 1924.
Patrologiae Graecae, ed. J. P. Migne, Paris, vols. I, II and V, 1886, 1894.
The Apostolic Fathers, ed. K. Lake, Loeb Classical Library, 2 vols., London and New York, 1930.
Ancient Christian Writers, ed. J. Quasten and J. C. Plumpe, Westminster (U.S.A.) and London, vol. I, trans. J. A. Kleist, 1946, vol. VI, trans. J. A. Kleist, 1948.
The Library of Christian Classics, ed. J. Baillie, J. T. McNeill, and H. P. van Dusen, London, vol. I, *Early Christian Fathers*, trans. and ed. G. C. Richardson, 1953.
The Ante-Nicene Christian Library, ed. A. Roberts and J. Donaldson, vol. I, *The Apostolic Fathers*, Edinburgh, 1868.
The Apostolic Fathers, ed. J. B. Lightfoot, London, 1896.
Origen, *Contra Celsum*, trans. H. Chadwick, Cambridge, 1953.
Stenning, J. F., trans. and ed., *The Targum of Isaiah*, Oxford, 1949.

3. OTHER BOOKS AND ARTICLES

Abbott, A. E., *Paradosis* (*Diatessarica*, part IV), London, 1904.
Abrahams, I., 'Jewish Interpretation of the Old Testament', article in *The People and the Book*, ed. A. S. Peake, Oxford, 1925.
Albright, W. F., *From the Stone Age to Christianity*, 2nd ed., Baltimore, U.S.A., 1946.
Aytoun, R. A., 'The Servant of the Lord in the Targum', in *J.T.S.* vol. 23, 1922, pp. 172–80.
Bacon, B. W., *The Apostolic Message*, London, 1925.
Bacon, B. W., *The Story of Jesus and the Beginnings of the Church*, New York, 1927.
Barrett, C. K., *The Gospel According to St John*, London, 1955.
Barrett, C. K., *The Holy Spirit and the Gospel Tradition*, London, 1947.

Barrett, C. K., 'The Lamb of God', in *N.T.S.* vol. I, 1955, pp. 210–18.
Barrett, C. K., 'The Old Testament in the Fourth Gospel', in *J.T.S.* vol. 48, 1947, pp. 155–69.
Bauer, W., *Wörterbuch zu den Schriften des Neuen Testaments*, 4th ed., Berlin, 1952.
Bentzen, A., *Introduction to the Old Testament*, 2 vols., Copenhagen, 1948–9.
Bentzen, A., *King and Messiah*, London, 1955. Eng. ed. of original book in German, *Messias—Moses Redivivus—Menschensohn*.
Bernard, J. H., *The Gospel According to St John*, ed. A. H. McNeile, International Critical Commentary, 2 vols., Edinburgh, 1928.
Bigg, C., *The Epistles of St Peter and St Jude*, International Critical Commentary, 2nd ed., Edinburgh, 1910.
Black, M., 'The "Son of Man" in the Old Biblical Literature', and 'The Son of Man in the Teaching of Jesus', in *E.T.* vol. 60 (1949), pp. 11–15, 32–6.
Bonner, C., *Melito's The Homily on the Passion*, ed. and trans., London and Philadelphia, 1940. Studies and Documents, vol. 12.
Bousset, W., *Kyrios Christos*, 3rd ed., Göttingen, 1926.
Bowman, J. W., *The Intention of Jesus*, London, 1945.
Bowman, J. W., 'The Background of the term "Son of Man"', in *E.T.* vol. 59, 1948, pp. 283–8.
Box, G. H., 'The Value and Significance of the Old Testament in Relation to the New', in *The People and The Book*, ed. A. S. Peake, Oxford, 1925.
Brandon, S. G. F., *The Fall of Jerusalem and the Christian Church*, London, 1951.
Branscombe, B. H., *The Gospel of Mark*, London, 1937.
Brownlee, W. H., 'The Servant of the Lord in the Qumran Scrolls', in *B.A.S.O.R.* no. 132, 1953, and no. 135, 1954.
Bruce, F. F., *The Acts of the Apostles*, London, 1951.
Büchler, A., *Studies in Sin and Atonement*, Oxford, 1928.
Büchsel, F., 'ἀντί', in *T.W.N.T.* vol. I, p. 373.
Büchsel, F., 'λύτρον', in *T.W.N.T.* vol. IV, pp. 341–52.
Bultmann, R., *Die Geschichte der synoptischen Tradition*, Göttingen, 1931.
Bultmann, R., *Jesus and the Word*, London, 1935, trans. L. P. Smith and E. Huntress from 2nd ed. of *Jesus*, 1934.
Bultmann, R., *Theology of the New Testament*, vol. I, trans. K. Grobel, London, 1952.
Burkitt, F. C., *Christian Beginnings*, London, 1924.
Burney, C. F., *The Aramaic Origin of the Fourth Gospel*, Oxford, 1922.
Cadbury, H. J., *The Making of Luke–Acts*, London, 1927.

BIBLIOGRAPHY

Cadbury, H. J., 'The Titles of Jesus in Acts', pp. 354–75, in *Beginnings*, vol. v, 1931.
Cadoux, C. J., *The Historic Mission of Jesus*, London, 1941.
Carpenter, J. E., *The First Three Gospels*, London, 1906.
Carpenter, L. L., *Primitive Christian Application of the Doctrine of the Servant*, Durham, U.S.A., 1929.
Cave, S., *The Doctrine of the Person of Christ*, London, 1925.
Cerfaux, L., *Recueil Lucien Cerfaux*, vol. II, Gembloux, 1954.
Charles, R. H., *The Book of Enoch*, Oxford, 1893.
Cheyne, T. K., 'Servant of the Lord', in *Encyclopaedia Biblica*, ed. T. K. Cheyne and J. S. Black, London, vol. IV, 1903, cols. 4398–410.
Clarke, W. K. L., *Divine Humanity*, London, 1936.
Cook, S. A., 'Israel before the Prophets', and 'The Prophets of Israel', in *The Cambridge Ancient History*, vol. III, Cambridge, 1925, pp. 416–57.
Cooke, G. A., *Ezekiel*, International Critical Commentary, Edinburgh, 1936.
Creed, J. M., *The Gospel According to St Luke*, London, 1930.
Cullmann, O., *Baptism in the New Testament*, Studies in Biblical Theology, vol. I, trans. J. K. S. Reid, London, 1950.
Cullmann, O., *Peter: Disciple, Apostle, Martyr*, trans. F. V. Filson, London, 1953.
Dalman, G., *Jesus–Jeshua*, trans. P. P. Levertoff, London, 1929.
Daniel-Rops, H., *Israel and the Ancient World*, trans. K. Madge, London, 1949.
Davies, W. D., *Paul and Rabbinic Judaism*, London, 1948.
Denney, J., *The Death of Christ*, ed. R. V. G. Tasker, London, 1951.
Dibelius, M., *From Tradition to Gospel*, London, 1934, Eng. trans. from *Die Formgeschichte des Evangeliums*, rev. 2nd ed., 1933.
Dodd, C. H., *According to the Scriptures*, London, 1952.
Dodd, C. H., *The Apostolic Preaching and its Developments*, 1936, London, new ed., 1944.
Dodd, C. H., *The Epistle of Paul to the Romans*, Moffat New Testament Commentary, London, 1932.
Dodd, C. H., *History and the Gospel*, London, 1938.
Dodd, C. H., *The Interpretation of the Fourth Gospel*, Cambridge, 1953.
Dodd, C. H., *The Old Testament in the New*, Ethel M. Wood Lecture, London, 1952.
Dodd, C. H., *Parables of the Kingdom*, London, 1935.
Driver, G. R., 'The Hebrew Scrolls from the neighbourhood of Jericho and the Dead Sea', *Friends of Dr Williams's Library*, Lecture 4, Oxford, 1951.
Driver, S. R., *The Book of Daniel*, Cambridge, 1900.

BIBLIOGRAPHY

Driver, S. R. and Neubauer, A., *The Fifty-Third Chapter of Isaiah according to the Jewish Interpreters*, Oxford and London, vol. I, Texts, 1876, vol. II, Translations, 1877.

Duncan, G. S., *The Epistle of Paul to the Galatians*, Moffatt New Testament Commentary, London, 1934.

Dupont-Sommer, A., *The Jewish Sect of Qumran and the Essenes*, trans. R. D. Barnett, London, 1954.

Eissfeldt, O., 'The 'Ebed-Jahwe in Isaiah xl–lv in the light of the Israelite Conceptions of the Community and the Individual, the Ideal and the Real', in *E.T.* vol. 44, 1933, pp. 261–8.

Engnell, I., 'The 'Ebed Yahweh Songs and the Suffering Messiah in "Deutero-Isaiah"', in *B.J.R.L.* vol. 31, 1948.

Farrer, A. M., *The Glass of Vision*, Westminster, 1948, Bampton Lectures for 1948.

Fascher, E., 'Theologische Beobachtungen zu δεῖ', article in *Neutestamentliche Studien für Rudolf Bultmann*, Berlin, 1954, pp. 228–60.

Flemington, W. F., *The New Testament Doctrine of Baptism*, London, 1948.

Flew, R. N., *Jesus and His Church*, London, 1938.

Frankfort, H., *Kingship and the Gods*, Chicago, 1948.

Frost, S. B., *Old Testament Apocalyptic*, London, 1952.

Fuller, R. H., *The Mission and Achievement of Jesus*, London, 1954.

Ginsberg, H. L., 'The Oldest Interpretation of the Suffering Servant', in *V.T.* vol. 3, 1953, pp. 400–4.

Goguel, M., *The Life of Jesus*, trans. O. Wyon, London, 1933.

Gore, C., *The Reconstruction of Belief*, London, 1926. New ed., in one vol., of *Belief in God*, 1921, *Belief in Christ*, 1922, and *The Holy Spirit and the Church*, 1924.

Grant, F. C., in *The Interpreter's Bible*, part VII, ed. N. B. Harmon, New York, 1951, pp. 767 f.

Grundmann, W., 'ἰσχύω', in *T.W.N.T.* vol. III, pp. 402–5.

Guignebert, C., *The Jewish World in the Time of Jesus*, London, 1939.

Hegermann, H., *Jesaja 53 in Hexapla, Targum und Peschitta*, Gütersloh, 1954.

Héring, J., *Le Royaume de Dieu et sa Venue*, Paris, 1937.

Hooke, S. H., *Babylonian and Assyrian Religion*, London, 1953.

Hooke, S. H., 'The Origins of Early Semitic Ritual', *Schweich Lecture* 28, for 1935, London, 1938.

Hooke, S. H., *Prophets and Priests*, London, 1938.

Hooke, S. H., 'The Theory and Practice of Substitution', in *V.T.* vol. 2, 1952.

Hooke, S. H., ed., *The Labyrinth*, London, 1935.

Hooke, S. H., ed., *Myth and Ritual*, Oxford, 1933.

BIBLIOGRAPHY

Hoskyns, E., 'Jesus the Messiah', in *Mysterium Christi*, ed. G. K. A. Bell and D. A. Deissmann, London, 1930.
Hoskyns, E. and Davey, N., *The Riddle of the New Testament*, 3rd. ed., London, 1947.
Howard, W. F., *Christianity According to St John*, London, 1943.
Howard, W. F., 'Great Texts Reconsidered: Mark 10. 45', in *E.T.* vol. 50, 1939, pp. 107–10.
Hunter, A. M., *Paul and His Predecessors*, London, 1940.
Hunter, A. M., 'The Study of the New Testament', in *E.T.* vol. 46, 1945, pp. 265–9.
Hunter, A. M., *The Unity of the New Testament*, 2nd ed., London, 1944.
Huntress, E., '"Son of God" in Jewish Writings Prior to the Christian Era', in *J.B.L.* vol. 54, 1935, pp. 117–23.
Jackson, F. and Lake, K., eds., *The Beginnings of Christianity*, part I, 5 vols., London, 1920–33.
James, E. O., 'Sources of Christian Ritual', in *The Labyrinth*, ed. S. H. Hooke, London, 1935.
Jaspers, K., 'Die Auffassung der Persönlichkeit Jesu', in *Essays Presented to Leo Baeck*, London, 1954.
Jeremias, J., *The Eucharistic Words of Jesus*, trans. from 2nd German ed. by A. Ehrhardt, Oxford, 1955.
Jeremias, J., *The Parables of Jesus*, trans. S. H. Hooke, London, 1954.
Jeremias, J., 'ἀμνός', in *T.W.N.T.* vol. I, p. 342.
Jeremias, J. 'παῖς Θεοῦ', in *T.W.N.T.* vol. v, pp. 676–713.
Jeremias, J., 'Zum Problem der Deutung von Jes. 53 im palästinischen Spätjudentum', in *Aux Sources de la Tradition Chrétienne*, Mélanges offerts à M. Maurice Goguel, Neuchâtel, 1950, pp. 113–19.
Johnson, A. R., *The One and the Many in the Israelite Conception of God*, Cardiff, 1942.
Johnson, A. R., 'The Role of the King in the Jerusalem Cultus', in *The Labyrinth*, ed. S. H. Hooke, London, 1935.
Kennett, R. H., *The Servant of the Lord*, London, 1911.
Kissane, E. J., *The Book of Isaiah*, vol. II, Dublin, 1943.
Kittel, G., 'The Jesus of History', in *Mysterium Christi*, ed. G. K. A. Bell and D. A. Deissmann, London, 1930.
Klausner, J., *Jesus of Nazareth*, London, 1925.
Lake, K. and Lake, S., *An Introduction to the New Testament*, revised ed., London, 1938.
Lampe, G. W. H., *The Seal of the Spirit*, London, 1951.
Langdon, S., *The Babylonian Epic of Creation*, Oxford, 1923.
Lightfoot, J. B., *St Paul's Epistle to the Galatians*, 4th ed., London, 1874.

BIBLIOGRAPHY

Lindblom, J., *The Servant Songs in Deutero-Isaiah*, Lund, 1951.
Lods, A., *Israel from its Beginnings to the Middle of the Eighth Century*, trans. S. H. Hooke, London, 1932.
Lofthouse, W. F., 'Imitatio Christi', in *E.T.* vol. 65, 1954, pp. 338–42.
Lofthouse, W. F., 'Some Reflections on the "Servant Songs"', in *J.T.S.* vol. 48, 1947, pp. 169–76.
Loisy, A., *L'Evangile selon Marc*, Paris, 1912.
McNeile, A. H., *The Gospel According to St Matthew*, London, 1913.
McNeile, A. H., 'Our Lord's Use of the Old Testament', in *Cambridge Biblical Essays*, London, 1909, pp. 217–50.
Manson, T. W., 'The Life of Jesus: A study of the available materials', in *B.J.R.L.* vol. 27, 1943, pp. 323 ff.
Manson, T. W., *The Sayings of Jesus*, London, 1949.
Manson, T. W., *The Servant Messiah*, Cambridge, 1953.
Manson, T. W., 'The Son of Man in Daniel, Enoch and the Gospels', in *B.J.R.L.* vol. 32, 1950, pp. 171–93.
Manson, T. W., *The Teaching of Jesus*, 2nd ed., Cambridge, 1935.
Manson, W., *Jesus the Messiah*, London, 1943.
Michael, J. H., *The Epistle of Paul to the Philippians*, Moffatt New Testament Commentary, London, 1928.
Mitchell, H. G., Smith, J. M. P. and Bewer, J. A., *Haggai, Zechariah, Malachi and Jonah*, International Criticial Commentary, Edinburgh, 1912.
Moffatt, J., *The First Epistle of Paul to the Corinthians*, Moffatt New Testament Commentary, London, 1938.
Moffatt, J., *The Theology of the Gospels*, London, 1912.
Montefiore, C. G., *The Old Testament and After*, London, 1923.
Montefiore, C. G., *Rabbinic Literature and Gospel Teachings*, London, 1930.
Montefiore, C. G., *The Synoptic Gospels*, 2 vols., 2nd ed., London, 1927.
Montgomery, J. A., *Daniel*, International Critical Commentary, Edinburgh, 1927.
Moore, G. F., *Judaism in the First Centuries of the Christian Era*, 3 vols., Cambridge, 1927–30.
Mowinckel, S., *He That Cometh*, trans. G. W. Anderson, Oxford, 1956.
Mozley, J. K., 'Christology and Soteriology', in *Mysterium Christi*, ed. G. K. A. Bell and D. A. Deissmann, London, 1930.
Mozley, J. K., *The Doctrine of the Atonement*, London, 1915.
Myres, J. L., 'Persia, Greece and Israel', in *The Palestine Exploration Quarterly*, January–April, 1953.
North, C. R., *Isaiah 40–55*, Torch Commentary, London, 1952.
North, C. R., *The Suffering Servant in Deutero-Isaiah*, Oxford, 1948.
Oesterley, W. O. E., *The Evolution of the Messianic Idea*, London, 1908.

Oesterley, W. O. E., *The Jews and Judaism during the Greek Period*, London, 1941.
Oesterley, W. O. E., *Sacrifices in Ancient Israel*, London, 1937.
Oesterley, W. O. E. and Robinson, T. H., *Hebrew Religion, Its Origin and Development*, 2nd ed., London, 1937.
Otto, R., *The Kingdom of God and the Son of Man*, London, 1938, trans. F. V. Filson and B. L. Woolf from revised ed. of *Reich Gottes und Menschensohn*, 1934.
Peake, A. S., *The Problem of Suffering in the Old Testament*, London, 1904.
Pedersen, J., *Israel, Its Life and Culture*, 2 vols., London and Copenhagen, 1946–7.
Pfeiffer, R. H., *History of New Testament Times with an Introduction to the Apocrypha*, New York, 1949.
Plummer, A., *An Exegetical Commentary on the Gospel According to St Matthew*, 2nd ed., London, 1910.
Plummer, A., *The Gospel According to St Luke*, International Critical Commentary, 5th ed., Edinburgh, 1922.
Pritchard, J. B., ed., *Ancient Near Eastern Texts Relating to the Old Testament*, Princeton, U.S.A., 1950.
Rabin, C., *The Zadokite Fragments*, Oxford, 1954.
Rashdall, H., *The Idea of the Atonement in Christian Theology*, Bampton Lectures for 1915, London, 1920.
Rawlinson, A. E. J., *The New Testament Doctrine of the Christ*, Bampton Lectures for 1926, London, 1926.
Rawlinson, A. E. J., *The Gospel According to St Mark*, Westminster Commentary, 7th ed., London, 1953.
Rawlinson, A. E. J. and Parsons, R. G., 'The Interpretation of Christ in the New Testament', essay in *Foundations*, ed. B. H. Streeter, London, 1912.
Riesenfeld, H., *Jésus Transfiguré*, Copenhagen, 1947.
Rignell, L. G., 'Isa. lii. 13–liii. 12', in *V.T.* vol. 3, 1953, pp. 87–92.
Robinson, H. W., *The Cross of the Servant: A study in Deutero-Isaiah*, London, 1926.
Robinson, H. W., 'The Hebrew Conception of Corporate Personality', *Werden und Wesen des Alten Testaments*, *B.Z.A.W.*, 66, Berlin, 1936, pp. 49–62.
Robinson, H. W., 'Hebrew Psychology', in *The People and The Book*, ed. A. S. Peake, Oxford, 1925.
Robinson, H. W., *Redemption and Revelation*, London, 1942.
Robinson, T. H., *The Gospel of Matthew*, Moffatt New Testament Commentary, London, 1927.
Robinson, T. H., *Poetry and Poets of the Old Testament*, London, 1947.

BIBLIOGRAPHY

Rowley, H. H., *The Biblical Doctrine of Election*, London, 1950.
Rowley, H. H., *Israel's Mission to the World*, London, 1939.
Rowley, H. H., *The Rediscovery of the Old Testament*, London, 1945.
Rowley, H. H., *The Relevance of Apocalyptic*, 2nd ed., London, 1947.
Rowley, H. H., *The Servant of the Lord and Other Essays on the Old Testament*, London, 1952.
Rowley, H. H., *The Unity of the Bible*, London, 1953.
Ryle, H. E., *Philo and Holy Scripture*, London, 1895.
Schrenk G., 'γραφή', in *T.W.N.T.* vol. I, pp. 749–61.
Schürer, E., *A History of the Jewish People in the Time of Jesus Christ*, div. II, vol. 2, trans. S. Taylor and P. Christie, Edinburgh, 1885.
Schweizer, E., 'Discipleship and Belief in Jesus as Lord from Jesus to the Hellenistic Church', trans. H. F. Peacock, *N.T.S.* vol. II, 1956, pp. 87–99.
Selwyn, E. G., *The First Epistle of St Peter*, London, 1946.
Skinner, J., *Isaiah Chapters xl–lxvi*, Cambridge, 1906.
Smith, C. Ryder, *The Bible Doctrine of Salvation*, London, 1941.
Smith, G. A., *The Book of Isaiah*, vol. II, London, 1904.
Smith, S., 'Isaiah Chapters xl–lv', *Schweich Lecture* for 1940, London, 1944.
Smith, W. R., *Lectures on the Religion of the Semites*, 3rd ed., ed. S. A. Cook, London, 1927.
Snaith, N. H., *The Distinctive Ideas of the Old Testament*, London, 1944.
Snaith, N. H., *The Jews from Cyrus to Herod*, Wallington, 1949.
Snaith, N. H., 'The Servant of the Lord in Deutero-Isaiah', essay in *Studies in Old Testament Prophecy presented to Professor T. H. Robinson*, ed. H. H. Rowley, Edinburgh, 1950.
Snaith, N. H., 'The So-called Servant Songs', in *E.T.* vol. 56, 1945, pp. 79–81.
Stauffer, E., *New Testament Theology*, trans. J. Marsh, London, 1955.
Strachan, R. H., *The Fourth Gospel, Its Significance and Environment*, 3rd ed., London, 1941.
Strack, H. L. and Billerbeck, P., *Kommentar zum Neuen Testament aus Talmud und Midrasch*, Munich, 4 parts, 1922–8.
Swete, H. B., *The Gospel According to St Mark*, London, 1898.
Taylor, V., *The Atonement in New Testament Teaching*, 2nd ed., London, 1945.
Taylor, V., *The Gospel According to St Mark*, London, 1952.
Taylor, V., *Jesus and His Sacrifice*, London, 1937.
Taylor, V., *The Names of Jesus*, London, 1953.
Taylor, V., 'The Origin of the Markan Passion-Sayings', in *N.T.S.* vol. I, 1955, pp. 159–67.

Thornton, L. S., 'The Body of Christ in the New Testament', essay in *The Apostolic Ministry*, ed. K. E. Kirk, London, 1946, pp. 53–111.
Thornton, L. S., *The Common Life in the Body of Christ*, London, 1942.
Thornton, L. S., *Revelation and the Modern World*, and *The Dominion of Christ*, vols. I and II of *The Form of a Servant*, Westminster, 1950 and 1952.
Torrey, C. C., *The Apocryphal Literature*, New Haven, U.S.A., 1945.
Torrey, C. C., 'The Influence of Second Isaiah in the Gospels and Acts', in *J.B.L.* vol. 48, 1929, pp. 24–36.
Torrey, C. C., *The Second Isaiah*, Edinburgh and New York, 1928.
Turner, C. H., 'ὁ υἱός μου ὁ ἀγαπητός', in *J.T.S.* vol. 27, 1926, pp. 113–29.
Turner, H. E. W., *Jesus, Master and Lord*, London, 1953.
Wardle, W. L., 'Currents of Old Testament Study', in *The London Quarterly and Holborn Review*, vol. 160, 1935, pp. 436f.
Weiss, J., *The History of Primitive Christianity*, trans. and ed. F. C. Grant, London, 1937.
Wolff, H. W., *Jesaja 53 im Urchristentum*, 2nd ed., Berlin, 1950.
Workmann, G. C., *The Servant of Jehovah*, London, 1907.
Wright, C. H. H., 'The Pre-Christian Jewish Interpretation of Isaiah LII, LIII', in *The Expositor*, 3rd series, vol. 7, London, 1888, pp. 364–77, 401–20.

INDEX OF BIBLICAL, APOCRYPHAL AND OTHER ANCIENT WRITINGS

OLD TESTAMENT

(References here, though not always in the text, are given as in EVV, but where the original text or the Septuagint version differ greatly from the English, the reference to them is given in brackets.)

Genesis

3	140
6. 18	186
17. 2	186
21. 27	186
22. 2, 12, 16	70
26. 24	184
31. 44–54	186

Exodus

4. 22f.	183
6. 6	185
12–14	124
14. 31	184
15. 13, 16	185
21. 30	185
23. 20	181
23. 32	171
24. 3–8	186
28. 41	198
30. 12	185
31. 3	67
34. 12, 15	171

Leviticus

17–26	124
19. 20	185
25. 24–6	185
25. 51f.	185
26. 6	171
27. 31	185

Numbers

3. 12	77, 185
3. 46–51	185
18. 15	185
20. 14–21	43
21. 9	105
25. 12f.	186
28–9	195
35. 31f.	185

Deuteronomy

1. 16	199
1. 31	183
7. 6f.	199
7. 8	185
9. 26	185
9. 27	184
13. 5	185
15. 15	185
18. 5	199
21. 8	185
24. 18	185
32. 43	179
34. 5	184

Joshua

1. 1	184
8. 33	186
9. 6	186
24. 29	184

Judges

2. 1	186
2. 8	184
6. 34	67
11. 34	70

Ruth

General	61

INDEX OF BIBLICAL, APOCRYPHAL, ANCIENT WRITINGS

1 Samuel
10. 24	199
26. 16	198
31. 9	66

2 Samuel
1. 20	66
3. 18	184
4. 10	66, 181
5. 3	186
7. 12–16	171
7. 14	69
18. 19–31	66
18. 27	66, 181
22. 20	71

1 Kings
1. 39	198
1. 42	66, 181
19. 16	198

2 Kings
7. 9	66
11. 17	186

1 Chronicles
6. 49	184
10. 9	66
28. 6	69
29. 1	69

2 Chronicles
22. 7	199
24. 9	184
29. 10	171

Nehemiah
9. 7	199
10. 29	184

Job
General	140
1. 8	184
1. 21	175
2. 3	184
2. 10	175
11. 20	175
31. 39	175
42. 8	184

Psalms
General	158
2	11, 18, 70, 182
2. 7	69, 182
3. 3	192
9. 8	199
11. 6	189, 196
18	184
18. 9	68
20. 6	199
21. 1–6	192
21. 7–9	130
22	4, 164, 176, 189, 192, 197
22. 1	200
22. 6	94
23. 5	189, 196
28	192
28. 8	199
30	176, 192
32	140
36	184
37	197
40 (39). 9	66
44	173
44. 3 (43. 4)	71
45 (44. 1)	70
50. 15	192
54–7	197
60. 5 (59. 7)	70
64	197
67. 12	183
68 (67). 11	66
69	4, 164, 197
70–1	197
73	140
84. 1 (83. 2)	71
88	176
89. 3	186
89. 27	69, 182
96 (95). 2	66
102. 25 f.	79
105. 15	199
105. 42	184
108. 6 (107. 7)	70
118	189
118. 22 f.	97 f.
118. 22	94
127 (126). 2	70

INDEX OF BIBLICAL, APOCRYPHAL, ANCIENT WRITINGS

Psalms (cont.)

141. 8	175
142	197
144. 5	68
147 (146). 11	71
149. 4	71

Proverbs

6. 35	185
13. 8	185

Isaiah

General	30
2. 2–4	170
5. 1–7	169
5. 1	70
6. 5–7	181
6. 10–13	169
6. 10	106
9	54
9. 2	187
11	54
11. 2–4	68
11. 2	199
11. 11–14	170
20. 3	184
26. 17	183
27. 12	186
32. 15	68
35	12, 19, 33, 77, 86
35. 5f.	85
35. 6–7	34
35. 9f.	185
35. 9	34, 185
35. 10	33
40	27, 50, 51
40. 1f.	169
40. 2	33, 40, 175
40. 3–5	33
40. 3	67, 181
40. 9	40, 65, 66, 171
40. 11	33, 34
40. 12–31	59
40. 12–14	33
40. 27	34
40. 28–31	34
41	27
41. 1	33
41. 8–10	32
41. 8f.	48, 169
41. 8	169, 170, 184
41. 9	33, 169, 184
41. 10	115, 116, 170
41. 14	185
41. 17f.	33
41. 18f.	35
41. 20	35
42	11, 18, 27
42. 1–4	33, 64, 84, 169
42. 1f.	22
42. 1	9, 49, 68, 70–3, 107, 169, 182, 184, 199
42. 2	71
42. 5–9	33
42. 6f.	130, 132, 150
42. 6	38f., 80, 82, 84, 112, 115, 199
42. 7	107, 115
42. 10–12	33
42. 13	33
42. 16	33
42. 18–25	50
42. 19–25	170
42. 19	48, 184
42. 24f.	35
42. 25	33
43	27
43. 1	185
43. 5–7	33, 34, 35
43. 9	33
43. 10	48, 169, 176, 184
43. 14	185
43. 15	171
43. 19f.	33
43. 21	169
43. 22–8	170
43. 25	40
43. 27f.	32
43. 28	34
44	27f.
44. 1f.	48
44. 1	169, 184
44. 2	169, 184
44. 3–5	32, 40
44. 3f.	33

Isaiah (cont.)

44. 3	34, 68
44. 21	48, 169, 184
44. 22–4	185
44. 22	33
44. 23	33, 169
44. 26	33, 48, 184
45	28, 174
45. 1	199
45. 4	48, 169, 184
45. 13	185
45. 14	31
45. 21f.	169
45. 22f.	31
46	28
46. 12f.	33
47	28, 31, 32, 34, 175
48	28
48. 1–19	50
48. 9f.	169
48. 10	33, 35
48. 11	35, 170
48. 20	48, 184
49	28, 184
49. 1–6	33
49. 1	115
49. 3	49, 169, 184
49. 4	121
49. 5f.	31, 49, 79
49. 5	33, 169, 184
49. 6f.	132
49. 6	54, 80, 84, 107, 112, 150, 169, 176, 184
49. 7	32, 34, 40, 169, 184
49. 8	33, 38f., 80, 82, 115
49. 9–13	34
49. 12f.	33
49. 14–23	59
49. 14	34
49. 18	33
49. 19–26	175
49. 19–21	32, 34, 169
49. 22–6	31, 34, 180
49. 23	169
49. 24–6	32, 40, 169
49. 24f.	33, 73f., 184
49. 26	32
50	28, 53, 91, 148, 150
50. 1–3	32, 170
50. 1f.	35
50. 4–11	33
50. 4–6	169
50. 6–9	32, 130, 131
50. 6f.	169, 175
50. 6	4, 90, 91
50. 7–9	169
50. 8f.	123
50. 10	48, 184
51	28
51. 3	35
51. 4	40
51. 6	79
51. 7f.	34
51. 7	33, 40
51. 9–11	33
51. 10f.	185
51. 11	185
51. 12–16	33, 34
51. 15f.	40
51. 17–52. 2	59
51. 17–23	32, 97
51. 17–20	32
51. 17	196
51. 21–3	34
51. 22	169
51. 23	169, 175
52. 1–12	28
52. 3	125, 185
52. 6	33, 40
52. 7	65, 66, 116f., 181
52. 8	40
52. 13–53. 12	28, 50, 55, 56, 85, 96, 106, 110, 116, 117, 121, 126, 140, 151, 162, 194
52. 13–15	34, 169
52. 13	49, 105, 178, 184, 194
52. 14	194
52. 15	115, 116, 117
53. 1–12	35, 130
53. 1	103, 115, 116f.
53. 2f.	194
53. 2	129
53. 3	32, 34, 94, 169
53. 4–12	193
53. 4	22, 64, 83

INDEX OF BIBLICAL, APOCRYPHAL, ANCIENT WRITINGS

Isaiah (cont.)

53. 5	125, 130
53. 6	79, 125
53. 7–9	32
53. 7f.	22, 103, 107
53. 7	89, 103f., 113f., 124, 125, 126, 130, 191, 196
53. 8	113f., 129
53. 9	125, 131, 194
53. 10–12	169
53. 10	32, 74
53. 11–13	177
53. 11f.	9, 78f., 81
53. 11	74, 111, 121, 184
53. 12	3, 4, 8, 9, 22, 32, 64, 74, 79, 80, 82, 92, 94, 123, 125, 131, 151, 175, 178, 184, 186
54	28f., 59
54. 1–10	49
54. 1–8	33
54. 1–3	32, 169
54. 7f.	169
54. 8	33
54. 9f.	38, 40
54. 10	40
54. 11–17	40
54. 11f.	33
55	29
55. 3–5	35, 40
55. 3f.	38
55. 3	33, 34, 40, 171
55. 10f.	33
55. 12f.	33
56–66	77
56. 6	184
59. 21	68, 186
60. 6	66
61	3, 12, 13, 19, 86
61. 1f.	9, 64, 85, 132, 187
61. 1	66, 68, 199
61. 3	175
62. 4	71
62. 12	185
63. 9	185
63. 11	183
63. 17	184
64. 1	68, 183
65. 9	184

Jeremiah

General	31–40, 42, 44, 147, 149, 162
6. 26	70
14. 10	71
15. 9	175
15. 21	185
20. 15	66, 181
23. 3	186
25. 9	184
25. 15	189
27. 6	184
29. 14	186
30	31–3, 40
30. 8f.	37
30. 8	34
30. 10f.	170
30. 21f.	37
30. 22	171
31	31–3, 40, 171
31. 1	171
31. 8, 10	186
31 (38). 11	185
31 (38). 20	71, 72
31. 31–4	36
31. 31–3	186
31. 31	171
31. 32	39
31. 33	39, 171
31. 34	39
32	31–3, 40, 171
32. 35	170
32. 37	186
32. 38	171
32. 40	36, 39, 171
33	31–4, 40
33. 14–26	37
33. 16	171
33. 20f.	36, 39
43. 10	184
49. 12	189, 196
50 (27). 34	185

Lamentations

4. 20	199

Ezekiel

General	31–40, 42, 44, 142, 147, 149, 162

INDEX OF BIBLICAL, APOCRYPHAL, ANCIENT WRITINGS

Ezekiel (cont.)
11. 17	186
16	47
16. 60	171
20. 34, 41	186
28. 25	184
33	34
34	34, 40
34. 13	186
34. 23 f.	37
34. 25–31	36 f.
34. 25–9	39
34. 25	39, 171
34. 30	39
35	34, 40
36	34 f., 40
36. 28	171
37	34 f., 40, 47, 175
37. 15–23	37
37. 23	171
37. 25	184
37. 26 f.	36, 39
37. 26	39, 170 f., 171
37. 27	39, 171
39. 27	186

Daniel
General	60, 142–5, 160 f.
6. 20	184
7	143, 145, 160, 189
7. 1–8	143 f.
7. 9–18	143 f.
7. 12	160
7. 13	142
7. 17 f.	198
7. 17	142
8. 22	142
8. 24 f.	177
9. 11	184
9. 24–7	177
11. 33, 35	177
12. 3	53, 58, 179
12. 10	177

Hosea
General	30
2. 9–13	169
2. 18 (2. 20)	170, 171
7. 13	185
9. 1–9	169
11	170
11. 1	183
13. 14	185

Joel
2. 28–32	183
2. 28	68
2. 32	181

Amos
General	30
5. 18–20	169
7. 7–9	169
8. 10	70
9. 11–15	170

Jonah
General	61

Micah
General	30
1. 2–9	169
2. 12	186
3. 8	68
3. 9–12	169
4. 10	185
6. 4	185

Nahum
1. 15	66

Habakkuk
General	46, 140
3. 13	199

Zephaniah
3. 1	185

Haggai
General	170

Zechariah
General	170

INDEX OF BIBLICAL, APOCRYPHAL, ANCIENT WRITINGS

Zechariah (cont.)

1. 4–6	195
9. 9	53, 57
9. 11	82, 186
10. 8	185
10. 10	186
12. 10	53, 57, 70
13	189

Malachi

1. 11	61, 187
2. 17	71
3	183
3. 1	67, 181
3. 17	183
3. 24	54
4	183

JEWISH APOCRYPHAL AND PSEUDEPIGRAPHICAL WRITINGS

1 Baruch

General	58–61
1. 1–14	58
1. 15–3. 8	58
3. 9–4. 4	58
4. 5–5. 9	58

2 Baruch

General	58–61
14	59
14. 8	59
15	59
85	59

Ecclesiasticus

4. 10	183
48. 10	54, 179

1 Enoch

General	54, 57, 60, 142–6, 153f., 160f.
38. 1f.	144, 198
39. 6f.	144
39. 6	198
40. 5	144
43. 3–6	198
45. 3–5	144
45. 3f.	198
46	143
46. 1–4	144
46. 3	144
47	153f.
47. 4	199
48. 2–7	144
48. 4	145, 199
48. 7–9	199
48. 7	145
48. 10	144
49. 2f.	144
49. 3	199
51. 2–5	144
52. 4	144
52. 6, 9	144
53. 6f.	144
55. 4	144
60. 10	198
61. 5–8	144
61. 5	198
61. 10	144
62	199
62. 1f.	144
62. 5–9, 13–15	144
66. 1f.	198
69. 26–9	144
69. 27	198
70. 1	144
71. 14–17	144
89	196
105. 2	69

2 Esdras (4 Ezra)

General	58–61
3–10	59
4	59
7. 28f.	182
9. 38–10. 28	59
13. 32, 37, 52	182
14. 9	182

INDEX OF BIBLICAL, APOCRYPHAL, ANCIENT WRITINGS

2 Maccabees	
7. 37f.	179
7. 37	54

4 Maccabees	
General	60, 61
1. 11	179
6. 27–9	54, 57f., 78
6. 28f.	179
12. 7f.	179
17. 20–2	54, 57f., 78
17. 21f.	179

Psalms of Solomon	
11	180

17. 23–51	182
17. 30	182, 183

Testament of Joseph	
19	196

Wisdom of Solomon	
1–5	141
2. 12–20	54, 57f.
2. 12	197
2. 16, 18	183
3. 1–9	54, 57f.
3. 5f.	141
5. 1–5	53, 57f.
5. 5	183

NEW TESTAMENT

Matthew	
General	3, 4, 7, 148–50, 154
2. 16	192
3. 3	64, 67
3. 11	64, 67f.
3. 16	64, 67f.
3. 17	64, 68–73
4. 23	65, 66
5. 10–12	136
8. 6, 8, 13	192
8. 16f.	64, 83
8. 17	3, 22, 106, 168
9. 15	65, 92, 135
9. 35	65, 66
10. 17–23	136
10. 38	136
11. 5	3, 65, 66
11. 10	181
12. 17ff.	3
12. 17f.	22
12. 18–21	64, 70, 84, 108
12. 18	71, 72, 107
12. 29	64, 73f.
14. 2	192
16. 21	65, 92–7
16. 24	136
17. 5	64, 68–73
17. 9–13	200
17. 12	65, 93–7, 135
17. 18	192
17. 22f.	65, 92–7
20. 18f.	65, 92–7
20. 18	189
20. 21	137
20. 22f.	135
20. 22	65, 97
20. 23	136
20. 28	9, 64, 74–9, 135
21. 15	192
21. 33–46	135
21. 42	65, 97f., 190
22. 29	190
23. 11	185
23. 29–36	135f.
23. 32	136
23. 37–9	136
24. 9–14	136
24. 14	65, 66
24. 31	64, 79
24. 35	64, 79
26. 12	65, 98, 135
26. 13	65, 66
26. 21	64, 79f.
26. 24	64, 65, 79f., 98f., 135, 168, 190
26. 28	9, 64, 80–3, 135
26. 31	65, 99
26. 38f.	135

INDEX OF BIBLICAL, APOCRYPHAL, ANCIENT WRITINGS

Matthew (cont.)

26. 54	99, 190
26. 56	65, 99, 190
26. 63	64, 87–9
26. 64	88
26. 67f.	65, 89–91
27. 11	88
27. 12	64, 87–9
27. 14	64, 87–9
27. 19	111
27. 24	193
27. 26–31	65, 90f.
27. 38	65, 91f.

Mark

General	7, 148–50, 154
1. 1	64, 65–7
1. 2f.	64, 67
1. 8–10	67f.
1. 8	64, 148
1. 9–11	166
1. 10	64, 68, 148
1. 11	16, 64, 68–73, 182
1. 14	65, 66
1. 15	65, 66
2. 19f.	65, 92, 135
3. 7–12	84
3. 27	64, 73f., 148, 184
8. 31	8, 16, 65, 92–7, 100, 166, 196
8. 34	136
8. 35	65, 66
9. 7	64, 68–73
9. 9–13	200
9. 12f.	190
9. 12	8, 9, 10, 16, 65, 93–7, 98, 100, 166, 168, 196
9. 13	135
9. 31	8, 16, 65, 92–7, 122, 166, 196
9. 35	185
10. 29	65, 66
10. 32	189
10. 33f.	8, 65, 92–7, 196
10. 33	16, 100, 122
10. 37f.	137
10. 38f.	135, 166
10. 38	65, 97
10. 39	136
10. 42	75
10. 43f.	75, 185
10. 44f.	74
10. 44	74, 184
10. 45	3, 5, 8, 9, 10, 15, 16, 20, 23, 64, 74–9, 82, 93, 94, 135, 166, 189, 199
12. 1–12	135
12. 10f.	97f., 102
12. 10	65, 189, 190
12. 24	190
13. 9–13	136
13. 10	65, 66
13. 27	64, 79, 148
13. 31	64, 79
14. 8	65, 98, 135, 166
14. 9	65, 66
14. 18	3, 20, 64, 79f., 98
14. 21–4	23
14. 21	3, 20, 64, 65, 79f., 94, 98f., 135, 190
14. 22	82, 189
14. 24	5, 8, 9, 10, 64, 80–3, 166
14. 27	65, 99, 102, 189
14. 34–6	135
14. 36	166
14. 49	65, 99
14. 61	64, 87–9
14. 62	88, 199
14. 65	65, 89–91
15. 2	88
15. 5	64, 87–9
15. 15–20	65, 90f.
15. 27	65, 91f.
15. 28	168, 190
15. 34	200
16. 15	65, 66

Luke

General	3, 7, 148–50, 154
1. 19	65, 66
1. 54	107, 108
1. 69	107, 108
2. 10	65, 66
2. 32	64, 84, 194
2. 43	192
3	183

INDEX OF BIBLICAL, APOCRYPHAL, ANCIENT WRITINGS

Luke (cont.)

3. 4	64, 67
3. 16	64, 67f.
3. 18	65, 66
3. 21f.	64, 67f.
3. 22	64, 68–73
4. 16–21	64, 85
4. 17–21	9
4. 18f.	85, 148, 187
4. 18	3, 65, 66
4. 21	13, 190
5. 34f.	65, 92, 135
7. 7	192
7. 22	3, 64, 65, 66, 85f., 148
7. 27	181
8. 1	65, 66
8. 51, 54	192
9. 6	65, 66
9. 22	65, 92–7
9. 23	136
9. 31	200
9. 35	64, 68–73
9. 42	192
9. 44	65, 92–7, 166
9. 48	185
11. 21f.	73f.
11. 22	184
11. 47–51	135f.
12. 45	192
12. 49f.	16, 65, 99
12. 50	97, 135, 166
13. 32ff.	166
13. 32f.	16, 65, 99f.
13. 33	136
13. 34f.	136
14. 27	136
15. 26	192
16. 16	65, 66
17. 25	65, 100, 166, 189
18. 31–3	65, 92–7
18. 31	189, 190
20. 1	65, 66
20. 9–19	135
20. 17	65, 97f.
21. 12–19	136
21. 22	190
21. 33	64, 79
22. 20	64, 80–3
22. 22	64, 65, 79f., 98f., 135
22. 27	74–9
22. 37	3, 8, 9, 10, 14, 22, 64, 86, 101, 149, 151, 164, 166, 168, 184
22. 41f.	135
22. 63f.	65, 89–91
22. 66–9	88
22. 70	88
23. 3	88
23. 9	64, 87–9
23. 11	65, 90f.
23. 33	65, 91f.
23. 34	166
23. 47	111
24. 21	186
24. 25–7	65, 100f., 137
24. 26f.	200
24. 26	189
24. 27–45	190
24. 27	190
24. 32	190
24. 44	190
24. 45–7	137
24. 45	190
24. 46	190

John

General	151f.
1. 14	192
1. 18	71
1. 23	67, 181
1. 29	103f., 126
1. 32f.	67f.
1. 34	68
1. 36	103f., 126
3. 14	103, 105f., 137
4. 51	192
8. 28	103, 105f.
8. 54	192
10. 11, 15, 17	166
12. 7	98
12. 27f.	137
12. 32	103, 105f., 200
12. 37f.	103, 106
12. 38	105, 117
12. 40	106
13. 31f	192

INDEX OF BIBLICAL, APOCRYPHAL, ANCIENT WRITINGS

John (cont.)

15. 20	136
17. 1	105
17. 4f.	192
18. 22	89–91
18. 33–8	88
19. 1–3	90f.
19. 9	87–9
19. 18	91f.

Acts

General	3, 8, 150f., 154, 158
1. 16	193
2. 14–39	197
2. 22–39	118–20
2. 23f.	138
2. 23	137
2. 36	138
3	154
3. 12–21	118–20
3. 13–26	197
3. 13	17, 107–10, 167
3. 14f.	138
3. 14	107, 111f.
3. 18	107, 112, 137
3. 26	17, 107–10, 167, 193
4	154, 193
4. 10–12	197
4. 25–30	192
4. 25	107, 108
4. 27–30	107–10
4. 27	17, 167
4. 28	137
4. 30	17, 167
5. 30–2	197
5. 41	139
7	138
7. 51f.	138
7. 52	107, 111f.
7. 55f.	138
8	13, 127, 150
8. 32–5	107, 113f.
8. 32f.	4, 22
8. 32	3, 4, 103f., 193
8. 35	193
9	115
9. 4f.	139
9. 15f.	116
9. 16	139
10. 36–43	197
10. 36	3
13	116, 150
13. 17–41	197
13. 26–41	118–20
13. 27–9	107, 112
13. 46f.	107, 114–16
13. 47	127
17. 2f.	107, 112
17. 2	193
17. 3	137
17. 11	193
18. 9f.	115, 116
18. 24, 28	193
20. 12	192
22. 7f.	139
22. 14	107, 111f.
26	116, 150
26. 14f.	139
26. 16–18	107, 114–16
26. 18	127
26. 22f.	107, 112, 137
26. 23	114f.

Romans

1. 24, 26, 28	122
4. 25	122, 138, 195
5	196
5. 1	122
5. 6–11	197
5. 8	137
5. 9	122
5. 12–21	122
5. 18	195
5. 19	122
6	196
6. 1–11	197
6. 16f.	194
7. 4	197
8. 16–18	139
8. 17	139
8. 32f.	123
8. 32	122, 137
10. 15f.	116f.
10. 16	115, 116
15. 20f.	115
15. 21	116, 117

INDEX OF BIBLICAL, APOCRYPHAL, ANCIENT WRITINGS

1 Corinthians

1. 23	178
5. 5	122
11. 23–5	80
15	117–19, 197
15. 3 ff.	17, 197
15. 3 f.	197
15..3	116, 117–20, 138
15. 11	118
15. 24	122

2 Corinthians

4. 10	139
4. 17	139
5. 15	197
5. 21	122
6. 2	115
6. 4–10	139
11. 23–9	139

Galatians

1. 4	137
1. 15	115
2. 20	122
4. 3	194
4. 21–30	138 f.
5. 11	139
6. 12	139

Ephesians

5. 2	122
5. 25	122

Philippians

1. 29	139
2. 1–11	197
2. 5–11	116, 120 f.
3. 10	139

2 Timothy

2. 11 f.	139

Hebrews

General	3, 151–3
2. 9	197
2. 10	137
9. 7	123, 195
10. 12 f.	197
9. 25	123
9. 26	138
9. 28	123 f.
11	138
11. 26	138, 200
12. 2	197

1 Peter

General	1, 3, 4, 151–3, 196
1. 10 f.	124
1. 18 f.	124 f.
1. 19	103 f.
2	13, 22, 127
2. 21–5	17, 124, 125
2. 22–4	22, 130
2. 22	131
2. 24	131, 138
3. 18	111
5. 1, 10	139

1 John

1. 7	138
2. 1	111

Revelation

General	126
5. 6	126

OTHER ANCIENT WRITINGS

Barnabas, Epistle of	
5	199
5. 1 f.	130, 131
5. 13 f.	130, 131
6. 1 f.	130, 131
6. 1	108
9. 2	108
14. 4	132
14. 6–9	130, 132
Clement of Alexandria	
Stromateis VI, 15, 128	129
Clement of Rome	
16. 1–17	130, 199
59. 2, 3, 4	108

INDEX OF BIBLICAL, APOCRYPHAL, ANCIENT WRITINGS

Didache
9. 2   108, 192
9. 3   108
10. 2, 3   108

Diognetus, Epistle of
8. 9, 11   108
9. 1   108
9. 5   130, 132f.

Josephus
Bel. Jud. 5. 9   178

Justin
Dialogue with Trypho 111   196

Martyrdom of Polycarp
14. 1, 3   108
20. 2   108

Melito
Homily on the Passion 64   196

Origen
Contra Celsum
1. 54f.   199
1. 55   180

Peter, Acts of, 23f.   129, 199
Peter, Preaching of   129, 199

Polycarp, Epistle of
8   199
8. 1f.   130f.

Shepherd of Hermas
Sim. 5   130, 132

INDEX OF
HEBREW AND ARAMAIC WORDS

אִישׁ	142	כָּבוֹד			105 f.
אָשָׁם	77	נָתַן			122
בָּזָה	94	עֶבֶד	3, 74, 104, 107–10, 120, 184, 194
בָּחַר	70	עָרָה			121, 175
בְּרִית	81 f. 170 f.	פָּדָה			76 f., 185
בָּשָׂר	65–7, 148	צֶדֶק			111, 122
גָּאַל	76 f., 185	צָלַח			71
חָפֵץ	71	רַב			78 f.
טָלֶה (טַלְיָא)	104, 126	רָחֵל			103
יָדִיד	70	רָצָה			71 f.
יָחִיד	70	שָׁאַר (שְׁאָרָה)			143
יַקִּיר	71	שָׁפַךְ			82

INDEX OF GREEK WORDS

ἀγαπητός	68–73
αἷμα	81f.
ἁμαρτία	82, 117–19, 123
ἀμνός	103f., 124f., 126, 191
ἀντί	77
ἅπαξ	123
ἀποδοκιμάζω	94
ἀρνίον	103, 126
γράφω, γραφή	95, 113, 119f., 190, 193
δεῖ	95, 105
διαθήκη	81f.
διακονέω	74
δικαιόω, δίκαιος, δικαιοσύνη	110, 111f., 122f., 150
δοξάζω, δόξα	105, 110, 192
δουλεύω, δοῦλος	74, 120, 184, 194
ἐκλεκτός	70
ἐκχύνω	82
ἐμπτύω	90f.
ἐξουδενόω	94
εὐαγγελίζομαι, εὐαγγέλιον	65f., 148
εὐδοκέω	68–73
ἰσχύω	184
κενόω	121
λατρεύω	74
λυτρόω, λύτρον	76–8, 124f., 185
μαστιγόω	90f.
μέλλει	95
μονογενής	71
παῖς	3f., 22, 70, 74, 104, 107–10, 120, 126, 127, 150, 184, 200
παῖς Θεοῦ	14f., 17, 108–10, 193
παραδίδωμι	3, 79f., 94f., 110, 122f., 137, 186
περιοχή	113
πολύς	78f., 82f., 122, 123
πρόβατον	125, 126, 191
πρόσωπον	90f.
προσδέχομαι	71
ῥύομαι	76
υἱός	68–73, 109
ὑψόω	105, 192

INDEX OF MODERN AUTHORS

Abbott, A. E., 80
Aytoun, R. A., 180

Bacon, B. W., 18, 167
Barrett, C. K., 104, 181, 191, 192
Bauer, W., 191
Bentzen, A., 57f., 170, 174, 176, 199
Bernard, J. H., 184, 191
Bigg, C., 195
Billerbeck, P. (*see* Strack, J. L.)
Black, M., 178
Bousset, W., 4, 92, 188
Bowman, J. W., 11–13, 18–20, 182, 187
Box, G. H., 165, 183
Brandon, S. G. F., 197
Branscombe, B. H., 188
Brownlee, W. H., 177, 178
Bruce, F. F., 192
Büchler, A., 56
Büchsel, F., 185, 186
Bultmann, R., 5, 92, 166, 168, 185, 188
Burkitt, F. C., 1, 3, 15f., 109, 164, 186
Burney, C. F., 191

Cadbury, H. J., 4, 21f., 86, 192, 193
Cadoux, C. J., 9, 182, 183, 184, 186, 187
Campbell, J. Y., 182
Carpenter, J. E., 2
Carpenter, L. L., 17f., 182, 183, 186, 187, 188, 192, 193, 194, 195
Cave, S., 196
Cerfaux, L., 115f., 121, 193, 194
Charles, R. H., 180
Clarke, W. K. L., 181
Cook, S. A., 175
Cooke, G. A., 170f.
Creed, J. M., 164, 187, 192
Cullmann, O., 17, 18, 182, 183, 192, 199

Dalman, G., 184, 187
Davey, N. (*see* Hoskyns, E.)
Davies, W. D., 177, 179
Denney, J., 182, 184, 185

Dibelius, M., 164, 188
Dodd, C. H., 20, 21–3, 104, 168, 172, 182, 183, 184, 186, 187, 188, 189, 190, 191, 192, 194, 195, 196, 197
Driver, G. R., 178
Driver, S. R., 198
Driver, S. R., and Neubauer, A., 173f.
Duncan, G. S., 195
Dupont-Sommer, A., 178

Eissfeldt, O., 168, 172
Emmet, C. W., 179
Engnell, I., 6, 57f., 165, 168f., 176, 180

Fascher, E., 189, 196
Flemington, W. F., 181
Frankfort, H., 171, 176
Friedrich, G., 181
Frost, S. B., 174, 179, 180, 198
Fuller, R. H., 16, 93f., 181, 182, 184, 185, 186

Ginsberg, H. L., 177
Goguel, M., 189, 191
Gore, C., 196
Grant, F. C., 188
Grayston, K., 183
Grundmann, W., 184
Guignebert, C., 181

Hegermann, H., 55
Hirsch, E. G., 182
Hooke, S. H., 173, 176
Hoskyns, E., and Davey, N., 1, 6–8, 181
How, J. C. H., 179, 190
Howard, W. F., 183, 184, 191
Hunter, A. M., 194, 195
Huntress, E., 182

Jackson, F., and Lake, K., 2–6, 9, 13f., 20, 21, 22, 80, 86, 154, 166, 167, 186, 188
James, E. O., 6

Jeremias, J., 14f., 81, 126, 179, 182, 183, 186, 187, 188, 189, 190, 191, 192, 193, 194, 195, 197
Johnson, A. R., 172, 173, 176

Kennett, R. H., 179
Kissane, E. J., 168, 169, 172, 176, 185
Klausner, J., 179

Lake, K., and Jackson, F. (*see* Jackson, F.)
Lake, K., and Lake, S., 193
Lampe, G. W. H., 181, 182
Langdon, S., 176
Lightfoot, J. B., 190f.
Lindblom, J., 169, 170, 174f., 180
Lods, A., 173
Lofthouse, W. F., 169
Loisy, A., 182

McNeile, A. H., 188
Manson, T. W., 15, 168, 181, 198, 199
Manson, W., 10f., 145f., 177, 180, 182, 184, 185, 188
Michael, J. H., 194
Milligan, G., and Moulton, J. H., 195
Mitchell, H. G., 179, 190
Moffatt, J., 168, 182, 184, 194
Montefiore, C. G., 164, 178, 182, 187, 191
Montgomery, J. A., 198
Moore, G. F., 178, 179, 181, 198
Moule, C. F. D., 189
Moulton, J. H., 183, 189
Moulton, J. H., and Milligan, G., 195
Mowinckel, S., 169, 170, 173, 174
Mozley, J. K., 185

Neubauer, A., and Driver, S. R., 173f.
North, C. R., 13f., 48–51, 166, 168, 171, 172, 176, 177, 178, 182, 189
Nyberg, H. S., 172, 176

Oesterley, W. O. E., 168, 170, 173, 181
Otto, R., 9, 184, 186, 187, 198

Pedersen, J., 172, 173
Pfeiffer, R., 180

Plummer, A., 181, 188, 192
Pritchard, J. B., 176

Rabin, C., 178
Rashdall, H., 23, 184, 185, 187
Rawlinson, A. E. J., 182, 184, 185, 188, 192
Riesenfeld, H., 176, 180
Robinson, H. W., 13, 42, 166, 175, 179, 181, 182, 185
Robinson, T. H., 170, 197
Rowley, H. H., 169, 172, 173, 176, 179, 198
Ryle, H. E., 178

Sanday, W., 182
Schrenk, G., 190
Schürer, E., 179
Schweizer, E., 200
Selwyn, E. G., 124, 196
Smith, C. R., 173, 174
Smith, S., 170, 172, 177
Smith, W. R., 183
Snaith, N. H., 168, 169, 185
Stählin, G., 194
Stanton, V. H., 179
Stauffer, E., 178f., 191, 195, 197, 198
Stenning, J. F., 178
Strachan, R. H., 191
Strack, J. L., and Billerbeck, P., 177, 178, 179, 181
Streeter, B. H., 164
Swete, H. B., 182, 183

Taylor, F. J., 185
Taylor, V., 8f., 13f., 98f., 126, 128, 182, 183, 184, 185, 186, 187, 188, 190, 191, 192, 194, 195, 198
Thornton, L. S., 94, 186, 191, 194, 195
Torrey, C. C., 177, 179f., 180, 182, 193
Tritton, A. S., 173
Turner, C. H., 183
Turner, H. E. W., 15f., 182, 183

Wardle, W. L., 172
Weiss, J., 168
Wolff, H. W., 9f., 168, 179
Wright, C. H. H., 180

INDEX OF SUBJECTS

A
Allegory, 50, 98, 174f.
Aquila, 55, 194
Atonement, 23f., 47, 54, 56, 78, 83, 91, 110, 133, 151, 155, 168, 196
Day of, 123f.

B
Babylonian ritual, 35, 48
Baptism of Jesus, 9, 11, 13, 15, 16, 18, 19, 67, 72f.
Barnabas, 114
Bath Qôl, 11

C
Caesarea Philippi, 17, 92, 159
Corporate Personality, 42–5, 49, 142, 145, 160, 172, 173
Covenant, 35–40, 42, 76, 81f., 123, 132, 161, 170f.
Cross and Crucifixion (*see* Death of Jesus)
Cyrus, 29, 40, 51, 170, 174

D
David, 36–40, 44, 75, 81, 108, 109, 156, 157
Dead Sea Scrolls, 56, 177, 178
Death of Jesus, 23, 24, 55, 91, 101, 105, 106, 119, 134–8, 163, 197
his foreknowledge, 1–24, 63f., 92–102, 134–7, 153
as ordained by God, 5, 7, 86, 95f., 122, 134f., 137, 150, 152, 166

E
Early Church
Judaistic element, 3, 14, 16, 17, 23, 109, 192
Hellenistic element, 2–5, 14, 16, 23, 109f., 154, 192
Eleazar, 54
Elijah, 54, 135f., 162

Eucharist, the, 104
Exile, the, 31, 46, 48, 50, 58
Return from, 27–40, 44, 45, 48, 50, 51, 60, 76, 147
Exodus, the, 76, 162, 172
Second, 68, 76, 161, 185

F
Fall, the, 140
'First Man', the, 57f.
Form Criticism, 8
Four-document hypothesis, 8

H
Healing miracles, the, 3, 4, 16, 83, 84, 85, 86, 148f.

J
Jerusalem, Fall of, 586 B.C., 31, 32
John the Baptist, 3, 9f., 12, 13, 66, 67, 73, 85, 104, 148, 161, 181
Josephus, 56, 178
Judgement, the, 59, 142–4, 153, 161

K
Kerygma, 110, 117–20, 121, 127, 137, 138, 150f., 152, 197
Kingdom of God, the, 16, 100, 173
Kingship, 37f., 43–5, 142, 171, 173, 176

L
Lamb of God, 4, 103f.
Last Supper, the, 9, 14, 16
'Lives of the Prophets', 141

M
Messiah
and the Son of Man, 10, 12f., 19f., 56–8, 142, 145f., 159f., 162, 177
and the Servant, 6, 11–13, 18–20, 55–8, 145f., 148, 149, 177
sufferings and death of, 4, 6, 55, 56f., 148, 177, 178, 179

228

INDEX OF SUBJECTS

Messiah (cont.)
  'of the Remnant', 11f., 18f.
  in popular thought, 11f., 15, 18, 43, 45, 69, 159, 161, 173, 182
  in the thought of Jesus, 10–12, 13, 19, 69, 88, 159–62, 182
  and redemption, 23f.
  Jesus proclaimed as, 109
Midrash, 56, 179, 182
Moses, 75, 81, 100f., 105, 109, 112, 132, 138, 156, 157, 162

N
Nationalism, Jewish, 31, 60f.

O
Origen   154

P
Paschal Lamb, 104, 124, 126
Passion predictions (see Death of Jesus)
Paul, as Servant, 114–16
Peshitta, 55
Peter, 92, 118–20, 129, 159f.
  Petrine theory, 16–18
Philip, 3, 113, 127, 150
Philo, 56
Priesthood, Levitical, 36, 77
  of Jesus, 123f., 151
Prophet and prophecy, 12, 14, 18f., 25f., 30f., 47, 101, 112, 124, 127, 141

R
Rabbinic literature, 12, 53, 56
Remnant, the, 18f., 72f., 81, 143, 145, 153, 160, 161
Resurrection of Jesus, 5, 14, 17, 23, 106, 114f., 118–20, 138
Restoration or Return (see Exile, Return from)
Righteous and righteousness, 111f., 144–6, 153f.

S
Scripture, use of, 2, 9, 10, 21–3, 83, 86, 129, 149
Servant
  identity of, 41ff.
  in Jewish literature, 53ff.
  in Synoptic gospels, 62ff.
  in early Church, 103ff.
Shealtiel, Apocalypse of, 59
Sin (see Atonement)
Solomon Astruc, 173f.
Son of God, 69, 72f.
Son of Man
  and 'First Man', 57
  in Daniel, 142f., 153f., 160f.,
  in 1 Enoch, 54, 142–6, 153f.
  and the Messiah, 10, 12f., 19f., 56–8, 142, 145f., 159f., 162, 177
  and the Servant, 2f., 5, 8, 9, 12f., 15f., 19f., 96f., 98, 145f., 177
  sufferings and death of, 78, 92–7, 98f., 100, 134–7, 153, 159–62
  and exaltation, 10, 16, 100, 105f., 137, 153, 159–62
Spirit of God, 11, 19, 67f., 73, 118, 148
Stephen, 138
Suffering
  of Israel, 30, 46f., 49, 50, 58–61, 148
  of Jesus, 134f., 137f., 152f.
  of his predecessors, 135f., 138f.
  of the disciples, 136f.
  of the early Christians, 139
  of the righteous, 56, 140f., 143, 153, 200
  of the Servant, 10, 29, 46, 148, 150, 158f., 175
  in Jewish thought, 140f., 153f.
  and exaltation, 46, 58–61, 100f., 105f., 120f., 136f., 138, 153, 159–62
Symmachus, 55

T
Talmud, 56
Tammuz cult, 176
Targum, 53, 55f., 57, 58, 63, 175, 178, 180, 182
Tell-el-Amarna letters, 173
Temptation, the, 11, 166
Theodotion, 55, 71, 142, 183
Transfiguration, the, 9, 16, 100, 162

U
Universalism, prophetic, 31, 60f., 79, 84, 163

INDEX OF SUBJECTS

V

Vicarious suffering, 3, 19, 23, 45, 46, 48, 54, 56, 60f., 128, 155f., 159, 163, 178f.

Vulgate, 142

Z

Zadokite Fragments, 56